Close to Home

Who votes for radical right parties and why? This book argues that the increasing popularity of the radical right in Europe originates in community bonds: strong ties to one's locality motivate support for the radical right. These parties use nostalgic themes and symbolic politicking to idealize community, defend local autonomy, and ultimately draw local identity into the electoral realm. While other explanations of the radical right's popularity typify supporters as victims of macro-economic shifts and strains, the author's account explores people's day-to-day experiences that link local connections to political decisions. The analysis also raises questions about the political implications of different formal authority structures such as the level and nature of power devolved to local units. The localist model of radical right support illuminates the psychological, social, and institutional conditions and processes that render people's feelings about their cities, towns, and villages relevant for politics.

Jennifer Fitzgerald is co-author of *Partisan Families* (Cambridge 2007), awarded the International Society of Political Psychology's Alexander George Book Award for best book in political psychology. Her other accolades include a Fulbright Award to conduct research in France, the University of Chicago's Morton Kaplan Prize, and teaching awards at the University of Colorado where she is Associate Professor of Political Science. Her research has been published in the *Journal of Politics*, *Comparative Political Studies*, *Political Behavior*, *World Politics*, *Electoral Studies* and *International Migration Review*, among other journals.

Cambridge Studies in Public Opinion and Political Psychology

Series Editors
Dennis Chong, *University of Southern California and Northwestern University*
James H. Kuklinski, *University of Illinois, Urbana-Champaign*

Cambridge Studies in Public Opinion and Political Psychology publishes innovative research from a variety of theoretical and methodological perspectives on the mass public foundations of politics and society. Research in the series focuses on the origins and influence of mass opinion, the dynamics of information and deliberation, and the emotional, normative, and instrumental bases of political choice. In addition to examining psychological processes, the series explores the organization of groups, the association between individual and collective preferences, and the impact of institutions on beliefs and behavior.

Cambridge Studies in Public Opinion and Political Psychology is dedicated to furthering theoretical and empirical research on the relationship between the political system and the attitudes and actions of citizens.

Books in the series are listed on the page following the Index.

Close to Home

Local Ties and Voting Radical Right in Europe

JENNIFER FITZGERALD

University of Colorado, Boulder

CAMBRIDGE
UNIVERSITY PRESS

CAMBRIDGE
UNIVERSITY PRESS

University Printing House, Cambridge CB2 8BS, United Kingdom

One Liberty Plaza, 20th Floor, New York, NY 10006, USA

477 Williamstown Road, Port Melbourne, VIC 3207, Australia

314–321, 3rd Floor, Plot 3, Splendor Forum, Jasola District Centre, New Delhi – 110025, India

79 Anson Road, #06-04/06, Singapore 079906

Cambridge University Press is part of the University of Cambridge.

It furthers the University's mission by disseminating knowledge in the pursuit of education, learning, and research at the highest international levels of excellence.

www.cambridge.org
Information on this title: www.cambridge.org/9781108421539
DOI: 10.1017/9781108377218

First published 2018

Printed in the United States of America by Sheridan Books, Inc.

A catalogue record for this publication is available from the British Library.

Library of Congress Cataloging-in-Publication Data
Names: Fitzgerald, Jennifer, 1972– author.
Title: Close to home : local ties and voting radical right in Europe / Jennifer Fitzgerald.
Description: New York, NY: Cambridge University Press, 2018. |
Series: Cambridge studies in public opinion and political psychology |
Includes bibliographical references and index.
Identifiers: LCCN 2018016146 | ISBN 9781108421539 (hardback)
Subjects: LCSH: Political parties – Europe. | Right-wing extremists – Europe. |
Radicalism – Europe. | Political campaigns – Europe. | Europe – Politics and government.
Classification: LCC JN94.A979.F57 2018 | DDC 324.2/13094–dc23
LC record available at https://lccn.loc.gov/2018016146

ISBN 978-1-108-42153-9 Hardback

For Eric

Contents

Figures

Tables

Acknowledgments

This research originated in my doctoral dissertation many years ago so I have nearly two decades' worth of thanking to do. I must start by acknowledging the late Alan Zuckerman, who was my academic mentor and advisor throughout and beyond my years at Brown University. His deep commitment to the highest-quality, methodical, unbiased, innovative research was always inspiring and sometimes intimidating. But he balanced out his high expectations with generous mentorship and supportive collegiality. At Brown I also learned so much from other members of the faculty: notably, Wendy Schiller, James Morone, and Linda Cook. My fellow graduate students made me smarter and kept me motivated. I am particularly indebted to Jason Barnosky, Josip Dasović, Carrie Nordlund, and Catherine Corliss. Patti Gardner is another person at Brown to whom I am grateful for all of her guidance and support.

In the Department of Political Science at the University of Colorado at Boulder I have been lucky to be surrounded once again by smart, interesting, and supportive people. The faculty were welcoming and helpful from my first days on campus. In particular, David Brown, Andy Baker, David Leblang, Sven Steinmo, Ken Bickers, Susan Clark, Scott Adler, and Joe Jupille have all been wonderful mentors. Jenny Wolak, Carew Boulding, and Vanessa Baird (a.k.a. the P.C.) have helped me so much with this project (and so many other things) at various stages and in various ways. I don't care to imagine what I would do without such incredible colleagues and friends. Thanks, too, to Pavel Bacovsky and Hannah Paul for assistance with the manuscript and to Duncan Lawrence for collaborating with me on a related piece of this research. I am grateful to Rachel Austin and Velina Dinkova for transcription and translation assistance.

Scholars Martin Schain, Nonna Mayer, James Hollifield, Sophie Body-Gendrot, and Romain Garbaye took the time to learn about my research and to provide advice on the study of French politics and the radical right. Geneviève Michaud from the Centre de Données Socio-Politiques at Sciences Po helped me access French electoral data. My field work in France benefitted from the help of a number of people and institutions. Research funding came from the University of Colorado and the French Fulbright Commission. Sciences-Politiques in Bordeaux, notably Vincent Hoffmann-Martinot, supported my Fulbright proposal and hosted me during my time in France. The faculty and staff at Sciences Po Bordeaux helped to make my stay a pleasant and productive one. And I am profoundly grateful to the mayors and council members of French communes who welcomed me and provided invaluable insight into life in the Gironde. Alain and Annie Calletier and Hervé Battistan were fantastic hosts and friends during my 2008 stay in Bordeaux. In France I also benefitted from the company of my troupe of "research assistants": Francis and Andrea Rodriguez, Angelo and Joan Pugliesi, Jo and Kyle Kutchey, Jennifer Bernsen, Rhonda Faulkner, Caroline Hybels, Darcy Hoff, and Pam Seymour.

I am grateful to the Swiss Household Panel experts at the Swiss Foundation for Research in Social Sciences (FORS), for their panel survey data and assistance with it. Notably, Ursina Kuhn and Marieke Voorpostel have been very supportive and helpful. Back in the US, Christine Kearney and Rafaela Dancygier generously shared data with me. Scores of other scholars have given me great ideas, read various chapters and helped with this project in different ways. I must single out David Art, Marc Hooghe, Hilde Coffé, Eric Gonzalez-Juenke, Amber Curtis, Moonhawk Kim, Carl Berning, Erik Amnå, Gary Freeman, Sidney Tarrow, and Irfan Nooruddin.

Cambridge University Press has been wonderful over the years. Lewis Bateman was supportive from the early days of this project; Robert Dreesen has provided valuable advice and shepherded the manuscript through the review and production processes expertly. I am grateful to anonymous reviewers who read the manuscript for Cambridge and provided essential feedback. Ruth Boyes, Céline Durassier, and Joanna Pyke were very helpful with the manuscript, and I am indebted to James Kuklinski and Dennis Chong for accepting this book into their series.

Finally, I am humbled by the support of my family and am thrilled to have the opportunity to express this in print. John and Fay Fitzgerald are just incredible people all the way through. They are giving and smart and funny and adventurous; lucky for me they are my parents. Kevin Fitzgerald, my brother, makes the world a better place with his big heart, sharp mind, and unusual take on things. JoAn and Joe Kindsvater, Dawn Kindsvater-Doyle and Roger Doyle, the late Isabel Kindsvater and Mark Potter, the Peters-Kisskalt-Rodriguez clan, and all the Fritches have provided many years of support and encouragement. I owe so much to the late Evelyn Margaret MacLean Potter (a.k.a. Gram) for the beautiful and powerful example she set for all of us. Wow, is she missed. As is Bradford Lee Potter, whose cherished book collection got me reading and kept me reading. These thanks would be incomplete without acknowledging my dad's parents, Patrick Francis Fitzgerald and Bridget Herlihy Fitzgerald. They migrated to Detroit from Ireland in the 1920s, coming in search of work and to create a better life. What an extraordinary thing to do and what extraordinary people they were.

I dedicate this book to my husband, Eric Adam Kisskalt, with gratitude, admiration, and love. He is generous, thoughtful, brilliant, and hilarious, and this book would not exist without his steadfast support.

I

Electoral Disorder, Social Change: An Introduction

Elections in advanced democracies have become increasingly unpredictable in recent years. New political elites and former pariah parties are gaining popularity while traditional, mainstream parties and leaders lose support. Perhaps most notably, Europe is in the midst of its most tumultuous electoral era since the inter-war years. Unconventional parties with leftist, rightist, and ideologically ambiguous platforms attract voters in political contests across the continent.[1] Vote shares of Europe's establishment parties such as left-leaning Social Democrats and right-leaning Christian Democrats are in precipitous decline in many countries. Election campaigns are increasingly confrontational, suggesting that the post-war commitment to political consensus among political parties has weakened. As challenger parties grow in popularity, they stand to further transform the nature of political competition and policy making. They also stand to alter political systems for decades to come as young generations enter a very different political environment than the one that ushered their elders into democratic citizenship.

The electoral ascent of radical right parties makes for particularly gripping headlines. These parties' campaigns hinge on anti-immigrant, anti-European Union, anti-globalization, and anti-establishment themes. High-profile examples range from the immensely successful Swiss People's Party, the winning party in Switzerland's last several legislative elections, to the National

---

[1] In Spain an upstart party on the left, Podemos, has risen to be the third largest party in the country since its founding in 2014 by a political scientist. On the right, the United Kingdom Independence Party (UKIP), established in the 1990s, engineered a successful referendum in favor of Britain's withdrawal from the European Union. Italy's Five Star Movement is the recent creation of a comedian-turned-blogger-turned-populist. It received more votes than any other party in the 2013 lower house legislative elections. The Five Star Movement defies definitive classification in traditional left-right terms. These parties are examples of the many movements contributing to electoral disorder in Europe.

Front in France, which has experienced ups and downs over several decades, to the nascent but un-ignorable Golden Dawn in Greece, which brands itself in stunning neo-Nazi style.[2] Even in Sweden, a country widely believed to be immune to modern political extremes, the Sweden Democrats have a fast-growing constituency. In most west European countries and increasingly in some east European states, radical right parties attract significant vote shares in national contests.[3] Sometimes they obtain seats in governing coalitions. Even when they do not ascend to governance, their very presence in politics pushes national dialogues and public policies to the right.

As these electoral shifts shake up modern democratic politics, they pique popular curiosity and energize academic discourse. Many ask: what explains these historic developments? This book provides new insights into citizens' decisions to vote for radical right parties. I ask: why do certain people at certain times in certain places decide that a radical right party or candidate merits their electoral support?

In big-picture historical terms, today's radical right phenomenon has been linked by many experts to a widespread unmooring in modern politics. People do not feel connected to political parties like they did in the decades following World War II when the basic parameters of partisan competition were established.[4] Partisan dealignment – a process through which citizens have become progressively detached from traditional political parties (Dalton and Wattenburg 2000) – and the ascent of new electorally competitive parties represent two sides of the same coin.[5]

While both the dealignment trend and the rise of new parties are distinctly political in nature, they are rooted in broader, societal developments: people's weakening ties to traditional social groupings that for decades aligned with mainstream political parties. Group-based models of voting have shaped our understanding of electoral behavior in Europe (Lipset and Rokkan 1967) and the United States (Campbell et al. 1960) as citizens traditionally view politics through various lenses – typically defined by class and religion. The process of approaching vote choice as members of defined social groups

---

[2] In recent legislative elections in these countries (in 2014 in Sweden, 2015 in Switzerland and Greece, and in 2017 in France) the Sweden Democrats received nearly 13 percent of the vote, the Swiss People's Party received nearly 30 percent of the vote, the French National Front about 9 percent of the vote in the second round (over 13 percent in the first round), and Golden Dawn received over 6 percent of the vote.

[3] They have also achieved success in European Parliament elections and many sub-national elections at municipal and regional levels.

[4] Lipset and Rokkan (1967) developed the "freezing hypothesis" that explains the post-war contours of Western European partisan debate in terms of deep-seeded social cleavages that originated in the 1920s.

[5] See Dassonneville and Hooghe (2018) on the consequences of partisan dealignment for broader political orientations. Ezro et al. (2014) make this case in reverse: connecting strong partisan attachments with very limited opportunities for extremist parties to compete electorally.

promoted stability in voter behavior for decades, resulting in relatively fore-seeable electoral outcomes. Most notably, trade unions and their related social classes have traditionally synched in ideological terms with center-left parties while (typically Catholic) Christian churches and their religious communities have sided with center-right parties. As membership in unions and churches and their attendant social groups wanes,[6] support for mainstream left and right parties becomes less socially rooted in a traditional sense and less habitual.

Observing such trends, one might surmise that the era of social group-based voting that was once a powerful, stabilizing phenomenon in democratic socie-ties is drawing to a close. Indeed, this is what some commentators and scholars have argued, referring to major segments of today's democratic electorates as "adrift."[7] The contemporary voter, according to this interpretation, is detached from foundational social groupings of modern life and increasingly inclined to make political judgments according to his or her own, idiosyncratic cri-teria. Instead of approaching elections from particular social positions, people now make choices at the polls that are motivated by attitudes on specific policy issues and attraction to particular political leaders (Ivarsflaten 2008, Stone 2017).

While the image of a detached, unpredictable, issue-focused voter may accu-rately capture the reality of electoral choices for some individuals, one fact of life stands in sharp tension with this interpretation of contemporary society as highly atomized: human beings have a psychological need to belong to social groups. It is natural – some would argue imperative – for individuals to locate themselves within defined social collectives. This attachment provides a source of identity, self-esteem, and well-being. Thus, as groups that formerly structured a significant portion of social life lose their stabilizing powers, other forms of belonging can be expected to take their place. In certain situations, these enhanced feelings of alternative group belonging will be salient for politics.

So what is happening in terms of group attachment and politics is not simply an unmooring; it is also a re-mooring. Thus, to understand large-scale transformations in society and politics, we should be on the look-out for types of group belonging that are on the rise in terms of personal salience and polit-ical salience. This approach will allow us to think differently about how var-ious dimensions of social ties shape electoral choices.

In this book I introduce, develop, and test what I call the localist theory of radical right voting: an account of unconventional electoral behavior that is motivated by people's feelings of attachment to their local communities. I argue

---

[6] See Sarlvik and Crewe (1983) on the declining relevance of social class, and Pollack (2008) on religious decline.

[7] For a journalistic account of voters adrift, see Cowell's (2010) essay in *The New York Times* and Doggett's (2017) Agence France-Presse article. A classic scholarly source of this argument is Andeweg (1982). A modern empirical study is van der Meer et al. (2013); they argue that voter volatility stems from the emancipation of European voters from traditional partisan structures.

that those individuals with the strongest sense of belonging to their localities find the programs of radical right parties particularly appealing. In addition to contributing a fresh account of the radical right phenomenon, I mark a path toward a fuller understanding of the ways different facets of people's social identities shape their vote choices in modern elections.

To date, the connections people feel to their local areas have not attracted careful attention in research on voter behavior. This is an oversight because so many factors signal that people's ties to their localities fuel the rise of radical right parties. To identify a few: these parties often get started by appealing to local pride in local elections, their success levels vary markedly by locality even in national contests, and they often promise to protect the political autonomy of local communities. These observations suggest that there is great potential in exploring the connections between politically relevant local attachments and radical right voting. As such, they set the stage for my consideration of Tip O'Neill's famous adage, "all politics is local," as it relates to the raucus electoral politics of the twenty-first century.[8]

To the extent that the concept of "the local" features in studies on the subject, scholars ask whether community characteristics such as foreign-born population size or unemployment rate predict support for radical right parties. Studies also examine the ways in which participation in community organizations and the resultant gains in social capital relate to radical right support. To date, these studies provide conflicting accounts of whether and how locally oriented factors can motivate support for the radical right, thus inspiring further exploration into the ways the local connects to the politically radical.

In the rest of this introductory chapter, I devote attention to radical right parties in order to clarify the nature and dynamics of their politics. I also consider alternate theories of radical right support, summarize my argument, and outline the chapters of the book. But first, I draw attention to the phenomenon of localism. Myriad observers point to the rise of local attachments and the implications of those attachments for many facets of life, but we know very little about how these trends influence politics.

THE RISE OF LOCALISM

People feel the need to belong; they crave membership in defined social collectivities and they find security when rooted in bounded communities. Scholars from Durkheim to Maslow to Tajfel make this observation. A sense of belonging provides positive self-identity, distinctiveness, and self-esteem (Livingston et al. 2008). Yet key facets of modern social change threaten individuals with anonymity. In an increasingly homogeneous, high-tech world there is great potential for people to sense that they don't matter. Many feel disempowered,

---

[8] I am grateful to an anonymous reviewer for Cambridge University Press for drawing this connection.

indistinct, and unanchored. It comes as little surprise that one Gallup poll after the next shows how stressed, anxious, and pessimistic many people are these days, particularly in Europe.[9]

One way to mitigate these negative effects is to seek refuge and empowerment in the locality. Small-scale communities can offer a sense of belonging and a sense of place; research in psychology bears this out. In the local arena individuals can feel connected with a group that distinguishes them in a visible way and provides the basis for feelings of pride and efficacy (see Bess et al. 2002), and a key source of identification can be the locality (Wilton 1998, Kingston et al. 1999, Forrest and Kearns 2001). Community psychologists Forrest and Kearns articulate the logic for this (re)localizing reflex as it relates to neighborhoods:

> Intuitively, it would seem that as a source of social identity the neighborhood is being progressively eroded with the emergence of a more fluid, individualized way of life ... On the other hand, globalizing processes may have the opposite effects. As the forces which bear down upon us seem to be increasingly remote, local social interaction and the familiar landmarks of the neighborhood may take on greater significance as sources of comfort and security. (2001: 2129)

Thus, in response to the march of globalization, people retreat to small-scale, local groups that provide a much-needed sense of membership. Numerous commentators and researchers have noticed this very trend: the backlash against anonymity prompts a renaissance of the local. Some identify this as a world-wide phenomenon; Friedman (2000) and Barber (1996) narrate the retreat to local traditions for security in the face of globalizing forces. Indeed, there are plenty of manifestations of increased localization in today's world; localist economic movements in scores of countries exemplify the trend. The heightened visibility of "buy local," "food sovereignty," and "shop small" movements characterize small-scale life in many countries, particularly in the global north (Weatherell et al. 2003, Ayres and Bosia 2011). These movements have been found to boost feelings of community attachment among residents (Mitchell 2007), blossoming in response to a global system that is perceived as distant, depersonalized, and uncontrollable (see Hess 2009).

Academic work from a range of disciplines further emphasizes the importance of small-scale "place" in addition to the notion of community. From sociology comes a narrative that highlights the continued relevance of particular places for individuals:

---

[9] Many Germans are stressed and anxious: www.gallup.com/businessjournal/190049/high-cost-worker-burnout-germany.aspx?g_source=anxiety&g_medium=search&g_campaign=tiles.
Many Greeks (followed by Bulgarians, Romanians, and Portuguese) are extremely pessimistic about the direction of their lives: www.gallup.com/businessjournal/159605/combating-greece-desperate-loss-hope.aspx?g_source=stress%20europe&g_medium=search&g_campaign=tiles (see also Fitzgerald, Curtis, and Corliss (2012)).

Could it be that place just does not matter anymore? I think it does. In spite of (and perhaps because of) the jet, the 'net, and the fast-food outlet, place persists as a constituent element of social life and historical change. (Gieryn 2000: 463)

We can find corroborating observations in political science, as well:

Modern life has not erased the importance of place … It may have, instead, increased the need for people to draw boundaries, to more crisply define their geographic community … and to behave in ways that signal their place-related identities … People are often proud of where they are from, and they continue to want you to know it. (Cramer 2016: 240, fn. 12)

Additional political science research shows that local attachments are on the rise in a range of European countries (Sellers and Lidström 2012). There is also a growing narrative about the political roots of the localist retreat, emphasizing that it is in part in response to a perceived lack of control and a feeling of distance from loci of power. Starr and Adams, for instance, find processes of "relocalization" to include "the practice of local sovereignty and the refusal of distant authority" (2003: 21) in response to globalization.

Altogether, economic, social, and political localism is on the rise, and this trend has high levels of support from many corners. Indeed, there is a strong case to be made that tightly knit communities are especially well suited to meet the challenges of the day, making it possible for residents to cooperate and solve common problems and to insulate themselves from the strains of modern life. Yet there are those who criticize localist movements. One line of disapproval warns against social fragmentation. For instance, human geographers uncover the ways that localism can devolve into divisive and potentially unjust spatial or local "fetishism." The concept of "defensive localism" has been developed in recognition of the fanaticism that characterizes some localist movements (Winter 2003, DuPuis and Goodman 2005). There can be economic costs, too. "Buy local" movements are criticized by economists as inefficient for the market, and place attachment can reduce incentives for young people to seek out better job opportunities elsewhere (Green and White 2007).

Furthermore, a person who links his or her self-esteem and identity to the local community is in a position to feel personally threatened if they perceive the locality to be under threat. Just as globalization pushes people to invest reflexively in their local areas, it also threatens to undermine what makes each locality special. The distinguishing character and status of a local community are things that locals who care will want to preserve. So the positive psychic benefits of community are counter-balanced by the potential negatives that come from perceived threat. As a result, local attachments today put individuals in a precarious position with respect to their status and, ultimately, their sense of place in the world. When local identities are strengthened and drawn upon, a powerful local "us" can become the basis for intense political views.

It seems we have a solid understanding *that* localism is on the rise, and we also have compelling intuitions as to *why* it is on the rise. Yet while the psychological and economic implications have attracted scholarly attention, we have little knowledge of the *political effects* of localism. Some work has connected globalism's social disruption to changes in modern politics. For instance, according to Eric Hobsbawm (2007), the impersonalizing forces of globalization push people to invent mental connections to social groups, thereby reinforcing the rise of identity politics. As I read this collection of signs, the increasing importance of local attachments and their connection to new trends in electoral behavior merit careful examination.[10]

Stepping back from the enhanced value of localities in the lives and psyches of individuals, one also observes a parallel trend toward the heightened political relevance of local units in many democratic societies. For instance, while national governments and the EU elicit low levels of citizen trust, local governments enjoy relatively high levels of public confidence. In a range of countries, people have positive views of their local authorities and know a great deal about them. At the same time, national leaders increasingly recognize the capacities of sub-national collectivities for addressing modern problems and respond by empowering local governments.[11] The practice of devolving power to local authorities has been taking place across democratic systems for the past few decades (Loughlin 2001, Jeffery 2006). This makes the localities increasingly meaningful in political terms, enhancing the politicization of local identities, considerations, and issues.

In tension with this overall trend toward devolution, territorial restructuring in certain countries threatens the autonomy of some local communities. In efforts to streamline bureaucratic processes and achieve greater efficiency in public service delivery, some national governments institute agglomeration schemes. These reforms "clump" previously distinct and relatively autonomous municipalities – most often those located in sparsely populated rural areas – into merged units. Such practices may ultimately improve the quality of life in affected communities, but they also spur intense debate about the status of the locality – and thus the value of people's local identities – in today's world. Through this mechanism, too, the local can become increasingly salient for politics.

Building on all of these insights, this book investigates the *electoral* implications of this turn toward the local, which have been largely overlooked. I find that today's passion for all things local and localities' enhanced political salience have contributed to the growth of radical right parties.

---

[10] Eatwell (2000) makes an adjacent observation about the way identity politics is promoted by globalization.

[11] The European Union's guiding principle of subsidiarity – that all policy should be made at the lowest sensible level of governance – is consistent with this shift in authority to sub-national units.

THE RADICAL RIGHT AND DOMINANT ACCOUNTS OF ITS SUCCESS

Radical right parties are meaningful electoral challengers in many European countries; common themes emphasized by these parties include sharp curtailment of immigration, autonomy from the European Union, extremely tough law and order stances, and pointed criticism of mainstream political parties. More broadly, they aim to represent those citizens frustrated by modernization and globalization – and the societal strains these trends have wrought. Their ultimate goal is to undo the perceived damage that has accompanied modernization (Minkenberg 2000). Radical right rhetoric paints a picture of a "better" time characterized by less diversity, more safety, intact sovereignty, greater affluence, and elevated status. They invite voters to share their nostalgic vision and to join them on the quest for a return to the past.

It is their rhetoric – that is imbued with nostalgia – that helps to distinguish the radical right from other kinds of parties, particularly those on the ideological right. Many center-right parties have taken firm positions on some of the same issues such as immigration and the European Union. But it is the backward-looking view of societal developments that sets the radical right apart. Populism is a key aspect of their appeals, as well. They claim to carry the mantle of the true citizenry, bringing the people's unfiltered voice directly into the political arena (Mudde 2004). They blend this populism (which by definition is ideologically neutral) with rhetoric that holds mainstream politicians responsible for societal shifts in the wrong direction: becoming increasingly diverse and increasingly hamstrung by superordinate agreements, diluting the power of the people. They charge ruling elites with incompetency and mismanagement at best, rampant corruption at worst.

While the advent of these parties sets the backdrop of this study, there are significant dimensions of variation that require attention. Most obviously, their electoral shares in national elections are highly inconsistent across countries. Switzerland has the most electorally successful radical right party; countries hosting robust support for these parties also include Austria, Denmark, and France. In other countries such as Germany, Greece, Hungary, and Sweden, the radical right has only recently gained traction with voters. In contrast, there are other national contexts in which there is no national-level representation for the radical right to date: Portugal, Ireland, and Spain, for instance. The cross-national variation has been well studied, but is not fully explained. The major accounts in this vein of research point to the role of national electoral systems and the dimensions of competition (or lack thereof) among political parties. These factors surely matter, but they don't tell the whole story, and they are not well suited to explaining shifts over time. The temporal dimension is particularly important since it can help to push our explanations beyond the identification of where the radical right does well toward a better understanding of why.

We also do not know enough about the reasons for variation across different communities within countries. It is well documented that support for these parties is very patchy in a geographical sense. Some cities, towns, and villages turn out en masse for these parties; in other places they fare poorly at the polls. Yet this diverse electoral geography presents an unsolved puzzle. Even less clear is why those sub-national patterns change over time – what draws residents of a particular community toward the appeals of radical right parties in certain election years and not others? Again, we lack sufficient theoretical tools to make sense of this variation.

Finally, academic studies leave lingering questions about the reasons people decide to support these parties and the reasons they decide not to. A substantial literature has generated insights into the profile of a typical radical right supporter. We know that statistically speaking he is male with relatively low socio-economic status (which involves factors such as education, skills, and other personal resources) (Betz 1993). The typical supporter also tends to take a negative view of modern developments such as large-scale immigration, associating the arrival of newcomers from other countries with domestic strains in economic, cultural, and social life (Rydgren 2008).

The most-likely supporter also lives in (or close to) areas that have been affected by modern changes such as economic decline and immigrant-related diversity (Rink et al. 2009, Valdez 2014). Straddling the individual-aggregate divide are accounts informed by theories of social capital; the argument is that individuals who invest in social capital (through participation in civil society) and those communities rich in social capital will not find the radical right particularly appealing (Coffé et al. 2007). It is those individuals who do not partake in these (trans)formative activities and who do not live in associationally vibrant communities who will support the radical right.

Knitting together these accounts yields an image of the stock supporter of radical right parties. We have established the most-likely profile, but we do not have a full enough sense of the range of motivations that propel citizens toward these parties. Add this to the fact that people move in and out of the radical right voter category over time (meaning they sometimes choose to vote radical right but at other opportunities they choose other parties or opt to not vote), and the profiling approach becomes less useful. Simply put, our current characterization of the radical right voter and his motivations is too narrow for the complexity of the decision to support one of these parties.

Moreover, the increasing size of radical right vote shares requires a wider net in terms of theorizing the factors and processes that connect voters to radical right platforms. When these parties only represented the fringes of society, a few key characteristics went a long way in making sense of the movement. But today the radical right has become increasingly popular among less likely supporters such as women and those who situate themselves on the left side of the political ideology spectrum. The radical right landscape has shifted in other ways, too. Early support tended to come from areas (towns, cities, neighborhoods) that had been immediately affected by the societal shifts associated with globalization. Today, there is rising support in areas that are quite different in nature: communities with little-to-no experience with immigration or post-industrial decline. Increasingly, areas that are rural, ethnically homogeneous, and economically prosperous host significant levels of radical right support in many countries. So while the existing accounts provide insight into a significant portion of the radical right electorate, they cannot address the motivations of many supporters. Furthermore, we have little understanding of when and where certain characteristics or motives will become salient enough to prompt a radical right vote choice. The analysis in this book yields new-found understanding of the diverse, broadening, and unstable coalition that is the radical right electorate.

To unearth some of the more nuanced aspects of radical right support, I examine variation in support for these parties at the individual level (why do some people vote for these parties while others do not?), at the municipal level (why do these parties receive higher levels of support in certain localities than in others?) and at the national level (why do these parties have more electoral success in some countries than in others?). I also consider the dynamics of radical right support over time: what explains shifts in support at the individual, local, and national levels? The analysis spans over thirty democratic countries, integrating surveys from advanced industrial democracies with data on key institutions and other societal characteristics. Couched in a broad-based analysis of radical right support in a range of countries, I devote particular attention to this phenomenon in France and Switzerland.

THE LOCALIST THEORY OF RADICAL RIGHT SUPPORT: A SUMMARY

I argue that local attachments underpin and motivate radical right support.[12] A sense of closeness to one's community involves a strong feeling of pride in the area and positive views of its residents. It also includes a desire for the locality to have status and some autonomy. "Localism" represents these ideals, establishing the basis for celebration and defense of the local community. Individuals can be characterized by their sense of closeness to their communities, and whole communities can be characterized by their levels of local pride and local rootedness.[13]

---

[12] By "local" I mean a defined, relatively small territorial arena in which people live. For measurement purposes, I focus on the municipality, the lowest administrative unit in most democratic state structures. When survey respondents answer questions about the local, it's possible they think smaller – as in a neighborhood, development, or estate – or even bigger – as in a metropolitan area that includes more than one municipality. But overall the term "local" refers to small-scale community that resides beneath the country and its constitutive regions.

[13] A community high in local cohesion is one characterized by feelings of closeness to the locality and its residents. I develop this concept more fully in Chapter 6.

For individuals and communities with powerful local attachments, I find, the radical right is an especially attractive partisan option.

The radical right is the beneficiary of these localist sentiments for a few reasons. Most importantly, these parties employ rhetoric that appeals to localists. They applaud a traditional version of community, warning voters that their local areas are threatened by encroaching state authorities, supranational governance, ethnic diversity, and lack of economic protections. Some of them even campaign on a pro-devolution platform, promising to guard or enhance local autonomy. More broadly, themes of sovereignty, territorial integrity, and belonging are central to radical right appeals. And though the group that is most directly invoked and celebrated is the nation, local attachments are generally complementary to national ties. Thus, by evoking these kinds of communal ideas, they attract voters who feel rooted and connected to a particular local place. In other words, by stressing themes of "we" and "us," these parties open the door to a plurality of ways that people conceptualize themselves as members of different social groups. Localist impulses naturally align with these in-group appeals.

Beyond drawing the central connection between localism and radical right support at the individual level and the community level, I identify several additional patterns that inform our understanding of electoral behavior. Three key aspects of the analysis are described in some detail below. These are the distinctions between active participation in and cognitive attachment to local communities, the ways that gender and ideology relate to localism, and the political salience associated with institutional design and shifts in formal authority.

Deconstructing Local Ties: Social Capital versus Localism

The ways in which people are connected to their localities has not escaped the attention of researchers who study the radical right. As noted above, some existing work investigates the effects of social capital on radical right support. Social capital refers to the intangible public goods that stem from citizen participation in social and civic life. Joining organizations, attending church, spending time with neighbors, and playing on local sports teams are aspects of many people's locally oriented activities. These activities are generally expected to promote pro-democratic values and minimize the draw of radical right and other extremist groups. Yet an alternative interpretation of the role of social capital in shaping the fortunes of such parties asserts that the social bonding that occurs in tight-knit communities can engender defensive and extremist political behavior. Research on the electoral impacts of such behaviors has not yet achieved consensus as to whether and how local ties relate to radicalism.

I contend that some of the murkiness in this area of research stems from the profound differences between the psychological and sociological dimensions of local engagement as they relate to voter behavior. In my analysis I distinguish these two aspects of local ties and consider them separately and in interaction with each other. I find that the positive feelings people have toward their communities – on the one hand – and their actual participation in community life – on the other – have divergent implications for radical right voting. This demonstrates quite clearly that not all local ties are alike.

I use the term "localists" to describe those who *feel* strongly tied to their local communities. Having very positive sentiments toward the locality and the people in it can make the radical right appealing. In contrast, routine engagement in community life wards off the appeals of these parties; when people invest their time and energy into participating in civil society and neighborhood life, the radical right is not so enticing an option. Moreover, it is feelings of attachment *net* the actual routine social interaction that benefits radical right parties. When people avoid routine social and organizational activity, but still feel very positively tied to their local communities, they are powerfully primed to consider radical right programs alluring.

Communities can be similarly characterized according to how cohesive they are in the aggregate and according to their levels of associational dynamism. These patterns parallel those at the individual level with the most cohesive communities, characterized by strong feelings of solidarity among residents, turning out at higher rates to support the radical right. In contrast, in the most associational communities, with vibrant civil societies, one finds the opposite.

I also find that neighborly relations have similarly distinct psychological and sociological components that relate differently to radical right support. On the psychological side, feeling positive about your neighbors and feeling willing to help them out with things are associated with support for the radical right. Alternatively, social patterns such as routinely spending time with your neighbors and routinely helping them out with things do not have this radicalizing effect. This distinction between the social dimensions of local participation and the psychological dimensions of imagining oneself as a member of a particular local community is important for understanding how local ties relate to the radical right and to political behavior more generally. By separating the two theoretically and empirically, I adjudicate between theories that would predict positive implications of community engagement for healthy democratic systems and those that would predict more undesirable consequences.

Who Are the Localists That Vote Radical Right? Gender and Left-leaning Ideology

Local attachments' radicalizing effects are especially powerful among certain subsets of citizens. These tend to be the kinds of voters who are not captured by existing theories of radical right support. Consider the motivations underpinning the female radical right vote. As described above, one personal feature that is highly predictive of a vote for such a party is gender. Men are more likely to support these parties than are women. What's interesting is that this trait seems to matter for the radical right vote independent of a long list of characteristics that tend to be associated with gender (such as issue positions and employment type). Even when researchers account for factors such as these, women are still statistically less likely to vote for radical right parties.

The confounding gendered dimension of radical right support suggests that women may approach the decision to vote for one of these parties differently than men. In other words, the difference in far-right-wing voter patterns distinguishing most women from most men is not simply quantitative in nature, but also qualitative. I find that women are particularly likely to be motivated to sympathize with and support the radical right based on their feelings of local attachments: the influence of local ties on radical right support is particularly visible for women. This finding addresses a lingering area of uncertainty in the literature on radical right support; it also underscores the importance of identifying different kinds of motivational pathways to particular electoral choices.

Another puzzling new constituency of radical right supporters is comprised of individuals who traditionally vote for left-wing parties. Voters who line up ideologically with far right parties should vote for those parties; the logic is straightforward. If we want to understand a radical right vote choice among far right ideologues, we should step back and examine the origins of their issue positions. In contrast, increasing numbers of people who skew left in terms of politics choose to vote for radical right parties, and this electoral decision begs explanation. To make sense of this choice, I consider whether these left-leaning, far-right-voting people feel closely tied to their local communities. It turns out that they do. Those individuals who situate themselves ideologically in the center or left of center are particularly likely to take a localist pathway to radical right support. With these conditional aspects of my analysis, I can account for some of the more perplexing dimensions of the radical right vote.

Under What Conditions Is Localism Most Politically Potent? Examining Political Salience

In different social and political contexts, certain aspects of people's group attachments can become triggered and made relevant. When a particular aspect of one's identity becomes politically salient, it can shape political behavior, such as vote choice. In the literature on voting we have much to learn about when and for whom a certain identity component will open a pathway to a particular partisan choice.

Social psychological research has shown the flexibility of different aspects of an individual's sense of self across different social arenas. Decades ago Leon Festinger, in asking about the conditions under which feelings of group belonging shape voting, put this issue on the scholarly agenda:

It has been emphasized many times by psychologists, sociologists, and anthropologists that the feeling of belonging to groups is an important determinant of the behavior of individuals in our culture. Most people would agree about the importance of group membership in the life of individuals. People join clubs, are proud of their country, are proud of their city, feel themselves identified with various groups or classes of people ... An individual's behavior or the behavior of a group is not equally influenced by group belongingness or group identification in all activities. Sometimes an individual's behavior seems to be very strongly influenced by a particular group belongingness (e.g., being a Catholic) while at other times this behavior determinant seems to be relatively absent. Likewise, sometimes individuals react towards each other with or without reference to a particular group belongingness of theirs (e.g., that a person is or is not Jewish). An understanding of the factors which affect the degree to which we are influenced by group belongingness in various situations seems to be extremely important for an understanding of the whole question (1947: 155).

In line with Festinger's questioning, some exciting research from political science demonstrates the role of political entrepreneurs in raising the salience of particular forms of belonging in their efforts to attract votes (e.g. Posner 2004). Studies of media content contribute to our understanding of issue salience as it relates to the radical right broadly and immigration attitudes in particular (Lubbers and Scheepers 2001, Schlueter and Davidov 2013). Yet these top-down approaches do not explain why certain people at certain times would be influenced by such appeals or information channels while others would not.

Toward a more comprehensive understanding of political salience of certain social identifications, I find that the radical right does best where the locality is politically salient. This local salience is enhanced by electoral institutions and state structures.[14] The positive link between strong community attachments and radical right support that I identify is most powerful where local elections are proximal to national elections, local elections result in locally chosen governing officials, local units have significant authority, and local units have recently forfeited authority. I find that these electoral and state institutions – which vary over time, across countries, and even within countries – shape the relevance of local belonging for national political contests. In developing this aspect of my argument, I supply an institutional explanation to account for the varying fortunes of extremist parties. Importantly, the institutional changes on which I focus are ongoing across democratic countries with little understanding of their effects on citizens' voting habits. Through the development of the localist theory of radical right support, I illuminate conditions under which

---

[14] Local salience is defined as the political relevance of the locality. A context characterized by high local salience is one in which locally rooted considerations are of import for politics. In such a situation, people draw on their feelings and thoughts about their local communities when they make political judgments and choices. For instance, an electoral context with a high level of local salience is one in which voters approach their partisan selections as members of their local communities. This factor, I find, moderates the relationship between local attachments and radical right party support. I develop this concept in Chapters 5, 6, and 7. Local salience's conditioning effects are illustrated in Chapters 5 and 6; its direct effects on radical right electoral support are shown in Chapter 7.

certain aspects of a person's identity become relevant for his or her electoral choices.

This book supplies an analysis that is sensitive to the intimate sphere of the local community as it informs a person's sense of self. By connecting the value of local attachments to radical right party support I provide an explanation of this major trend in modern politics that can account for portions of variation across individuals, over time, and across space.

THE PLAN OF THE BOOK

Why do some people support radical right parties while others do not? Why do some communities host higher levels of support for these parties than other communities? Why do they fare better in some countries than in others? What explains the timing of shifts in support for these parties? These are the questions that motivate the analysis. For cases, I draw on data from across Europe, and where the data are available I integrate other advanced democracies from North America and Oceania. Specific countries of intense interest are Switzerland and France. For evidence I assemble a range of datasets to compare individuals, communities, and countries. I am also sensitive to the timing of radical right support at each level of analysis; panel survey data and time series cross-sectional data permit examination of dynamic patterns in party preferences of individuals and electoral support levels at various levels of aggregation. The evidence comes from a wide variety of sources such as surveys, censuses, and electoral results. I also leverage previously assembled comparative datasets such as the Database of Comparative Institutions and the Comparative Manifestos Project database, and I use information that I collected myself, including details of local life that I learned during field work in southwestern France. I conclude this introduction with a summary of each coming chapter.

Chapter 2 develops the localist account of radical right support. I first assemble theories of voter behavior and social psychology to motivate the conceptualization of a voter who is rooted in social groupings but also relatively flexible in his electoral choices. From there I construct the theoretical case for localism, grounding it in insights from existing work. This structures my theorizing on people's ties to their local communities as a source of radical right support. Specifically, I describe and consider the competing expectations derived from two distinct analytical approaches. Theories rooted in the mass society tradition and reinforced by the mainstream social capital literature predict that local connections will diminish right-wing radicalism. In contrast, theories developed in social psychology and buttressed by dark-side social capital accounts portend such ties to enhance the appeal of radical right parties. I discuss the fundamental tension between these competing accounts, but I also identify complementarity. Each is useful in making sense of the ways that social engagement – broadly defined – relates to radicalism.

In this chapter I also establish a framework for studying the question of political salience: under what conditions will local attachments be particularly relevant for right-wing electoral politics? Research by comparative politics scholars and social psychologists supplies the basis for my construction of a theory of local political salience. Local ties are most politically relevant when and where the locality has significant authority and autonomy, when and where the locality has recently lost substantial power, and when and where local elections are temporally proximal to national elections. In this chapter I also devote attention to questions of national identifications as they relate to the radical right.

Chapter 3 is the first empirical chapter. It outlines competing explanations of radical right support, notably the modernization losers thesis that underscores the import of vulnerable socio-economic status as well as attitudinal theories that emphasize specific views on high-profile issues. I also fold into the discussion institutional theories that prioritize the role of countries' political structures, such as the nature of electoral competition, and contextual theories on the role of immigrant presence and unemployment. I then test these hypotheses against the prediction that local attachment motivates radical right support, as described in Chapter 2. Using European Values Study data from twenty European countries in conjunction with the Swiss Selects survey, the Swiss Household Panel survey, and the French Political Barometer, I model support for the radical right via simple logit models and hierarchical logit models. I find that there is a positive correlation between local attachment and radical right support. This result comports with the expectations from social psychology. Yet in line with mass society theories I also find that people who participate in associations of civil society are less supportive of the radical right on average. These results highlight the different ways that social engagement relates to far right vote choice. I also draw on these surveys to provide a broader sense of what it means to be a localist; it involves feeling like one belongs to the local area, identification with the local community, and preference for local political authority.

Chapter 4 takes a closer look at who these locally oriented radical right voters are. For which individuals is localism a likely motivator of radical right support? Using the European Values Study and the Swiss Selects survey, I provide the results of a series of interaction models. I find that localism is most predictive of radical right support among those individuals for whom standard explanations of this phenomenon fall short. Namely, women and political centrists and leftists are those most likely to take a localist path to radical right support. Frustration with immigrants does not enhance the connection between local ties and radical right support, but distrust of the European Union does. The theme of neighboring also arises in this chapter: locally tied individuals who also feel like they would help their neighbors if asked are especially likely to support the radical right. In contrast, those localists who actually *do* help their neighbors on a routine basis are especially *un*likely to support the radical right. This pair of results emphasizes the competing dimensions of social engagement in terms of how they relate to radical right support: feelings of closeness promote such voting proclivities while actual interactions and aid counter this force. These findings help to refine the localist model of radical right support. They also signal that the locally rooted account represents a novel pathway to the radical right, helping to explain why certain unlikely far right supporters find their way to these parties.

Chapter 5 offers a closer inspection of neighborly ties as they relate to radical right voting. What kinds of neighboring patterns promote far right support? Using Swiss Household Panel survey data, individuals' preferences for the Swiss People's Party (SVP) are modeled over twelve years. Annual surveys make it possible to trace affinities for all the major Swiss parties, comparing their over-time trends and predictors. From year to year, strong ties to neighbors make the SVP more appealing (and they do not boost support for any other major party). Memberships in organizations, in contrast, diminish the appeal of these parties.

This chapter also provides a nuanced investigation into the political implications of neighborly ties, disaggregating affect toward neighbors from interactions with them. The dimensions of neighboring that drive SVP support are: feeling on good terms with a large number of neighbors and getting emotional support from neighbors. The dimensions of neighboring with no independent effects are: frequency of spending time with neighbors and getting practical support from neighbors.

Models including context-specific interactions also demonstrate that neighboring is most potent for fueling radicalism in the types of communities that host the most local cohesion among residents. This chapter also considers the institutional factors that make neighboring – and hence local ties – especially salient for voting in national elections. I find that the positive neighboring-SVP link is strongest in areas where the localities are electorally empowered (meaning they elect their own local legislatures) and in areas where localities have recently lost independent authority through municipal fusions. This introduces the theme of salience to the empirical analysis. There is nothing obviously political about neighborly ties, but certain institutional features and shifts can enhance their relevance for electoral contests.

Chapter 6 picks up on the themes of local political salience and the importance of local cohesion for extreme right support. This is a case study of the 2002 French presidential election in which Jean-Marie Le Pen (in)famously advanced to the second round, beating out the Socialist Party candidate to get there. This was also the election in which Le Pen's support began to grow in rural areas in contrast to the post-industrial centers that had until then fueled his electoral successes. By leveraging data on Le Pen support in the previous presidential election, I model changes in his popularity over time by commune. What explains extreme right support at the sub-national level in France? Looking across French municipalities (called communes), with a special emphasis on the southwestern Aquitaine region, I examine the predictors of Le Pen support rates. This chapter shows that deeply cohesive communes host high levels of Le Pen support while localities with many associations are less supportive.

I also find that Le Pen benefitted from the process of intercommunality, through which certain powers are reallocated from individual communes to intercommunal councils that make binding decisions for communal members. Communes grouped into these larger collectivities since the previous presidential election saw higher (increased) support for Le Pen. This effect is particularly strong among communes high on a scale of local cohesion, reinforcing confidence that this result is about communal ties. Furthermore, communes that recently lost authority to intercommunal councils were particularly drawn to Le Pen if there was also a relatively sizeable foreign-born local population. These findings signal that radical right support is rooted in local pride and motivated by frustration with profound changes in local life and diminishing communal status.

Chapter 7 further explores and expands the notion of local political salience. I ask: what explains variation in extreme right electoral success rates across countries and over time? Comparing thirty OECD countries over thirty-plus years, I test the thesis that radical right support levels in national legislative elections are correlated with certain institutional features of a country's localities. I find that radical right parties do best where and when local elections are proximal to national elections. These results are robust to controls for other institutional and societal predictors that alternative accounts emphasize. Furthermore, where and when localities are especially independent (in terms of electing their own community leaders, controlling purse strings, and making policy), the radical right does best. These results underscore the importance of the local arena for radical right politics. I also show that these salience-boosting characteristics of localities are becoming more common over time as national governments devolve power to sub-national authorities. This suggests that the locally rooted trends I identify are likely to persist and strengthen in the future.

Chapter 8 summarizes the findings of the book and considers some large-scale and more defined transformations that have shaped today's social and electoral arenas. In devoting attention to such trends, which are associated with things such as patterns of socializing and news consumption, local authority shifts, electoral timing, and information included on cars' license plates, I point to areas for future research illuminated by my study. In doing so, I also propose a localist interpretation of the 2016 "Brexit" referendum in which UK citizens voted to leave the European Union, and I comment on the applicability of the localist theory to the vote for Donald Trump in the 2016 US presidential election. More broadly, I advocate for studies that take seriously themes such as place, change, and status for understanding electoral behavior.

While the focus of this book is on the radical right and its connection to localism, I also supply insights into a series of more expansive, critical areas of political behavior. These include:

- why people support the political parties they do,
- the implications of strong (local) identities for electoral behavior and outcomes,
- the conditions under which certain aspects of identity become politically relevant, and
- how political devolution and other shifts in authority structures shape political behavior.

2

Theorizing Localism and Radical Right Support

In this chapter I present the theoretical framework for my argument. I integrate literature on themes such as social identity, mass society, social capital, political salience, and state structures to construct a foundation for empirical inquiry, drawing from a range of disciplines such as political science, sociology, psychology, and geography. The localist theory I develop is one that connects people's community ties to the electoral choices they make. I start by outlining competing perspectives on voter behavior; I then draw attention to the local dimension of electoral choice. This sets up the theoretical debate over the impact of community and social ties on radical right support and my argument for a disaggregated examination of local ties. Finally, I develop an approach for studying the political salience of local (and conceivably other) attachments.

STABILITY AND CHANGE IN VOTER BEHAVIOR

Today's electoral disorder – the rise of outsider parties and the decline of mainstream parties – prompts scholars to revisit some central theories of voter behavior. This gives us an opportunity to consider how useful the dominant models are for explaining recent trends. In light of modern developments, it makes sense to think about different theories of voter motivations in terms of how well they are able to account for stability and change over time. The two main sets of theories of voter behavior are: (1) structural in nature and (2) individual-based. These two approaches offer distinct interpretations of the ways regular people relate to the political realm.

Structural theories emphasize the importance of social groups. Class, religion, neighborhood, and family have traditionally served as the structural building blocks of advanced democratic societies. When participating in an election, an individual uses his or her social position(s) as a point of departure.

One's political profile, so to speak, is shaped by the interests, identities, and values of the group or groups to which one belongs.[1] Per this understanding, certain social positions render electoral choice rather predictable. This interpretation of political behavior aligns with the longtime stability of party systems – "frozen" as Lipset and Rokkan (1967) observed – which reflected the social and political reality of inter- and post-war decades. This process has traditionally translated to large vote shares for the mainstream center-left, for instance, on the part of working-class citizens, and center-right parties that benefit from wealthier and more religious constituencies. As such, we tend to think about structural accounts as having the greatest purchase on vote choice in times of relative political stability. Generally speaking, they predict support for established, moderate parties.

The main alternative approach to explaining voter behavior focuses less on social collectivities and more on individuals. People's characteristics, such as education level, gender, and attitudinal configuration, are the key factors expected to predict their vote choice. Whether these studies are driven by economic (Downs 1957) or psychological (Inglehart 1997) interpretations of human motivation, they depict a free-standing and free-wheeling electoral participant. Voters make electoral decisions relatively independently, using their own set of considerations when choosing to vote for particular parties or candidates.[2] These theories seem better suited than structural narratives to explaining unconventional voting behavior and electoral instability over time. A voter unfettered by strong social group influences is likely to engage in electoral choices that do not conform to the ordered expectations described above. As such, when seeking to explain support for new, extremist parties, scholars typically turn in this individualistic direction for theoretical guidance.

If it is true that social structures account for stability while individuals' traits, calculations, and feelings are crucial for explaining change, then structural theories are not well equipped to account for the increasing popularity of radical right parties. Indeed, one reason that social structure is not such a common consideration in work on radical right support is that these parties tend to attract voters from all of the social groups that we typically think of as politically relevant (Betz 1993, Zaslove 2004).

Structural theories of voter behavior are also challenged by the abundant evidence that the social groupings that once shaped electoral choice are becoming less prominent in society. The declining impact of social class, for instance, has been well documented (e.g. Sarlvik and Crewe 1983).[3] One could reasonably argue that if traditional social structures were still such dominant forces in people's lives, we would not have the kind of electoral upheaval we

---

[1] See, for instance, Berelson et al. (1954), Zuckerman et al. (1994).
[2] See also Dalton (1984), Franklin et al. (1992).
[3] Though other work reminds us not to fully discount the influence of these structures (Elff 2007, Botterman and Hooghe 2012).

see today. The core logic of such an account is that people are less connected to each other than they once were, and this unmooring results in new voting trends. What matters more than social group membership, many contend, are specific attitudes (about immigration, about the EU) and individuals' reactions to economic strains that stem from large-scale, global processes.

Yet some recent research on radical right support signals the potential of social structure to account for shifting electoral tides. On the subject of class, many workers still approach the voting booth as members of the working class, but now they select radical right parties that promise to protect their jobs and way of life (Kitschelt, with McGann 1995) and that appeal to their collectivist mentality. On the matter of religious groups, many Christians are still guided by their religion in their vote choice, but now they vote for the radical right due to its tough rhetoric on Islam out of concern for the challenge it poses to a Christian community. This choice takes the place of traditional votes among the religious for mainstream confessional parties of the center-right (Immerzeel et al. 2013). In relation to the family, intergenerational influence – considered a bulwark of electoral stability – still happens. But when it comes to radical right and other rising parties, influence flows from the younger generation to their parents (Fitzgerald 2011). These findings call for refinement of how we expect structural theories to relate to radical right support and electoral change more broadly.

To understand democratic electoral behavior in times of flux, it makes sense to appreciate the virtues of both the structural and the individual approaches. The strength of structural theories lay in their recognition of the embeddedness of the human experience. The benefit of individual theories is that they attribute a high level of agency to voters. Because we know that both observations reflect reality, it is important that we draw upon both in our theorizing. As of late, individualistic accounts of electoral choices take center stage. This limits the progress scholars can make in explaining large-scale shifts in voter behavior. To better understand electoral disorder as a social phenomenon, structural theories with more dynamism are necessary.

I propose that to accomplish this, we stand to benefit from thinking differently about what belonging looks like in today's world. It makes sense, given Europe's complex social landscape, to broaden in our analyses the set of politically relevant groupings to which people can belong. I identify the locality – or small-scale community – as a crucial collectivity that serves as the basis for radical right support. Over time the locality has risen in importance, particularly for individuals who feel disoriented in a globalizing world. This sense of local belonging has unidentified political consequences, and this restricts our comprehension of large-scale political developments.

I contribute to our understanding of voter behavior by developing a perspective that is structured but also fluid. Individuals feel more or less rooted in and attached to their local communities, these communities host varying levels of local attachment, and the political salience of localities varies across space and time. Through a localist account of radical right support, I connect these stable and dynamic themes to people's electoral choices.

I also submit that behavioral theorizing would benefit from greater sensitivity to the distinctions between actual connections among citizens and the emotional or mental connections individuals have with particular places and social collectivities. This means distinguishing interpersonal engagement from emotional ties to social groups. Another way to put this is that our understanding of sociological membership should always be clearly distinct from psychological membership in conceptual and empirical terms. Routine, face-to-face engagement with others and participation in social organizations are well-studied phenomena; we have learned a great deal about their political implications. But feelings of connections to neighbors and identification with local communities are less understood. Unfortunately, the two concepts are sometimes collapsed into one in academic treatment of social engagement and social ties. This leads to confusion and limits our knowledge of the political implications of belonging.

We can also improve our understanding of processes through which certain group memberships become more or less politically salient. For which kinds of individuals and under which conditions are particular feelings of belonging relevant for electoral choices? This is an area of inquiry that stands to be significantly expanded. Some would argue that political parties cue certain aspects of voters' group identifications when stumping for votes. While this may be true, there are structural factors that have less visible implications. Here I identify several ways that foundational state and electoral institutions (such as decentralization of authority and electoral timing) make local attachments particularly salient for politics. My exploration of local political salience delivers an account of the radical right's unsteady electoral march across space and over time.

Altogether this study pushes past the dominant accounts of radical right support that conceptualize individuals as free-floating and unrooted. I demonstrate that changes in community life have occurred in past decades, and I consider the ways life is lived at the local level. Moving in the direction of locally embedded individualism yields deeper understanding of a more rooted voter than most individual theories conceptualize. But we also dislodge the individual from an overly static conceptualization of group-based belonging.

I offer an explanation of radical right support that emphasizes embedded micro-level processes. Individuals make up their own minds about political parties, often changing their partisan preferences from one year to the next. But the individual is characterized by his or her level of connection to the local community and these connections are conceptualized in careful terms.[4] My research identifies a likely radical right supporter as a lover of her community

---

[4] I follow those who paved the way for this kind of work. Notably, Alan Zuckerman established a high standard for theorizing a democratic citizen whose partisan choices are shaped but not fully determined by his or her social environment (see, for instance, Zuckerman 2005). Zuckerman's

who is not socially engaged with organizations or neighbors. Furthermore, in different places at different times, community ties are more or less salient for politics. This account integrates insights from structural and individual theories, and it identifies patterns that show how group belonging operates in dynamic fashion.

THE LOCAL COMMUNITY AND EXTREMISM

Research from a range of disciplines signals that the local arena is a particularly influential one for politics. Studies of political behavior demonstrate that neighborhoods and other small-scale social aggregations host distinctive patterns of voting and other kinds of political participation (Johnston 1972, Morgenstern and Swindle 2005). Electoral geography in many ways paved the way for these insights, developing an early understanding of how space and politics are connected (see Cox 1969, Agnew 1987, Pattie and Johnston 2000, Johnston and Pattie 2006). As place relates to the far right, electoral geographers were among the first to identify the distinct spatial patterns of voting in inter-war Germany. O'Loughlin et al. (1994) examine the electoral rise of Hitler's NSDAP in the 1930s, finding that diverse local contexts (and broader regional ones) host varying rates of Nazi support.

Radical right party support in the modern era is also highly variable by locality. As Golder notes in a recent review article:

Most studies of far right support focus on the national level … [yet] national-level support for the far right hides significant subnational variation. Across constituencies, far right support ranges from 4.97% to 31.50% in France, 0% to 44% in the United Kingdom, and 0.30% to 5.08% in Germany. Similar or higher levels of variation are seen within constituencies … [Some] randomly selected constituencies indicate that far right support ranges from 0.07% to 32.12% in Kettering, 0% to 50% in the third constituency of Aude, and 1% to 3.5% in Odenwald-Tauber. This variation is incredibly local. The median area of a commune in France is just 4.14 square miles, and there are communes in our chosen constituency with 0% far right support bordering communes with more than 25% far right support. This localized variation raises questions about what is being captured by national measures of far right support and about the usefulness of theories that focus solely on national-level, or even regional-level, characteristics. (2016: 491)

Golder (2016) also notes that factors often expected to account for variation in radical right party support – such as electoral institutions, quality of candidates, and inter-party dynamics – cannot explain local-level variation, at least in French presidential elections.[5] Additional political science research demonstrates that radical right electoral support varies by locality in a

---

careful scholarship develops a probabilistic understanding of the ways social groups influence a person's partisan choices.
[5] I return in Chapter 6 to the sub-national French electoral puzzle that Golder spotlights.

range of countries such as Sweden (Rydgren and Ruth 2011), the Netherlands (Berning and Ziller 2017), Belgium (Poznyak et al. 2011), France (Schain et al. 2002), and Switzerland (Fitzgerald and Lawrence 2011).

Furthermore, numerous studies point to the local dimension of radical right appeals. Many radical right parties grew out of particular local arenas (see Bréchon and Mitra 1992, Eatwell 2000, Goodwin 2012). The French National Front benefitted from early local successes in Dreux, Marignane, Vitrolles, Orange, and Toulon (Hainsworth 2000). The Belgian Vlaams Blok built on electoral support in Antwerp (Swyngedouw 2000); the Swiss People's Party took off electorally in the city of Zürich. Case studies detail movements with slogans such as "Toulon for the Toulonnais" by France's National Front (Veugelers 2012) and "Vienna for the Viennese" by Austria's FPÖ (Morrow 2000).

There is also a radical right policy dimension that complements voters' local affinities. Many of these parties advocate devolution of powers to sub-national governments. One example of this is the Lega Nord (LN) in Italy, which is founded on a sub-national platform that distinguishes the north from the south and exalts the local community. The LN, according to Zaslove, paints the "local as ideology: an autochthonous civil society ... The Lega embraces the local as good and morally pure, claiming that this purity has been corrupted and colonized by the state and its allies" (2011: 98). The party also stokes fears that globalization and immigration will ultimately destroy local cultures and local identities (2011: 121, 140).[6] The LN is not alone in the use of such an approach. Radical right parties often campaign for limiting the powers of states in general (Carter 2005: Ch. 2) and empowering sub-national governmental units (Ennser 2012).[7]

This emphasis on the sub-national and often – more specifically – the local dovetails with a strong strain of anti-elite, anti-mainstream, anti-system rhetoric employed by radical right parties. Studies by Ignazi (2003), Zaslove (2011), and others demonstrate the adoption of such themes in party appeals. These dynamics may signal a resurgence of center-periphery cleavages that in the past have proved to be highly politically salient (Lipset and Rokkan 1967, Inglehart 1977). Some scholars have observed the rise of the center-periphery divide relative to other cleavages such as the left-right ideological divide (Alonso 2012).[8] Clearly, "peripheral" does not equate solely to "local," but the

---

[6] Local identifications are also key to LN support. As compared to supporters of other right-of-center Italian parties, LN voters are the most closely tied to their towns (but not necessarily their regions) (Bulli and Tronconi 2012: 81).

[7] Zaslove (2011) observes that the Lega Nord in Italy emphasized such a theme during an anti-tax protest in the 1990s. The party urged that "Citizens [northerners] should either simply not pay their taxes or else pay them to the local municipal government" (2011: 135).

[8] According to Alonso, "During the 1990s, centre-periphery issues became more relevant again while the saliency of left-right issues in peripheral parties' manifestos dropped from 37 per cent in the 1980s to 27 per cent during the 1990s, an indication of pro-periphery radicalization as well as of diversification into new issues such as the environment and valence issues such as

growth of a rift between national and sub-national elements sets the stage for local attachments to become increasingly politically potent. They thus become better fodder for the appeals of radical right groups with anti-mainstream, anti-system platforms.

With respect to the role of people's local ties in shaping their likelihood of supporting a radical right party, the evidence points in two different directions. One line of analysis signals that those who are particularly connected to their localities should find these parties appealing. So, too, should communities characterized by strong local ties. Alternatively, there is another vein of research that suggests local ties predispose people to fend off the appeals of radicals. Here, I present these two streams of literature and consider their relationship.

Socio-psychological Perspective: Local Ties Strengthen Radical Right Politics

There is good reason, corroborated by good research, to expect that local attachments can invigorate political extremism on the right. The more closely tied people are to their communities, the more they will want to defend them. Forces such as Europeanization, market liberalization, and immigration are processes that can heighten defensiveness of the local. Radical right parties – which campaign on combatting these trends – offer much to the citizen who approaches electoral politics from the position of a community member.

The idea that local ties underpin support for radical right parties finds theoretical grounding in social psychology and environmental psychology. From social psychology come the insights that a sense of belonging is key to deriving positive self-esteem (Turner et al. 1994) and that identification is especially important when a person feels threatened (Ethier et al. 1994). Notably, Social Identity Theory posits that individuals by nature situate themselves psychologically within social groups, and they derive self-esteem from the social status of such groups (Tajfel and Turner 1979, Tajfel 1981, Turner et al. 1994). For purposes of dignity, distinctiveness, and pride, individuals self-categorize into various social collectivities.

Complementary predictions specific to the power of local belonging can be derived from Place-Identity Theory (Proshansky 1978, Low and Altman 1992), developed by social psychologists and environmental pyschologists. Place identity is the aspect of a person's self-conception that is defined by the environment in which he or she lives. It tends to be associated with physical surroundings (Proshansky et al. 1983), which are understood as backdrops for people's experiences, conceptions, and memories. Per this theory, places are imbued with deeply symbolic meanings; people can form strong emotional

government efficiency ... The saliency levels reached during the 1990s remained mainly constant well into the 2000s with a slight decrease of the left-right issues to 26 per cent and a slight increase of the centre-periphery issues to 19 per cent" (2012: 210). As one cleavage and its constituent groups decline in importance, one or more takes its place.

attachments to specific locations. Place identity sits alongside other aspects of self-categorization such as social class and partisanship. Yet political science has not devoted as much attention to this kind of belonging. Exceptions include Kathy Cramer's study that establishes place (rural communities in Wisconsin) as a starting point for making sense of politics (Walsh 2012, Cramer 2016) and Cara Wong's exploration of the role that place plays in shaping Americans' political attitudes (Wong 2010).

Scholars who identify a dark side to social capital (Portes and Landolt 1996, Maloney et al. 2000, Chambers and Kopstein, 2001) provide more direct support for the expectation that feeling attached to a particular locality motivates radical right support. Community engagement can yield exclusionary attitudes that are compatible with the goals of radical right movements which seek to undo key features of the modernization process and usher life back to a better, simpler time. Specifically, through bonding social capital, individuals who are closely connected to their local communities can translate this attachment into an exclusionary mindset (Putnam 2000). From this theorizing comes a prediction that those who feel tied to their communities are particularly likely to support radical right parties.

Empirical evidence points in this direction: areas with the most social cohesion are often times the places where radical right support is greatest. Looking back to the rise of the Nazi party in inter-war Germany, Hamilton (1982) argues that the most cohesive communities voted at the highest rates for the Nazis. Allen's (1965) classic case study of the Nazi rise in Nordheim and Satyanath et al.'s (2013) comparison of 100 German towns identify the ways that social ties were useful vehicles for expanding NSDAP support. Examining Swiss municipalities in more recent times, Duncan Lawrence and I find that local social cohesion has significant (positive) contextual effects on the likelihood of an individual supporting the Swiss People's Party and on the level of support that party receives in a particular area (Fitzgerald and Lawrence 2011).

Socio-structural Perspective: Local Ties Weaken Radical Right Politics

Distinct from the political psychology point of view, there is a socio-structural perspective on the link between community engagement and radical right support. This account is rooted mainly in mass society theory and posits that local ties *reduce* the appeal of radical parties. From this direction, the rise of the radical right can be blamed on the erosion of social connections among citizens.

Social theory is rich with accounts of the ways that traditional community bonds have disintegrated on the path to modernity. Tönnies (1887), Weber (1922), and Parsons (1968) examine the distinctions between traditional community rooted in close, interpersonal ties and modern society in which social connections are less habitual and less intimate and in which life is lived on more individualistic terms. As classical community bonds have weakened over time, fluid, anomic societies have emerged as context of much human existence. Isolation and anomie are core concepts in this literature (Durkheim 1897), as is their attitudinal correlate, loneliness (Wirth 1938). People these days are on average less connected to one another (Lane 2000). They are less likely to get together with their neighbors (Putnam 2000), they are less trusting of others (Fukuyama 1999), and they are more inclined to prioritize the practical over the moral (Redfield 1960) than are those who lived in previous eras.

Similarly, people's lives are less structured by critical social institutions than they once were. As noted above, churches with empty pews want for members, unions are in decline, and mainstream political parties do not hold the social position they once did (Katz and Mair 1995). Just as neighborhoods and communities fail to knit individuals into a collective social fabric, the decline of societal institutions leaves people adrift in society. This is the narrative of mass society theorists such as Kornhauser, who connect these atomizing trends to the rise of extremist groups in society. Because they are less insulated from the mobilizing efforts of radical elites, today's citizens are especially vulnerable to the predatory efforts of far-right political entrepreneurs. The connection to a local community should render an individual less disposed to radicalism, not more.

This social disintegration hypothesis receives support among academics who study the extremism that exploded in the first half of the twentieth century (Arendt 1951, Kornhauser 1960). More recently, others find empirical evidence connecting weak societal integration to support for today's radical right parties (Falter and Schumann 1988, Mayer and Perrineau 1992, Van der Brug and Fennema 2007). For instance, in Belgium, Vlaams Blok/Vlaams Belang support is highest among those who feel socially isolated (Billiet and De Witte 1995), for those with few close friends (Vanhoutte and Hooghe 2013, Rydgren 2009), and for those who reside in localities with relatively weak associational networks (Coffé et al. 2007).[9] Based on these works, one can hypothesize that individuals who are least connected to society through social ties and institutional structures are especially likely to support radical right parties. In aggregate terms, one can expect that areas with less social cohesion[10] and weaker institutional structures are especially likely to host support for these parties.

---

[9] Others find no evidence of such a relationship between social (dis)integration and radical right support (Rydgren 2011, Werts et al. 2013), while Berning and Ziller (2017) find that social trust at the individual and neighborhood levels weakens the appeal of radical right parties.

[10] Social cohesion is a multifaceted concept (see Botterman et al. 2012). From sociology we get the understanding that a social collectivity is characterized by high structural social cohesion when members are interconnected: "A collectivity is structurally cohesive to the extent that the social relations of its members hold it together" (Moody and White 2003: 106). A broader, related concept is social solidarity, which includes structural cohesion along with a subjective sense of community (Puddifoot 1996). In this book, I use the terms "local cohesion" and "local solidarity" interchangeably. Disaggregating this community-level concept is beyond the present

Social capital has a role to play on this side of the theoretical divide, as well. Upbeat versions of the social capital narrative support the logic that local ties should minimize radical right support. Social engagement is found to promote pro-democratic, trusting, tolerant values (Putnam 1993, Brehm and Rahn 1997, Cigler and Joslyn 2002, Hooghe 2003, Li et al. 2005, Keele 2007). Logically, then, these values should diminish the appeal of radical right political programs, which pursue goals that conflict with such norms.

Integrated Approach: The Dynamics of Belonging

The socio-psychological narrative charges community ties with fueling the rise of radical right parties. The socio-structural account credits community ties with weakening the appeal of these same parties. One interpretation of this theoretical pairing is that the predictions derived from these accounts contradict one another. Along these lines, my study ultimately weighs in on the debate over which account better captures the effects of community ties. On balance, the socio-psychological account of locally rooted radical right support receives the most consistent support in the chapters that follow.

However, a more nuanced read of these theoretical approaches yields a sense of complementarity between the two. *Feeling* connected to the locality is the emphasis in the psychological perspective; *being* socially connected to the local community is the emphasis in the structural account. In other words, local attachment and local pride represent attitudinal ties to the locality while organizational participation and routine engagement in neighborhood networks represent behavioral ties to the locality. The former should boost political radicalism; the latter should undermine it. This distinction can also be drawn at the community level. Where residents feel the most connected through high levels of local pride, local unity, and positive orientations toward neighbors, there should be more radical right support. And where people are actively connected through networks and organizations, there should be less radical right support.

These different dimensions of local ties may be related, but they are also distinguishable. The basis for making such a distinction between how people feel and how they act comes from Richard LaPiere's (1934) foundational theorizing on the "attitude-behavior gap." LaPiere's personal observations and subsequent research revealed that people's attitudes did not always correspond to their patterns of behavior.[11] Immerzeel et al. (2013) find evidence in support of drawing these conceptual boundaries at the individual level: religiosity boosts

---

study due to data limitations. But from a theoretical standpoint I emphasize the affective, psychological dimensions of the concept.

[11] LaPiere (1934) was the first to demonstrate empirically that those with racially biased attitudes often did not act on those feelings when engaging with persons against whom they held negative views. See also Deutscher (1966).

the likelihood of a person supporting a radical right party while churchgoing weakens the radicals' appeal.

These distinctions between feelings and actions have also been made with respect to people's local attachments. Kasarda and Janowitz (1974) developed the concept of community attachment that is used by researchers today. They established three key components of community attachments: (1) a formal participatory dimension that denotes an individual's engagement in formal organizational life of the locality, (2) an interpersonal dimension that taps routine connections with other community residents, and (3) an affective sentiments dimension that represents people's feelings about the community. The first two dimensions are about actual participation in community life, while the third is strictly sentimental. Trentelman summarizes the relevant concept: "Community attachment ... considers connections between residents and their communities ... It is typically used as a measure of sentiment regarding the community one lives in and an indicator of one's rootedness to one's community" (2009: 201). Trentelman also distinguishes community attachment from place attachment, which are complementary concepts. She explains that to place scholars, the community is one of a number of possible social spaces to examine. To community sociologists, place attachment is one of a number of relevant relationships linking people to their communities (see Corcoran 2002). I find both concepts useful in the theorizing here.

By examining these two dimensions of community ties side-by-side, I establish how each relates to radical right party support and how they interact. In doing so I model the behavior of individuals in a way that is sensitive to the community embeddedness they feel and experience. In the end, both the socio-psychological and socio-structural accounts receive support in my analysis. The very specific nature of a theorized link between community attachment and political support for extremists requires consideration of local political salience, to which I now turn.

SALIENCE OF LOCAL IDENTITIES

Feeling connected to a local area is not necessarily relevant for politics to all people in all places. Plenty of people love their neighbors and their localities but this certainly does not perforce make them radicals. Therefore, I ask, under what conditions would community ties be especially relevant for electoral behavior? When would an individual draw on his or her feelings about the locality when deciding how to vote? What factors link the local to the political in people's minds? I rely primarily on two sets of literature to craft expectations about local political salience: from a range of psychology (sub) fields and from the political science federalism literature. Local attachments – not unlike attachments to groups defined by commonalities in social class or religion – rise and fall in political salience. Here I develop my argument on the factors that enhance local group salience: electoral institutions and authority structures.[12]

The Political Psychology of Salience

Local ties, community attachment, and rootedness are terms that connote feelings of connection to certain geo-social areas and their residents. They also typically go hand in hand with a sense of solidarity with other members of a particular community. Research from several disciplines signals that these collective attachments can be important for people's self-conceptions and self-esteem (Low and Altman 1992, Dixon and Durrheim 2000, Spinner-Haley and Theiss-Morse 2003). Social psychologists Simon and Klandermans itemize five basic needs addressed by feelings of group membership: belongingness, distinctiveness, respect, understanding, and agency (Simon and Klandermans 2001).[13] From environmental psychology comes the observation that place identities are strong emotional bonds that are important for the ways people think of themselves: "Individuals do indeed define who and what they are in terms of such strong affective ties to 'house and home' and/or neighborhood and community" (Proshansky et al. 1983: 61).

We also know from political science that collective identities can be important motivators of political engagement (Fowler and Kam 2007, Huddy and Khatib 2007, Dostie-Goulet et al. 2012). The behavioral implications of these kinds of politicized group identifications addressed in existing work relate to collective action and social movement participation and in some cases decisions to participate in elections. The central lesson learned from such research is that individuals who identify with social groups are especially likely to participate in collective action on behalf of those groups and that feelings of group cohesion serve as a resource for groups pursuing political objectives (Klandermans 2002).

---

[12] I argue elsewhere that national institutions shape the very definitions of the "political" that individuals hold (Fitzgerald 2013).

[13] Simon and Klandermans write: "... collective identity confirms that one belongs to a particular place in the social world. At the same time, it also affords distinctiveness from those other social places (or people) to which one does not belong. It further signals that one is like other people, though not necessarily like all other people, so that one can expect respect, at least from these similar others (which in turn is a necessary precondition for self-respect or self-esteem). Moreover, collective identity provides a meaningful perspective on the social world from which this world can be interpreted and understood. Finally, collective identity signals that one is not alone but can count on the social support and solidarity of other in-group members so that, as a group, one is a much more efficacious social agent ('Together we are strong!')" (2001: 321). The term "collective identity," they explain, is akin to the concept of social identity, but they prefer the former for purposes of theoretical precision and clarity.

Yet we simply do not know enough about the conditions under which certain dimensions of people's self-conceptions are activated and made salient in the political arena. To fill this lacuna in our knowledge we can draw on various disciplines' insights into the dynamics of different kinds of attachments and aspects of people's social identities. From social psychology comes knowledge about the kinds of social situations (for instance, finding one's self in the minority in some sense) that might prompt a particular identity aspect to become relevant to an individual (Taylor and Fiske 1978, Oakes 1987, Huddy 2001). From sociology we learn how people flexibly assume certain social roles when voicing opinions about politicized topics (Eliasoph 1998). And political psychology research underscores the import of group cohesion and the salience of group attachments for certain social identities to matter for politics (Huici et al. 1997, Huddy 2003, Wong 2010, Citrin and Sears 2014).

Similarly, there is work in a Marxist vein from political science on the role of group consciousness for motivating group behavior, particularly collective action. As Miller et al. explain,

Group identification connotes a perceived self-location within a particular social stratum, along with a psychological feeling of belonging to that particular stratum. Group consciousness, on the other hand, involves identification with a group and a political awareness or ideology regarding the group's relative position in society along with a commitment to collective action aimed at realizing the group's interests ... Clearly then there is no theoretical reason to expect a simple direct relationship between group identification and political participation. (1981: 495)

They argue that when people perceive their group to be downtrodden, they experience a sense of relative deprivation. It is this sense that their group's relatively low status is illegitimate that motivates collective behavior such as taking part in demonstrations or joining group-based organizations.[14] Miller et al. also note that "A sense of group consciousness may also vary from individual to individual, over time, and across strata, depending on the existing social conditions" (1981: 495). Through their theorizing they connect people's feelings of group belonging, which tend to be relatively stable over time, with the more uneven tendency toward political action.

The politicization of identities has also been explored in psychology. Lauren Duncan's work connects feelings of belonging with broader political developments and contexts. She develops the concept of "personal political salience," which she defines as the "overall propensity to attach personal meanings to social events" (Duncan and Stewart 2007: 145). Duncan and Stewart cite Crosby (1976) who identifies relative deprivation as an important ingredient in channeling group identity into political relevance and action. Furthermore, in a rare look into the development of a politicized group identity motivating far-right participation, Duncan and Stewart find through

---

[14] See also Gurr (1970) on the more violent implications of relative deprivation.

biographical research of a German neo-Nazi that perceived illegitimate sub-ordination of one's group and a sense of power discontent are important to the politicization of group identities (Duncan 2010). Together, these works contribute concepts and mechanisms such as minority status, social situation, group consciousness and identification, relative deprivation, power discontent, and personal meaning to the set of tools developed for understanding political salience of group attachments.

But relative to our understanding of how these sorts of fluid, social, and/or personal factors shape the ways people relate to and engage in politics, our knowledge of when specific attachments will be relevant in particular electoral contexts is thin. More specifically, these literatures do not produce generaliz-able expectations for the implications of group attachments for vote choice.

This is an exciting area of behavioral research to which comparative politics stands to contribute. Notably, comparativists can offer insights into the role of institutions and other structural factors at the national level in raising or low-ering the relevance of particular group attachments in politics. Some relevant work focuses on ethnic politics, an area of study that reminds us of the complex, fluid nature of cultural identities (see Laitin 1986). For example, research into the political salience of tribal, etho-linguistic, and racial group memberships for voting behavior in certain African countries finds that institutions shaping the nature of electoral competition are important conditioning factors (Posner 2004, 2005, McLaughlin 2007). This gels with other research that shows how electoral institutions can affect the salience of inter-ethnic tensions for elec-toral behavior (Lijphart 1977, Horowitz 1985). These studies point toward a conditioning role of electoral design and institutional contexts more broadly in making group attachments of various kinds more or less relevant for politics. To begin integrating these diverse insights, I focus on the ways such factors can influence the political salience of socio-territorial group attachments and direct them toward pro-radical voting tendencies.

Electoral Institutions, Authority Structures, and Salience

One particular aspect of electoral systems that may influence territorial attachment salience is the relative timing of elections for different levels of governance. We know that holding different levels' elections (such as local- and national-level contests) at the same time can influence turnout (Lijphart 1997) and outcomes (Schakel 2011). In this study, I posit that electoral timing influences the political salience of local attachments and thereby boosts the popularity of the radical right in Europe. If local attachments are good for rad-ical right politics, then they should be especially influential when the locality is foremost in the minds of voters. The expectation is that when local and national elections are held simultaneously or in close temporal proximity to each other, the radical right will do best because the locality is a chief con-sideration for voters at such a time. This hypothesis is explored in Chapter 6 using French municipal data and in Chapter 7, which looks across countries over time.

Elections do not only differ with respect to their timing, they also vary in terms of their meaningfulness. Therefore, another aspect of my institutional argument is that the locality is more politically salient – all else equal – if the locality itself has elections that are impactful. This impact can come in the form of the independent election of a mayor and/or residents' selection of a local council or parliament. The idea is that where and when people think of the locality in political terms, they will most easily connect the local with the political realm. For instance, I reason that where and when local issues are the subject of debate in meaningful electoral contests, the local and the political fuse in a powerful way.

Other comparative work suggests that state authority structures stand to have powerful electoral effects. Take, for instance, historical analyses that trace the process of state-building and its attendant nation-building throughout the nineteenth and twentieth centuries in Western Europe (Anderson 1983, Hobsbawm 1994, Caramani 2004). State strength and the political relevance of national attachments have gone hand in hand in Europe. Shifting downward to sub-national authority structures, other work finds that regional identifications are reified and more politically relevant when authority is decentralized (Marks 1999). In particular, some argue that devolving powers to regional government units enhances demands for greater regional independence and territorial secession (Brancati 2006, Erk and Anderson 2009). Combined, these studies suggest that political units with higher levels of authority will host more politically salient attachments to those units. Though most work considers such implications of national and regional authority levels, Sellers and Lidström (2012) stand out for considering the attitudinal impact of devolving power to municipal governments. They find that in countries where local communities have gained political authority, feelings of attachment to the locality strengthen. Building on these insights, I examine the extent to which local authority levels relate to radical right vote shares. Where and when the municipality is particularly powerful, it should be especially relevant to the ways people think about politics. For considerations about the local community to matter in voters' decision-making processes, there must be conditioning factors that make people's attachments to their communities politically relevant. I propose that local authority levels constitute just such a factor.

Another dimension of authority structures that stands to enhance the political salience of the locality is the formal loss of community autonomy. Government reform programs that diminish municipal authority often shift formal powers to higher levels of decision making. In Switzerland, for instance, agglomeration (the merging of separate municipalities into new, larger municipalities) is the dominant mode of local power reform. In the French case, restructuring processes create intercommunal councils that make decisions for sets of municipalities. Authority shifts in France can also take the shape of agglomeration (as is the norm in Switzerland) though this is less common to date than intercommunality. I argue that this erosion of local independence raises the political salience of local attachments as individuals deal with losses in local status and local autonomy.

To summarize, I identify two broad institutional features that can influence the political salience of territorial attachments: electoral institutions and authority structures. When constructed and changed in certain ways, these factors help people connect their local orientations to their vote choice in national elections. I theorize an interactive relationship when developing the salience argument: local attachments are most powerfully motivating for radical right support where and when the locality is politically salient. The institutional variables are conceptualized as moderators. This is the way I test the salience thesis in Chapters 5 (on Switzerland) and Chapter 6 (on France). In Chapter 7 I still rely theoretically on the local salience-boosting effect of local institutional features. But I test the thesis in direct terms, positing that the electoral and authority institutions identified also prove to have statistically independent effects on radical right party successes across countries and over time.

The Nation Is Not Enough

In urging reconsideration of the way group belonging relates to voter behavior, I acknowledge that some important work in this area has already been accomplished with respect to the radical right. Many would describe what we see in the ascent of radical right parties as the rise (or perhaps reawakening) of identity politics. As longtime social cleavages disintegrate, people seek alternate ways to belong. And they often settle on an exclusive version of the national community that is peddled by right-wing extremists (Skenderovic 2009, Goodliffe 2012, Halikiopoulou et al. 2012.). From studies of political behavior, the dimensions of national attachment that are most closely connected with radical right voting are identification with and pride in the nation as well as an understanding of the nation as an ethnic group (Billiet and De Witte 1995, Lubbers and Coenders 2017). The relevant scholarly emphasis on national affiliations as fueling the radical right makes perfect sense. Indeed, most definitions of radical right parties include a nationalistic component.

But focusing solely on people's feelings about the nation blinds us to the relevance of sub-national collectivities. Furthermore, if we were to focus exclusively on national attachments, we would miss a series of grassroots shifts that are taking place at the community level in advanced democratic societies. It may also be the case that people's concerns about diversity of the population and frustration with national elites and national institutions diminish the personal pride and self-esteem people can derive from the nation. Thus, taking the cue from the importance of nationalism, but not overstating its psychological dominance in people's identity repertoires, motivates fresh consideration of how territorial belonging on a smaller scale matters for radical right support.

As I illustrate in the pages that follow, local attachments are equally relevant – if not more relevant – to radical right support than national identifications.

IN SUMMARY

This chapter has established a theoretical framework for the localist account of radical right support. Structural theories and individualist interpretations of voter behavior are integrated in service of developing an understanding of people that is at once rooted and also fluid. Existing studies of radical right parties and their supporters point to a local-friendly set of themes in their rhetoric. This makes radical right parties logical beneficiaries of increasingly powerful and salient feelings of local attachment. Then from the socio-psychological school comes the perspective of social attachments and identities as potentially exclusionary, while the socio-structural approach motivates an expectation that routine social and institutional engagement with others can serve as an antidote to this darker side of local ties. Comparative politics supplies an understanding of the institutional factors that enhance the political salience of people's feelings about their localities. Integrating these insights yields a series of expectations about the relationship between community ties and radicalism,[15] providing a basis for the five main guiding hypotheses for this book. These are:

- Levels of local attachment are positively associated with radical right party support at the individual level.
- Levels of social and organizational participation are negatively associated with radical right party support at the individual level.
- Levels of local cohesion are positively associated with radical right party support at the community level.
- Where the locality is salient for politics (based on electoral timing and authority structures), local attachment will have a particularly strong positive association with radical right support.
- Higher levels of local salience (based on electoral timing and authority structures) are positively associated with radical right party support at the national level.

In the next five chapters I subject these dimensions of the localist theory to empirical tests, and each hypothesis receives support. Through the course of the analysis, I develop the localist theory of radical right support, identifying a motivation for voting radical right that other work has not addressed.

---

[15] The main implications of this study relate to the predictors of supporting radical right parties in national electoral contests. I also present ancillary evidence, however, suggesting that the account I develop relates to radical right support in sub-national and supra-national elections as well.

I also build into the account some flexibility, recognizing that the defining characteristics of localists are only relevant for politics at certain times in certain places.

The core insights of the localist theory of radical right support are two-fold, with one part focused on the psychological attachments of individuals to their communities and a second part that is institutional; certain institutional structures make local attachments politically salient. To the extent that a localist profile or model of a radical right voter emerges from my research, it is an individual who feels closely connected to his or her local community, who feels a strong sense of local belonging and identity, who has positive views of and feels emotionally linked to neighbors, who favors local political authority, and who lives in an area characterized by high levels of social cohesion and where local ties are politically salient.

3

Localism and Radical Right Support in Europe*

Are people with strong local attachments especially likely to support radical right parties? Or is it those individuals who feel disconnected from their localities and adrift in society who find these parties appealing? The previous chapter establishes that there are solid theoretical and empirical reasons for thinking that local ties matter for radical right voting. The purpose of this chapter is to establish whether a relationship exists between these two key factors and the nature of that relationship. I test the competing local attachment hypothesis at the individual level using survey data from the European Values Study (EVS) nested within countries. This makes it possible to test a range of theories of radical right party support, including theories geared toward explaining the vote choices of individuals and those theories that address the ways that national contexts can shape those choices. I then subject these multinational results to additional tests using several country-specific surveys from Switzerland and France.

To preview the central, resultant insight of this chapter: those who feel strongly attached to their localities are especially likely to support radical right parties. Furthermore, various aspects of local orientations such as preference for enhanced communal authority and the importance of the locality for a person's identity positively predict support for a radical right party. Organizational participation, on the other hand, diminishes the appeal of these parties. Altogether, these findings establish that local attachments are important sources of radical right party support.

---

* A version of this chapter was presented at the Annual Meeting of the American Political Science Association, Chicago, IL, August 29–September 1, 2013.

ELECTORAL BEHAVIOR AND VOTING RADICAL RIGHT

What explains vote choice in modern democratic elections? A substantial literature on partisan support in advanced democracies guides inquiry in this area. Over the past several decades, proximal theories of vote choice hinging on economic interests (Lewis-Beck 1983, Powell and Whitten 1993), political attitudes (Converse et al. 1969, Zaller 1992), socio-demographic characteristics (Tingsten 1937, Inglehart 1977, Norris 1999), and socio-contextual factors (Lazarsfeld et al. 1948, Pattie and Johnston 1998) have come to frame debates over the ways people choose which parties to support in democratic elections. These explanations emphasize factors relatively close in the causal chain to electoral choices.

Findings specific to radical right voters align closely with much of this broad body of research on party choice; indeed, previous scholarship yields accounts of radical right voting that support each of these theoretical approaches. Economic calculations, political attitudes, contextual environments, and socio-demographic traits all matter for radical right party support. For most of these sets of explanations, a myriad of indicators have been investigated in radical right studies, deepening our understanding of this contemporary phenomenon.

Yet decades of research on voting also signals that a priori to interests, attitudes, traits, and contemporaneous contexts kicking in, people hold deeper social orientations that are typically understood to be more remote in the causal chain and more foundational for their electoral choices (Lipset 1960, Campbell et al. 1960, Almond and Verba 1963, Wolfinger 1965). Social identities, for instance, shape the ways that individuals perceive their position in society and motivate their political reasoning. In deciding how he or she feels about a particular issue, or in determining how different political choices relate to his or her economic situation, or in absorbing the content of one's information environment, an individual does so from a particular position (or a set of positions) in society. These themes have not been effectively integrated into the radical right literature; I begin to remedy this here. Below, I summarize some key research on radical right voting then step back to consider the role of deeper orientations to society and politics in shaping these more proximal factors. An empirical test of these explanations follows.

EXISTING RESEARCH

A distinction between the two main approaches to studying the radical right is in order. Theories of radical right support tend to emphasize either the demand side or the supply side of the electoral equation. The demand side explores the traits and motivations of those citizens who choose to vote radical right. Supply-side theories focus more on the national systemic features of different countries' electoral systems and party systems and the nature and strategies of radical right parties, themselves. In this chapter, I include variables from both sides in my analysis, nesting individuals in their national contexts.

Demand Side Accounts

Economic Interests

Examination of economic interests shows that factors such as employment type and education level are linked to radical right party voting. This approach to understanding radical right support has been termed the "modernization losers" model or "socio-economic status" (SES) model to underscore the importance of economic developments in putting certain segments of society at a disadvantage in the market. These kinds of theories point to deeply structural social and economic shifts in modern society to make sense of large-scale changes in citizens' political preferences. Per the foundational narrative of the modernization losers account, low-skilled individuals who work in the industrial sector feel threatened by global economic shifts, and this insecurity motivates support for the radical right (Betz 1994).[1] Tests using survey data confirm this thesis: across a range of countries those who have relatively low levels of education, who work in low-skill jobs, and who are unemployed or fear unemployment are particularly supportive of radical right parties (Betz 1993, Mayer 1998, Lubbers and Scheepers 2001, Lubbers et al. 2002, Evans 2005, Arzheimer and Carter 2006, Savelkoul and Scheepers 2017.) There is also evidence that middle-level educational achievement is associated with radical right voting (Swyngedouw 1998, Arzheimer and Carter 2006).

Different versions of the socio-economic status account of radical right voting further underscore the importance of labor market position for shaping people's views on key political issues. Low-skilled workers, for instance, seek a sense of belonging and membership that they have lost due to the large-scale erosion of working-class institutions and social groups (Goodliffe 2012). They find it in a resurgence of an exclusionary version of nationalism offered by radical right parties. In alignment with the argument that class-based factors shape people's inclinations to vote for radical right parties is the connection between working-class status, low levels of education, and authoritarian attitudes among certain subsets of voters (Lipset 1981, Middendorp and Meloen 1990, Stubager 2008).

Another contribution in this area argues that labor market positions and experiences are important socializers, informing people's ideologies and ultimately their choices for radical right parties. Relevant findings are that – in addition to low-skilled workers – those whose occupations are classified as petit bourgeois are especially drawn to the radical right (Kitschelt, with McGann,

---

[1] See Flecker (2007) for a detailed critique of this hypothesis.

1995, McGann and Kitschelt 2005, Norris 2005). This argument and others in the socio-economic vein facilitate predictions about electoral behavior beyond the level of individuals and into the realm of social aggregations. A number of studies suggest that where economic structures leave laborers of various kinds particularly vulnerable to strains stemming from economic liberalism, radical right parties will receive greater vote shares. Evidence at the national and local levels suggests that, in certain cases, the prevalence of economic disadvantage (some would say the prevalence of modernization losers) in a defined area can benefit the radical right (Kitschelt, with McGann, 1995, Bowyer 2008). More generally oriented research on the contextual effects of class show that it can heavily influence voting patterns (Huckfeldt and Sprague 1995, Fisher 2000).

Socio-economic Context

On the theme of context, another approach to explaining radical right support is known as the socio-economic model. Under certain societal conditions – such as the significant presence of a large number of immigrants or high rates of unemployment – the radical right is expected to do especially well in elections. In some studies, national unemployment rates have been found to benefit radical right parties (Anderson 1996, Jackman and Volpert 1996). Similarly, existing work demonstrates that the percentage of the national population comprised of immigrants is positively associated with radical right vote shares (Anderson 1996, Knigge 1998, Lubbers et al. 2002, Swank and Betz 2003, Golder 2003b, Kessler and Freeman 2005).

However, these relationships are generally not found to be stable over time and across space. For instance, some work reveals a negative relationship between unemployment and radical right vote share at national (Knigge 1998), sub-national regional (Lubbers and Scheepers 2000, Dülmer and Klein 2005, Jesuit et al. 2009), and local (Coffé et al. 2007, Bowyer 2008) levels. Presence of immigrants in the national arena is also often found by some to be unhelpful for radical right parties (Kitschelt, with McGann, 1995, van der Brug et al. 2005, Arzheimer and Carter 2006). Other studies yield null or even negative results with respect to the link between immigrant presence and radical right support across a range of sub-national units (Kestilä and Söderlund 2007, Arzheimer and Carter 2009, Jesuit et al. 2009).[2]

---

[2] As developed further in Chapter 6, the presence of immigrants in the local arena is in some cases found to benefit the radical right; in other cases it does not. For instance, municipalities that have received high levels of immigrants, especially those from stigmatized groups such as Muslims, sometimes are more supportive of radical right parties (DeVos and Deurloo 1999, Mayer 2002, John et al. 2006, Bowyer 2008, Coffé et al. 2007, Green et al. 2015). But other studies find no such effects (Mayer and Perrineau 1996) or uneven effects over time (Kestilä and Söderlund 2007). Indeed, in some cases the areas that have no or nearly no diversity at all are the ones that are most supportive of radical right parties (Bowyer 2008). Still other researchers have identified

Political Attitudes

Another approach to accounting for radical right voting underscores the importance of people's attitudes on key political issues. These ideologically oriented theories identify particular stances on issues that align with these parties' programs. A well-documented attitude of import is a negative view toward immigrants and immigration (Ivarsflaten 2008, Rydgren 2008, Coffé and Voorpostel 2010). Anti-European Union sentiment is also an important driver of radical right voting. Case study and cross-national research shows that the EU's unpopularity creates a significant pool of potential supporters in countries that are members of the EU and even countries that are not, such as Switzerland (Swyngedouw 2001, Ivarsflaten 2008).

One also finds among radical right voters a deep sense of frustration with their political systems and political leaders (van der Brug and Fennema 2003). For instance, anti-government attitudes play a particularly strong role in support for the Golden Dawn in Greece whose voters are aggrieved with the country's political institutions (Lamprianou and Ellinas 2017). These observations have at some junctures fueled an understanding of radical right party support as a protest vote. Notably, some argue that growing alienation from and distrust in democratic political institutions motivates radical right support (Eatwell 1998, Swyngedouw 2001, Kessler and Freeman 2005).

Socio-demographic Traits

Socio-demographic traits of individuals have also been identified as relevant for radical right voting. Most notably, supporters tend to be more male than female (Givens 2004, Kessler and Freeman 2005, Fontana et al. 2006, Spierings and Zaslove 2015a). This is a relationship that I consider more carefully in the next chapter to better understand the gendered nature of the radical right vote. Age is another factor that is typically examined in studies of the radical right. Most work seems to find that the typical supporter is relatively young (Hainsworth 2008: 101–104, Mayer 2014). Others note that while the young-skewing electorate is the norm, it is not necessarily the case across countries (Minkenberg and Perrineau 2007). Still others have noted a shift over time through which an older radical right electorate has morphed into a younger one (Evans 2005). In a broader conceptualization of the way age relates to extremist voting, Inglehart (1997) posits that new generations will adopt non-traditional (post-materialist) political values, which for many will result in non-traditional vote choices such as radical right parties.

Socio-political Orientations

If we step back to consider the basic social positions from which people approach the task of making political choices, the above explanations of

---

a phenomenon in which localities that are close to high-diversity areas host the most radical right support (Bréchon and Mitra 1992).

radical right support supply a useful set of options. With respect to theories that emphasize economic interests, we can identify social class or perhaps occupational position as the starting point for some citizens as they navigate the political arena. Given an individual's position as a worker, business owner, professional, etc., he or she has the basis for establishing which political party best suits his or her economic needs. It is not clear whether an individual's economic location serves as a basis for social belonging or simply a starting point for utility calculation – this would depend on the specific theory – but overall we can see market location as a starting point for making political judgments.

While economic interests and grievances surely play a role in the advent of radical right parties, the bulk of studies on the subject signal that they do not play the starring role. Instead, cultural grievances associated with loss of group status and threats to collective identities have been found to be particularly powerful drivers of radical right party popularity. Theories that spotlight specific policy views, such as cracking down on immigration and reducing the supranational authority of the European Union, are thematically in line with this understanding.

A central aspect of these accounts is national identity, which emerges as an important part of theories crafted by Rydgren (2004), Ellinas (2014), and Goodliffe (2012) among others. Feelings of national belonging represent a key attitudinal component of radical right support. This does not seem to be debated, and for good reason since supporters tend to feel strongly attached to their national communities (Falter and Schumann 1988, Billiet and De Witte 1995, Lubbers and Scheepers 2000, Lubbers and Coenders 2017). Case studies demonstrate the prevalence of nationalist appeals within radical right party campaigns (Hainsworth 1992, Mudde 1999, Klandermans and Mayer 2006, Braunthal 2009, Skenderovic 2009, Ellinas 2014). Classic, well-known radical right slogans such as "French First!" (*les Français d'abord*) and newer arrivals such as "Hungary belongs to the Hungarians!" (*Magyarország a Magyaroké*) are clearly geared toward activating a specific form of social membership for political purposes. A sense of belonging to a national community, and a desire to protect the national community from perceived threats posed by immigration, globalization, market liberalization, and Europeanization, fuel radical right movements.

Despite what we have learned from these studies of the political implications of national identities, social group membership has been quite narrowly studied as it relates to radical right support. According to scholarly literature on group belonging and identification, social attachments can be numerous, over-lapping, and fluid (Laitin 1998, Brubaker 2004). Yet the only group membership theorized to matter for radical right support is national in nature. As I point out in the previous chapter, this limited view of social membership effects is particularly insufficient given that a diverse landscape of group attachments is so important for guiding political behavior in general and vote choice in particular in complex democratic societies (Berelson et al. 1954, Brand et al. 1993, Huddy 2003).[3]

As developed in the previous chapters, I expand the set of relevant group attachments in our analytical repertoire to include the locality. Numerous case studies of radical right support describe the ways in which radical right vote choice is rooted in people's feelings about their local communities; among these, Roger Eatwell's (1998) account stands out. In building the case for a more locally sensitive approach to studying right-wing extremism, he asserts:

> Economic factors should not be overstated. A study carried out in St. Denis by the Centre d'étude de la vie politique française in Paris found that FN voters did not primarily discuss economic issues or welfare competition. They tended rather to see immigrants in 'us' vs. 'them' terms ... In this case, the belief that elites had undermined national identity – and the quest to rediscover identity – seems crucial. One has to be someone before one can be rational. We need to probe human nature and behavior more carefully ... Thus hostility to Bengladeshis, or yuppies, in Millwall can be 'explained' not as racism or envy, but within a discursive strategy which posits a – largely mythical – holistic, rooted, communitarian life which is being destroyed by change. (1998: 30)

This passage signals that purely economic accounts of radicalism are not particularly influential; it also points to a sense that national elites have hollowed out what it means to be part of the nation by allowing immigration-related diversity to re-shape society. In turn, people seek a sense of belonging rooted in community. More broadly, Eatwell points to the importance of group belonging and its dynamic quality over time. The analysis I present below explores the effects of community ties on people's decisions to support radical right parties.

Supply-side Accounts

"Supply-side" political opportunity studies – as opposed to "demand-side" motivational theories – focus on certain institutions at the national level, sub-national level, or the party level to understand how these parties emerge and how they compete electorally. Institutions shown to impact radical right parties' electoral fortunes include electoral rules (Golder 2003a, Carter 2005), party system players and dynamics (Kitschelt, with McGann, 1995, Bale 2003), and party organizations (Art 2011). These kinds of studies ask: what makes it possible for radical right parties to attract and mobilize voters? While my line of inquiry is different (through what processes do individuals make the choice to support a particular party?), it is important to take supply-side theories into account to create a robust test of my demand-side theory.

---

[3] Perhaps there is potential for generational and gender-based groups to serve as foundations for interest-based motivations for radical right support, but these have not been developed to my knowledge.

Specifically I look at two main features of national systems to gauge the influence of these kinds of factors. First, I integrate into the analysis data on the electoral threshold, which denotes how difficult it is for a particular political party to gain representation (and by association, votes) in an election. More representative systems (such as those that use highly proportional processes to allocate legislative seats in the wake of an election) typically have particularly low electoral thresholds. Also folded into the threshold is any system-wide requirement that a party receive a particular percentage of the popular vote to qualify for legislative participation. The expectation is that – as for any party – the radical right will do better in low threshold systems (Jackman and Volpert 1996). Second, I consider the role of ideological polarization among parties, which indicates the programmatic diversity within the halls of government. This aligns with the thesis that where political parties of the right and left have converged, they leave space open to newcomers on the fringes of the ideological spectrum. This, in turn, creates an opportunity for upstart parties to enter the party system (see Katz and Mair 1995, Kitschelt, with McGann, 1995, Bale 2003).

DEFINING THE RADICAL RIGHT

I identify radical right parties in line with Mudde's (1996) tripartite conceptual definition; they are anti-globalization in terms of issue positions, authoritarian in their perspectives on power, and populist in their rhetoric. The term "right-wing populist," thus, also fits the cases and phenomena that I bring into my analysis.[4] For identifying the parties to include in the data I mainly follow Norris's (2005) classification. Norris draws on expert surveys by Lubbers and Huber and Inglehart to establish where parties stand ideologically and on immigration issues.[5] Parties that rate an eight or higher (on a ten-point left-right index) are categorized as a part of the radical right.[6] The process of adding newer radical right parties to the list adheres to this logic (and fits with the choices of Inglehart and Norris 2016). For instance, Norris includes the Austrian Freedom Party (FPÖ) in her 2005 analysis as the sole radical right party in Austria. Here, the Alliance for the Future of Austria (BZÖ) is also included because it is the splinter party formed in 2005 by Jörg Haider, the FPÖ's former leader.[7] Finland's True Finns (PS) is included on the basis of

---

[4] For additional definitional considerations see Mudde (1996) and Mondon (2013). While I integrate a great deal of literature on what have been termed "extreme right" parties, the understanding that they are by definition critical of democracy puts them on the fringe of my research. They are still relevant, but I cast a wider net than some versions of the "extreme right" classification would allow.

[5] For foundational data, see Lubbers (2000) and Huber and Inglehart (1995).

[6] See Norris (2005: 46–49) for details.

[7] Though Haider developed a more moderate public image as leader of the BZÖ relative to the image of the FPÖ, the two parties' platforms were quite similar and they competed for radical right voters (Luther 2009, Duncan 2010, Ensser 2012: 154).

Arter's case study (2010). The Dutch Party for Freedom (PVV) is characterized by some as a part of the radical right party family (van der Pas et al. 2011) or at least very close to it (Vossen 2011).[8]

Case studies of Jobbik in Hungary (e.g. Karácsony and Róna 2011) demonstrate that the party is a good fit for the analysis. In Bulgaria, National Union Attack (*Ataka*) has grown and been characterized by observers as belonging to this party family (Frusetta and Glont 2009). The remaining central and eastern additions to the case set are Croatian (Croatian Party of Rights – HSP), Czech (Czech Republicans – RMS), Latvian (National Alliance – TB/LNNK), Polish (League of Polish Families – LPR), Slovakian (Slovak National Party – SNS), and Slovenian (Slovene National Party – SNS). They are categorized as radical right or "nearby" (in the case of Latvia) the radical right in a party space study (Bustikova and Kitschelt 2009).[9] Minkenberg's work (2017) supports these classification decisions as they relate to Central and Eastern Europe, though he points out that in the east these parties are more vocal in their criticism of democratic institutions and more unapologetically racist.

CASE STUDIES: SWITZERLAND AND FRANCE

Switzerland and France are home to two radical right parties that have been relatively successful by continental standards: the Swiss People's Party (SVP) and the National Front (FN) in France.[10] Their messaging and policy prescriptions are quite similar in that they campaign against immigration, they condemn the European Union, and they vow to limit its influence,[11] and they come out very strongly on issues associated with law and order. In both cases they also sharply criticize political elites as being out of touch with regular citizens. Importantly for this study, the SVP and the FN stoke localist feelings of pride and fears of local denigration through their rhetoric. Here, I provide some historical and programmatic details of these two parties and consider the suitability of this case pairing for my study.

---

[8] See Mudde (2007) for a dissenting view. The existing literature identifies some additional, smaller radical right parties but these are excluded from analysis if the EVS data identify none of their supporters.

[9] The findings presented below are robust to exclusion of Latvian respondents as well as Dutch respondents. No one country's respondents drive the results.

[10] The SVP is the Schweizerische Volkspartei in German-speaking regions, the Union démocratique du centre in Francophone Switzerland, and the Unione Democratica di Centro and Partida Populara Svizra in the Italian and Romansh areas, respectively. The National Front in France is known as the Front National.

[11] The specific rhetoric on the EU differs between the two parties, however, since France is a founding, high-powered member of the supranational body while Switzerland has never joined it.

Swiss People's Party

Until recently, the Swiss political system was very stable. The early twentieth-century electorate seemed to have settled on three parties, each of which received roughly equal shares of the vote across elections. These were the Social Democratic Party, the Christian Democratic Party, and the Radical Democratic Party. They jockeyed for first place but overall held roughly the same amount of seats and authority, each receiving voter support in the high teens and twenties across elections. In 1971 a new, junior member of this partisan line-up emerged. The Swiss People's Party (SVP) received a significantly smaller share of electoral returns over its first two decades: on average about 11 percent of the vote. Switzerland for many years seemed to emblemize the frozen party systems hypothesis (Lipset and Rokkan 1967).

In the 1990s things changed. The SVP, originally established as a moderate-right agrarian party most successful in the German-speaking east, began its electoral ascent. Christophe Blocher rebranded the SVP as a party that aligns with most definitions of a radical right party: anti-immigration, anti-European Union, and anti-political establishment. It has also consistently campaigned for devolved authority to the cantons and communes. In 2001 Andreas Ladner observed, "The success of the Swiss People's Party ... in the 1990s is probably the most striking in the whole electoral history of the Swiss system ..." (2001: 129). Since then, the party has only expanded its national presence. It has been winning the popular vote since 1999 and has had the largest share of seats in the National Council since 2003. In 2015 it received over 29 percent of the vote (over 740,000 voters) and over 32 percent of the legislative seats. The next most successful party in this election, the Social Democrats, received less than 19 percent of the vote that year.[12]

The SVP comes out very strongly in defense of local customs and traditions throughout Switzerland. For instance, it reminds the Swiss that the high level of governmental devolution that empowers Swiss municipalities in a wide range of policy areas is a source of pride for the Swiss people. This allows it to integrate localism and nationalism in its appeals. It also appeals to those who feel connected to their local communities by describing the threat posed by other political parties. Its party platform reads:

The other parties reject federalism and shift more and more competencies from the cantons and the communes to the federal government in Bern – to the detriment of our children, of our families, and of our schools (p. 8) ... They threaten the essential units of society like the family, associations, foundations, churches, neighborhood relationships ... the communities of neighborhoods or villages, all forms of cohabitation that exist independent of the state. (UDC 2015: 95)

---

[12] Figure 5.1 in Chapter 5 depicts the SVP's electoral rise relative to that of other Swiss parties.

This characterization of the other Swiss parties as predatory agents of the state who aim to denigrate the local community allows the SVP to position itself as the sole force preventing this from happening. Furthermore, the SVP vows to provide financing to the communes which it says the other parties would choose to withhold, and its materials also criticize the federal government for its over-reach in areas of taxation and overall authority. Switzerland's decentralized democratic institutions work in the SVP's favor as it positions itself as the party that will preserve local autonomy.

Finally, as I cover in greater detail in Chapter 5, there have been significant shifts over time in the Swiss state's authority structures. Recent processes of agglomeration, through which small communes become grouped together into larger administrative units, have had an impact on people in certain parts of Switzerland. This process has the potential to politicize citizens' local attachments, which I posit benefits radical right parties. If this theory of mine reflects reality anyplace, it should be in Switzerland where the SVP campaigns on local autonomy, where localities have a tradition of significant formal authority, and where that authority is in many places being diminished.

National Front

The French National Front (FN) is in many ways a similar party to the SVP. It, too, campaigns against immigration, the EU, and mainstream politics. It has emphasized themes of traditional community and local autonomy over the years as well.[13] Jean-Marie Le Pen started the party in 1972, and over the decades its central themes have not changed. For many years it attracted a very small percentage of the vote in legislative elections. It received less than 1 percent of the popular vote in its first three National Assembly contests, but jumped to nearly 10 percent in 1986. Since then, its success in legislative elections has been inconsistent, dipping close to 4 percent in 2007, but then rising to nearly 14 percent in 2012, and holding relatively steady in 2017.[14]

But it is not the legislative elections that attract the biggest headlines for the FN. Jean-Marie Le Pen's stunning advancement to the second round run-off of the 2002 presidential elections shocked many within and outside France. The idea of the FN as a hopeless pariah party received reconsideration by many. Yet mainstream France rallied in the second round, holding Le Pen's vote share to approximately 18 percent. Placards emblazoned with "Vote for the crook, not the fascist" urged citizens to select center-right Jacques Chirac over far-right Le Pen for president.

Marine Le Pen, Jean-Marie's daughter, assumed control of the party in 2011. She boasted a strong third-place showing in the first round of the 2012

---

[13] The FN is generally critical of devolution processes in France, though, so its record on formal local autonomy is mixed.

[14] These are first-round figures from France's two-round electoral system. In 2018 the FN's official name became the National Rally (*Rassemblement National*).

presidential elections with nearly 18 percent of the vote. The FN then won the most votes of any party in the 2014 European Parliament elections in France with nearly 25 percent of the vote. In 2017 Marine Le Pen capped all of her previous achievements – as well as her father's – by advancing to the second round of the presidential election and receiving nearly 34 percent of the vote. Later in 2017 she won her first seat in the General Assembly as representative of the Pas-de-Calais eleventh district.

The National Front cues localist sentiments in more subtle – and one could argue inconsistent – ways than does the SVP. It campaigns in favor of a strong, central state, but at the same time it praises and idealizes the local community as an essential part of French life. In past years, when the party was under the control of Jean-Marie Le Pen, much of the platform was geared in favor of communities, particularly in rural areas (Le Pen 1993).[15] While one of his main slogans was "French first," Le Pen challenged the central government's dominance over policy areas such as social protection, and he criticized Parisian control of the transportation system. He vowed to ensure the survival of rural life and to preserve the French countryside. These are themes that would naturally appeal to local communities feeling threatened by contemporary developments.

Marine Le Pen's platforms contain similar themes that resonate with locally oriented voters. She advocates for retention and even restoration of authority of the communes (localities) in France and restoration of the prominence of local mayors in small and medium-sized towns and villages.[16] These appeals, it is important to note, contradict in big-picture terms her strong stance against the decentralization process stared in the 1980s in France. The FN today stands for a strong state despite (what some have called) pandering to those who seek to enhance the authority of the regions, in particular.[17]

Marine Le Pen advocates expanding public services in small towns. She also promises decentralized budgetary policies and signals support for rural populations in her messaging. One aspect of her campaigning stands out as providing a hook for locally oriented citizens: her central campaign slogan of "On est chez nous" translates to "We are at home." The broader message is one about France (presumably about drawing a distinction between those who belong in France and those who do not), but the connotation can be expanded to represent any understanding of "home" that a person holds.

---

[15] See Chapter 6 for more details of Jean-Marie Le Pen's programme.

[16] See www.frontnational.com/le-projet-de-marine-le-pen/. She advocates a simpler administrative structure than currently exists that keeps the central state, the departments, and the communes: "Revaloriser en conséquence le rôle et le statut des maires des petites et moyennes communes." (p. 2)

[17] For coverage of the inherent tensions within the FN's messaging on authority structures, see Graff (2015).

Enhancing the value of the French case study is the ongoing process of territorial reform that progressively shifts formal authority from the hands of municipalities to larger collections of municipalities (and implements additional inter-level shifts as well). This loss of autonomy, I contend, creates frustration and resentment on the part of some communal populations, boosts the political salience of local sentiments, and ultimately motivates voting for the radical right. Making the case that the FN is the beneficiary of this politicized localism, again, involves some slightly tricky navigation given that the party is critical of locally rooted elites who – the FN charges – have created local fiefdoms that violate the party's vision of a unified, uncorrupted France of the people. However, the argument I develop below reflects a layperson's sense of attachment to his or her commune and a sense that its status is in decline. This aligns well with FN rhetoric on governmental authority, which is sensitive to the integrity of the country's communes.

Case Pairing

The SVP and the FN are typically considered to be members of the same, radical right party family. This makes Switzerland and France a useful pair of cases for analysis in that the phenomenon under examination is similar enough to draw observations that apply to the radical right in both cases and to the many other instances of radical right parties and party support. Yet the differences between these two parties – and the two countries – render the insights derived from these case studies even more broadly applicable across a range of radical right cases. Three main differences stand out when surveying these two cases together.

The first difference is conceptual in that some scholars do not place them in the same radical right category (for instance, Statham and Koopmans 2009). Some of their visible differences are that the FN has a reputation for being more outspokenly xenophobic while the SVP uses relatively moderate language when discussing issues of ethnic diversity. Indeed, the FN has been tied ideologically to Europe's fascist past, while the SVP has avoided some of the more blatant anti-democratic components of right-wing extremism. Furthermore, the SVP is viewed by some as more populist in nature. These differences amount to some variation in style and substance between the two parties.

Second, their patterns of electoral success are quite different from each other. Both the SVP and the FN have seen their electoral fortunes shift and ultimately rise over time. Though in contrast to the SVP, the FN has seen more uneven success at the national level. As the SVP has achieved a relatively steady rise in popularity since the 1990s, the electoral fortunes of the FN over the past forty-plus years ebb and flow. Together, these parties offer an opportunity to explain different kinds of variation over time in radical right success: steady climb in the case of the SVP and fits and starts in the case of the FN.

Third, these two parties compete in very different contexts. With respect to their electoral systems, Switzerland and France represent nearly polar opposites: the SVP operates in a proportional system that has traditionally emphasized consensus in governing, and the FN in a majoritarian system that is much more competitive. Another key institutional difference between Switzerland and France relates to basic state structures: Switzerland is one of the most (if not the most) decentralized democracies in existence, while France represents a highly unitary system. In other words, governmental authority in Switzerland is highly devolved to sub-national units such as the municipality, while in France the power is relatively concentrated in the center. This makes for very different contexts in which to study the importance of local attachments and their politicization. This dimension of difference also shapes the structures of the parties, themselves. For instance, the SVP is a relatively decentralized and diverse party, with a more moderate wing that chafes against the newer radical faction. In comparison, the FN is centralized and internally coherent, in line with the unitary structure of French politics.

Each of these differences renders these two parties a useful case study pairing. An explanation that can account for support for the SVP and the FN generalizes to other radical right parties.

EVS DATA AND METHODS

Cross-national survey data provide insight into the relationship between local attachment and radical right party support. Surveys from twenty countries in which radical right parties compete in national elections make it possible to investigate the phenomenon of interest at the micro level. These data also allow for hierarchical modeling of radical right support, in that the roles of individual-level and country-level predictors are measured simultaneously. The analysis includes Western European countries typically addressed in radical right studies (such as Austria, Belgium, and Denmark), and it also brings Central and Eastern European countries (such as Croatia, Hungary, and Romania) into the analysis as few existing studies have done.

The models here draw on the European Values Study (EVS). Two waves of the survey provide snapshots of the correlates of individual-level radical right support.[18] The benefits of this survey for the present purposes are threefold. First, party support and local attachment are measured consistently across numerous countries. Second, important control variables are derived from the data, making it possible to subject the working hypotheses to a tough series

---

[18] The two waves that are used (Wave 3 in 1998–2000 and Wave 4 in 2008–2009) are selected because they contain the largest number of radical right supporters among available waves to date and because citizens are identifiable through a citizenship item, which I use as a filter. For survey details, see www.europeanvaluesstudy.eu/.

of tests. Third, there are enough countries with radical right supporters in the sample to make hierarchical modeling possible.[19]

The dependent variable is dichotomous, measuring whether or not an individual supports a radical right party. The question for the dependent variable comes in two parts: "If there was a general election tomorrow, can you tell me if you would vote?" If yes, "which party would you vote for?" Those who would vote for a radical right party are coded 1. Those who would not vote or who would choose another party are coded 0.[20] This prospective vote item provides a sample from twenty countries of over 36,000 individuals. About 2,500 (or 7 percent) of these individuals claim that they would support a radical right party.[21]

The key independent variable is a scale that represents how attached an individual feels to his or her locality.[22] It is derived from two distinct survey items. Item 1 asks, "Which of these geographical groups would you say you belong to first of all? Locality or town where you live, region of country where you live, [country], Europe, the world as a whole." Item 2 asks, "And secondly?" with the same set of options presented. The resultant scale used for analysis, termed *Local attachment*, has three values: 1=local area is the first choice, .5=local area is the second choice, 0=local area is neither the first nor the second choice. Figure 3.1, Panel A, presents the resultant descriptive pattern. Just over 45 percent of respondents (from the sample used here, containing only citizens of their country of residence) report that the group they belong to first of all is their locality.

From these two survey items also comes a *National attachment* variable that parallels the local one: 1=country is first choice, .5=country is second choice, 0=country is neither. For the sake of comparison between local and national attachments, respondents' answers on belonging to the country of residence are presented in Figure 3.1, Panel B. The country is a less popular top choice, with approximately 30 percent of respondents listing it first.[23]

---

[19] Countries included in the analysis and parties coded as radical right are listed in Appendix Figure A3.1.

[20] Removing non-voters from this sample does not affect results.

[21] In some countries, follow-up questions include "Which political party would you vote for – 2nd choice?" And for those who report that they would not vote in an upcoming general election: "Which party appeals to you most?" Though these questions identify additional individuals who could be characterized as radical right supporters, the fact that they are not consistently asked across countries and waves makes for a less comparable dependent variable. Therefore, the initial question is used for the main dependent variable. But running the models with an expanded measure that takes these additional questions into account yields substantively similar results.

[22] Community psychologists have developed the concept of community attachment, using feelings of connectedness to the local area and the people in it as measures of this sentiment (see Kasarda and Janowitz 1974, Lee et al. 2005, Middleton et al. 2005).

[23] Because this question requires respondents to rank order their geo-social attachments, the correlation between Local attachment and National attachment is -.49. This may be a natural way

Local preference: descriptive pattern

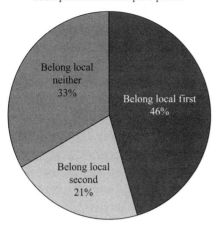

FIGURE 3.1 PANEL A
Source: European Values Study

National preference: descriptive pattern

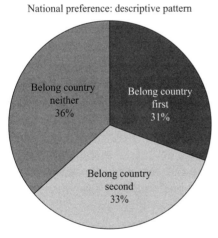

FIGURE 3.1 PANEL B
Source: European Values Study

that people think about their various attachments, but perhaps it is not. To assess the locally oriented hypotheses using a non-ranking instrument, additional datasets are useful. These data and
their measures are presented later in this chapter. It turns out that it does not much matter for
predicting radical right support how different levels of attachment are asked about; the results
tend to be substantively consistent regardless.

The popularity of the local varies across countries. Polish respondents are the most attached to their localities; 64 percent of the Polish sample identifies the locality as the geographical group they belong to first. In comparison, only 22 percent of Swiss make this claim (the lowest in the survey). The French stand in the middle with just under 40 percent feeling primarily attached to the local area. As for national group belonging, at the high end 43 percent of Finns select this option first and Germans represent the low end with approximately 13 percent stating that they belong to Germany first; 33 percent of French respondents feel national first, as do 30 percent of the Swiss.

A set of variables signifying socio-economic status represent theorizing associated with the socio-economic status (SES)/Modernization losers model. Education is divided into three categories: low, middle and high.[24] Low education level has been consistently shown to relate to greater likelihood of supporting a radical right party, and intermediate education level can have a similar effect. Dummy variables for *Education low* and *Education medium* are included in the models, leaving high education as the reference category.

Employment variables are also dichotomous. These predictors are based on a pre-coded variable in the EVS. A respondent is (x=1) or is not (x=0) in each of the following categories: *Working* (full- or part-time), *Retired*, *Homemaker*, *Student*, or *Unemployed*. The reference category is a mix of those who are not working and those who fit into a category labeled "other." Extant work finds that occupation is an important factor in predicting radical right support.[25]

Another set of determinants included in the models represent what has been called the "sociological model," which emphasizes the role of demographic characteristics. *Male* and *Age* make up this category. We know that men tend to be especially likely to support these parties, as do younger voters.

Organizational memberships represent participation in civil society. The relevant survey item reads, "Please look carefully at the following list of voluntary organisations and activities and say ... which, if any, do you belong to?" The options listed are: Social welfare, Religious, Education/arts/music/cultural, Trade unions, Political parties, Local community action, Third world development/human rights, Conservation/environment, Professional association, Youth work, Sports or recreation, Women's groups, Peace movement, Voluntary/health, and Other.[26] *Memberships* is a dichotomous variable indicating whether an individual belongs to any organization.

In addition to the geographical group attachment variables described above, other attitudinal variables are included in the models. *Distrust in parliament*

---

[24] This is a variable internally coded by EVS and intended to be comparable across countries. See http://info1.gesis.org/evs/variables for details.

[25] Alternate specifications of the models that include measures of the kind of work people do (service, manual, etc.) yield similar results. I use this more generic breakdown because it facilitates replication with the other surveys I use in this study. Models in Chapters 5 and 6 include specific occupational categories.

[26] For additional survey details, see www.europeanvaluesstudy.eu/.

and *Distrust in European Union* represent anti-government and anti-European orientations, respectively. The question wording for these is, "Please look at this card and tell me, for each item listed, how much confidence you have in them, is it a great deal, quite a lot, not very much or none at all?" Parliament and the European Union are among the specific institutions listed.

The EVS contains a number of questions on the topic of immigration. The one asked most consistently across countries and over time is included in the analysis. The survey item reads, "On this list are various groups of people. Could you please sort out any that you would not like to have as neighbours? Immigrants/foreign workers." If immigrants are mentioned by the respondent, the variable *Anti-immigrant* is coded 1; if not it is coded 0. Utilizing this variable to measure anti-immigrant sentiments establishes a particularly stringent test of the hypothesis that local attachment invigorates radical right support. If local attachment is merely a proxy for the way people view immigration, then including immigration attitudes specifically related to the neighborhood would eliminate any effect of local attachment. All of the survey variables are coded to run from 0 to 1.

Country-level variables characterize the national contexts during the year of each EVS survey. Existing research directed the selection of these variables (e.g. Golder 2003b, Kessler and Freeman 2005). *Immigration level* represents the percentage of the country's population comprised of non-citizens. These data are collected from OECD and individual countries' statistical offices (OECD 2010a). *Unemployment rate* is the percentage of the labor force that is registered as unemployed (OECD 2013).

Other work points to effects of additional factors at the aggregate level. Political opportunity structure theories predict that institutional contexts can affect the success of radical right parties. Carter (2005) emphasizes electoral rules and party system features in her account of radical right support at the aggregate level. Here, these factors are included to test their relevance for individual-level party choice. *Electoral threshold* indicates how high the electoral hurdle for representation at the national level is. This is the minimum percentage of votes that is required for at least one seat in the legislature. *Polarization* of political parties, some argue, precludes new fringe upstarts from locating open space on the ideological spectrum when mainstream, centrist parties do not converge in the center. The measure is the highest difference in values between the chief executive's party's ideological score (on a left-right spectrum) and the score of the most distant of the three largest governing parties or largest party in the opposition. These institutional variables come from the Database of Political Institutions (DPI) (Beck et al. 2001, Keefer and Stasavage 2003, Keefer 2012).[27] The expectation is that each of these contextual factors

---

[27] For additional information on these data, see: http://econ.worldbank.org.

is negatively related to radical right support. To address time-related factors, each model includes yearly dummy variables to account for survey year.

EVS RESULTS

The first models are simple logistic regressions with fixed effects by country. Then I present mixed effects multilevel logistic regression models; individuals are nested within their country contexts. Level 1 is the individual in these models; level 2 is the country. Coefficients (Coeff.), standard errors (S.E.), and statistical significance levels (Sig. or *) are reported in all tables for statistical models throughout this book.

Table 3.1 contains the results of three logit models. Because logit coefficients are not intuitively meaningful in terms of substantive effect, direction of sign and level of significance are most immediately useful. Model I is a basic test of the competing theses on the link between local attachment and radical right support. The relationship on balance is positive and statistically significant above the conventional .95 threshold. Those with strong local attachments (in this case, strong in relation to other geographical group attachments) are especially likely to support radical right parties. The only controls here are year and country variables.

Model II includes a series of socio-economic characteristics and socio-demographics. Age, Male, Memberships, education level, and employment variables perform largely as expected. The SES/losers model receives support; low- and mid-level-educated individuals are especially supportive of the radical right. Students make up the least supportive of the employment categories. Socio-demographics also behave as anticipated: young people and men are particularly supportive. These results fit the typical profile of a radical right supporter.

Model III contains additional attachment and attitudinal variables. National attachment, distrust of parliament, distrust of the EU, and anti-immigrant sentiments are positive, significant predictors of radical right support.[28] These findings are novel in that the evidence is derived from data that span across Europe, rather than only focusing on Western European countries. Thus, the relevant theories find support from a broader set of citizens than is typically considered. The findings are also further supportive of the notion that local ties motivate radical right support; community attachment's effects are robust to the inclusion of these characteristics.[29]

---

[28] Alternate versions of these models containing additional control variables (not presented) further demonstrate the robustness of the positive local attachment effect. These include Anti-Muslim attitudes, Left-right ideology, Level of pride in nationality, Post-materialism index, Support for greater respect for authority, Size of town, and West Europe. The substantive results do not change with these inclusions.

[29] When replicating these models using only the French sub-sample and then the Swiss sub-sample of the EVS, the results are quite similar despite the relatively small number of observations. In both cases the local attachment coefficient is positive and significant in the country-specific versions of Model I (bivariate) and Model II plus the addition of National attachment. But also in both cases once the attitudinal variables are introduced the Local attachment coefficients are

TABLE 3.1 *Support for radical right parties in 20 countries*

Logit models

Predictor	I		II		III	
	Coeff.	S.E.	Coeff.	S.E.	Coeff.	S.E.
Attachments/Attitudes						
Local attachment	.13	(.05) *	.09	(.05) *	.19	(.06) *
National attachment					.25	(.07) *
Distrust parliament					.93	(.10) *
Distrust EU					.80	(.09) *
Anti-immigrant					.70	(.06) *
Civic engagement						
Memberships (any)			−.12	(.05) *	−.03	(.05)
SES/Modernization losers						
Education low			.86	(.08) *	.75	(.08) *
Education middle			.58	(.07) *	.47	(.07) *
Occupational status:						
Full-/part-time			−.08	(.15)	−.20	(.14)
Self-employed			−.04	(.17)	−.15	(.17)
Retired			−.02	(.16)	−.12	(.16)
Homemaker			−.24	(.18)	−.17	(.17)
Student			−.70	(.18) *	−.70	(.17) *
Unemployed			−.03	(.17)	−.13	(.17)
Socio-demographics						
Male			.37	(.05) *	.38	(.05) *
Age			−.97	(.14) *	−.92	(.14) *
Constant	−5.49	(.20) *	−5.70	(.20) *	−6.76	(.27) *
N individuals	36,260		35,846		31,611	
−2Xlog likelihood	15,540		15,006		13,076	
Wald chi²	1,692	*	1,900	*	2,779	*

* p<.05. Models include dummy variables for each country and year of survey.
Countries: Austria, Belgium, Bulgaria, Croatia, Czech Rep., Denmark, Finland, France, Germany, Greece, Hungary, Italy, Latvia, Netherlands, Norway, Poland, Romania, Slovakia, Slovenia, Switzerland.
Source: European Values Study, filter variable = citizen.

only significant at the .90 cutoff instead of the conventional .95 threshold. The country-specific versions of Model I show that the probability of supporting the SVP in Switzerland increases .05 and of supporting the FN in France increases .02 as local attachments shift from their lowest to highest values. The Swiss results are more robust than the French results, suggesting that a locally rooted impulse to support the radical right may be more powerful in Switzerland than in France. These sub-sample models are available from the author.

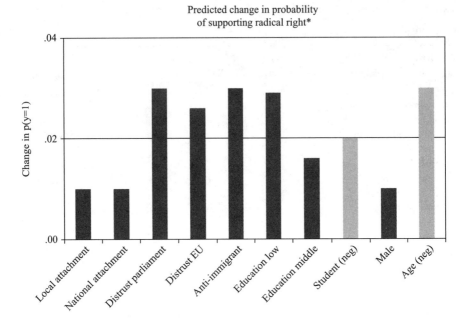

* Absolute values (moving each variable from its minimum to its maximum).
Based on Model III in Table 3.1.

FIGURE 3.2
Source: European Values Study

To better illustrate the relative strength of the statistically significant relationships, Figure 3.2 presents the predicted change in probability of supporting a radical right party associated with moving each statistically significant variable in Model III from its minimum to maximum score. The effects are relatively modest across the board, but it is important to remember that the mean value of this variable is approximately .07. The results show that (all else equal) an individual who claims his or her strongest sense of belonging is to the local area is one percentage point more likely to support a radical right party than an individual who does not identify the local area as one of their two closest geographical groups. This effect is similar in magnitude to those of National attachment and Male, factors that figure prominently in other studies of the radical right supporter.

Multilevel models provide an opportunity to control for country-level factors that are typically expected to affect support for relatively new, unconventional parties. This is an important step, particularly given that in this sample 37 percent of the variance in the dependent variable is attributable to the country level. Therefore, multilevel models are introduced into the analysis to examine the ways in which individual-level and national-level variables relate to the phenomenon of interest. Relevant contextual data for eighteen countries are available, so the number of countries drops by two. Table 3.2 presents the full model. Local attachment and most other individual-level variables significant in Table 3.1 remain so in this new specification. The substantive impact of Local attachment (calculated using Clarify) as the variable shifts from the minimum value to the maximum value is approximately .03 in this model. As for the contextual variables, two operate as would be predicted by political opportunity theories: Threshold and Polarization are negatively related to radical right support and their effects are statistically significant.[30] Immigration and Unemployment show significant, negative effects. These coefficients challenge theories emphasizing socio-contextual factors, but they conform to results reported in many other studies.[31]

SWITZERLAND AND FRANCE

To what extent does a strong local orientation characterize radical right supporters in Switzerland and France? As noted above, carving out the Swiss and French respondents from the EVS data yields models similar to the cross-national ones. In this section, I replicate the EVS models using nationally representative surveys from these two countries to further test the link between local attachment and radical right support. The surveys are: the Swiss Electoral Studies (Selects) survey, the Swiss Household Panel (SHP) survey, and the French Political Barometer (BPF) survey. The Selects survey asks a question about local attachment that is very similar to the EVS item, which is a benefit for replication of the multinational models. Through the other two surveys I introduce two additional local orientation measures to better establish the nature of a locally rooted radical right vote. These additional measures are: the importance of local identity to one's sense of self (found in SHP) and preference for increased local authority (found in BPF). Survey details beyond those presented in the text directly below are in Data Appendix 3.1. I use this collection of datasets because each of these surveys includes questions that tap into local attachments or locally oriented attitudes. And each includes at least one useful question on party support that either measures which party a person feels closest to or asks about prospective voting plans.[32]

---

[30] Additional electoral system factors were introduced in a series of alternate models; none produced significant results. These include: Proportional representation, Mean district magnitude, Electoral threshold (all for lower legislative bodies). When radical right parties are divided into different groups according to their message type (per Golder 2003b, Carter 2005), populist radical right parties (rather than neo-fascist parties) are most significantly supported by those attached to their localities.

[31] In this specification, no statistically significant interaction effect between immigration and unemployment levels is evident.

[32] There are other datasets that contain local attachment/local orientation variables that I do not use due to certain details of each survey. One is the International Social Survey Program, which

TABLE 3.2 *Support for radical right parties in 18 countries*

Hierarchical logit models

Predictor	Coeff.	S.E.	Sig.
Attachments/Attitudes			
Local attachment	.20	(.07)	*
National attachment	.16	(.08)	*
Distrust parliament	.97	(.12)	*
Distrust EU	.59	(.11)	*
Anti-immigrant	.75	(.07)	*
Civic engagement			
Memberships (any)	−.13	(.06)	*
SES/Modernization losers			
Education low	.70	(.08)	*
Education middle	.52	(.08)	*
Occupational status:			
Full-/part-time	−.29	(.16)	
Self-employed	−.21	(.18)	
Retired	−.19	(.17)	
Homemaker	−.20	(.19)	
Student	−.85	(.20)	*
Unemployed	−.11	(.19)	
Socio-demographics			
Male	.40	(.06)	*
Age	−.99	(.15)	*
Contextual factors			
Unemployment rate	−.54	(.08)	*
Immigration level	−.24	(.06)	*
Electoral threshold	−.17	(.09)	*
Polarization	−.35	(.20)	*
Constant	1.11	(1.24)	
N individuals	24,571		
N countries	18		
Wald Chi²	791		*
-2Xlog likelihood	10,428		

Models include dummy variables for survey years.

* p<.05. Countries: Austria, Belgium, Croatia, Czech Rep., Denmark, Finland, France, Germany, Greece, Hungary, Italy, Netherlands, Norway, Poland, Romania, Slovak Rep., Slovenia, Switzerland.

Source: European Values Study

asks about how close a person feels to his or her town or city but only includes a retrospective vote question for partisan choice. The European Social Surveys (in 2006 and 2011) contain a question about attachment to the local community and a question on which party a person prefers. However, there is no national attachment correlate and this is important to the analysis from a theoretical standpoint. There is also a more recent Selects survey (administered in 2012; I use the 2007 data here) that asks about local attachment, but it only does so of one-third of the sample.

The dependent variable from Selects used in the models below is the self-reported probability that a respondent will vote for the Swiss People's Party (SVP) one day.[33] In the SHP the measure asks which party one would vote for if there were an election tomorrow. The BPF asks the probability of a Le Pen vote in the upcoming presidential election and also the party to which the respondent feels closest.

Independent Variables

Swiss Electoral Studies (Selects)

Local attachment is measured by the 2007 Swiss Selects as: "People can feel attached to varying degrees to their commune, their canton, their linguistic region, to their country or to Europe. Please tell me to what extent you feel attached to … your commune." Options are: "very attached, quite attached, not very attached, and not at all attached."[34] This item is similar to the EVS local attachment measure in that it cues a geographic dimension of attachment. But rather than asking respondents to rank order their geo-group attachments, the Selects question gives them an opportunity to report their attachment levels separately to their commune, country, etc. This survey item also yields a National attachment variable: "Please tell me to what extent you feel attached to … your country (Switzerland)." The inclusion of this variable makes it possible to establish the relationship between Local attachment and SVP support when accounting for feelings toward Switzerland.[35] In the sample of Swiss-born respondents used here, 38 percent feel "very attached" to their commune while 61 percent feel this way about Switzerland.

The Selects survey also asks Swiss respondents about confidence in various institutions, including local authorities. The item reads, "Can you tell me how much confidence you accord to the following institutions and organizations, on a scale from 0 to 10, where 0 signifies 'no confidence' and 10 signifies 'full confidence'? … The political authorities of your commune …"[36] Including

---

[33] Selects contains a range of partisan measures, any of which could be used here. In the text I introduce the one that allows for a particularly substantive interpretation since it is a likelihood item. But regardless of which dependent variable one considers, the effect of local attachment does not vary much. See Appendix Table A3.2 for bivariate models of each available party choice measure.

[34] Author's translation. Original text reads: "Les gens peuvent se sentir attachés à des degrés divers à leur commune, leur canton, leur région linguistique, à leur pays ou à l'Europe. Veuillez me dire dans quelle mesure vous vous sentez attachés à … Votre commune … votre pays (la Suisse) … très attaché, assez attaché, assez peu attaché, pas attaché du tout."

[35] The descriptive breakdown of these variables appears in Figure A3.2 in the Appendix. The local attachment and national attachment variables are positively, significantly correlated at .28: local and national affinities are complementary to each other.

[36] Author's translation. Original text reads: "Pouvez-vous me dire quelle confiance vous accordez aux institutions et organisations suivantes: Sur une échelle allant de 0 à 10, où 0 signifie 'aucune confiance' et 10 signifie 'pleine confiance' … Les autorités politiques de votre commune …"

this measure in the analysis broadens the scope of the concept of interest. Is localism a purely psychological phenomenon or are there specific political aspects to it? Trust in local authorities is positively and significantly correlated with Local attachment. Of those who feel closest to their communes approximately 1 percent have no confidence in the local authorities while over 20 percent have full confidence in them. If this variable positively predicts radical right party support, our understanding of the relevant aspects of local orientations expands.

Swiss Household Panel Survey (SHP)

The Swiss Household Panel introduced in its sixteenth wave (in 2014) an identity question. It reads, "To what extent does membership in the following places constitute an important part of your identity? ... Membership in your commune of residence." Options range from "not at all important" to "very important" on an eleven-point scale.[37] This item also asks about membership in the whole of Switzerland, yielding a national identity variable.[38] While the EVS and Selects measures ask about local and national attachments, the SHP item specifically gets at different aspects of identity, broadening the scope of the concept of interest. As in the Selects survey, respondents are not asked to rank order their identity components. On a ten-point scale, the mean score for communal identity's importance is approximately 6. For national identity it is approximately 8.

French Political Barometer (BPF)

The BPF surveys French respondents (in 2007) and introduces to this analysis a different kind of local measure. It prompts, "In France, would you say that the following institutions have too much power, not enough power or [is it] as it should be?" One institution asked about is the commune (or municipality).[39] This item provides insight into a distinctly political aspect of people's feelings about their localities; it signals an inclination toward the local that is clearly political in nature as it is about governmental authority. Therefore, this serves as another useful probe of the boundaries of the relevant local orientations for radical right support.

---

[37] Author's translation. Original text reads: "Dans quelle mesure l'appartenance aux lieux constitue une partie importante de votre identité, si o signifie 'pas du tout' et 10 'très important'? ... l'appartenance à la commune de residence ..."

[38] Originally worded: "... l'appartenance à toute la Suisse ..." Other spaces are also asked about: canton, language group, rural-urban, and outside Switzerland. The communal and national identity variables are significantly, positively correlated at .36.

[39] Author's translation. Original text reads: "En France, estimez-vous que les institutions suivantes ont trop de pouvoir, pas assez de pouvoir ou comme il faut? – Trop – Pas assez – Comme il faut ... Les communes ..." Other institutions asked about include departments, regions, parliament, the president, and the parties.

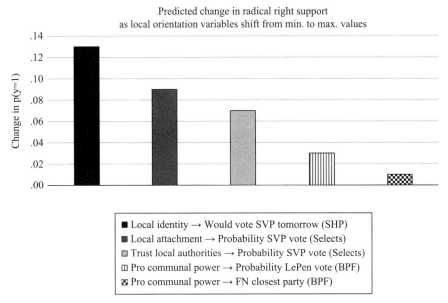

FIGURE 3.3

Models

Five models estimate the relevant relationships. All variables are coded to run from 0 to 1. I present the substantive results of bivariate specifications in Figure 3.3 for the sake of simplification since available covariates and controls vary by survey. Full models are printed in the Appendix (Tables A3.1 and A3.3–A3.6). Each bar in Figure 3.3 represents the predicted change in probability of supporting the radical right as the relevant predictor shifts from its minimum to maximum value. Each relationship is positive and statistically significant. I present the results in order of impact. Those Swiss with the strongest local identities have a .14 higher probability of supporting the SVP (if there were an election tomorrow) as compared to those with the weakest local identities. Local attachment is associated with a .09 increase and Trust in local authorities with a .07 increase in probability of someday supporting the SVP. The French communal authority measures have more modest effects, enhancing probability of support for Le Pen by .03 and probability of choosing the FN as the closest party by .01.

Once the non-attitudinal covariates are included in each of these models, each local orientation of interest retains statistical significance.[40] This demonstrates

---

[40] In Switzerland and France, radical right supporters are relatively young and male with comparably low levels of education. They also hold anti-EU, anti-immigrant, and anti-parliamentary attitudes.

a robust set of findings that are independent of occupational, associational, and demographic factors. With the introduction of attitudinal controls, the Swiss results for local orientations remain significant but the French results are less robust, falling slightly below the .95 threshold.[41]

DISCUSSION

The findings presented here answer some questions and generate others that are addressed in subsequent chapters. First, this chapter shows that there is a positive correlation between local attachment and radical right support in Europe. The relationship is robust to multiple factors representing extant theories of this phenomenon. Localists – those who feel strongly connected to their communities – tend to endorse radical right politics, all else equal. In contrast, citizens who participate in associational life are considerably less supportive of these parties as compared to the non-joining population. This emphasizes the divergent implications of specific aspects (psychological versus sociological) of social engagement for extreme right support. Disaggregating people's feelings about their communities from their routine social engagement is important for understanding the roots of radical right support.

Yet something important that these models cannot tell us is who these locally motivated radicals are. What kinds of people approach the choice to support the radical right on the basis of strong local attachments? A fuller understanding of the localist pathway to radical right support requires further analysis. One might also ask about the extent to which localists' traits or motivations have already been identified by previous research. Is local attachment a distinct starting point for finding one's way to the radical right or is it an offshoot of an existing theory? The next chapter uses interactive models to further illuminate the contours and assess the novelty of the localist approach.

A second contribution of this chapter is that it identifies various aspects of local orientations that matter for radical right support. This is made possible through leveraging the diversity of available survey measures to determine what localism means. There is evidence of a general place-based attachment (in the EVS and Selects), an identity component (in the SHP), a political trust dimension (in Selects), and an aspect that relates to political authority (in the BPF). Each of these predicts radical right support, comporting to expectations from theories based on psychology about the weight of group attachments and feelings of belonging. And while we see organizational memberships weakening the appeal of radical right politics, the models presented here do not directly address questions of actual social relationships with fellow locals. This seems

---

[41] Preference for enhanced local power is only predictive of FN support when anti-immigrant sentiments are not included in the equation. And this same preference for local power is significant in models of likely Le Pen support that do not include education controls.

important. The complexities of people's social lives require further attention to clarify how localism operates. The next two chapters (4 and 5) look into social relations more directly. I pay particular attention to distinctions between people's feelings and their actions to sort out the mechanisms at work.

Third, the results presented in this chapter hint that localism is stronger in some countries than in others. Where Swiss and French findings can be viewed side by side, Switzerland seems to host a more radically potent localism. Another way to state this is that in Switzerland, local communities and people's attachments to them may be more relevant for politics. Chapters 5, 6, and 7 look into the conditioning role of local political salience in detail.

4

Who Are the Localists that Support the Radical Right?

The previous chapter connects local attachment to support for radical right parties. Individuals who feel tied to their local communities and who favor local authority are especially likely to support the far right. In this chapter I explore the relationship further, seeking a better understanding of how the localist model operates. Specifically, I ask: for what kinds of people do local attachments translate into radical right support? Many Europeans feel tied to their local communities; recall that nearly half of European respondents to the European Values Study are more closely tied to their localities than to any other layer of society (see Figure 3.1 in Chapter 3). Yet in no country are so many people supportive of radical right parties; the most successful one to date is the Swiss People's Party, and it has not exceeded the 30 percent mark in national elections. These facts motivate the question: what factors sharpen or dull the effects of localism on radical right support?

I focus on three areas of theoretical and practical interest to investigate the contours of the localist pathway toward voting radical right. These are gender, social life, and political attitudes. What, I ask, can be said about the traits, routine behaviors, and political views of those locally tied individuals who support radical right parties? In other words, how do these factors relate to the key process of interest? Using the European Values Study and the Swiss Selects survey, I run interaction models to gain further insight into localism's link to radical right support.

To summarize the findings, localists who would vote radical right are especially likely to be women, to avoid associational memberships, to feel close to neighbors (but not to frequently help them), to be low on self-reported xenophobia and high on anti-EU sentiment, and to be of the center to center-left politically. These interactive results signal that the localist channel to radical right support is most frequently traveled by those individuals whose motivations are not well identified by dominant models of the phenomenon (which account for why strongly xenophobic, male, right-wingers would support the radical right). This chapter provides crucial insight into a distinct basis for radicalism, contributing to the conceptualization of the radical right constituency as "motivationally diverse" (see Cutts et al. 2011). In the pages that follow, I draw on existing literature to deduce expectations for how localism may relate to factors such as gender, participation in social activities, and political attitudes. For each of these traits, patterns of engagement, and viewpoints I also illuminate competing arguments and residual puzzles that characterize the existing literature. I then present the results of a series of interaction models and consider their implications.

GENDER

Women on average are less supportive of radical right parties than are men (Givens 2004, 2017, Evans 2005, Norris 2005, Ford and Goodwin 2010). The radical right gender gap has been well documented; two main sets of explanations exist. The first emphasizes occupational traits, asserting that economic interests vary by gender. Because men and women tend to have different job profiles, they have different perceptions of their own economic insecurity and of the extent to which they compete with immigrants in the job market (Perrineau 1997). Because males are disproportionately represented in low-skilled jobs, they are especially likely to be on the losing end of modernization and globalization. This, in turn, renders them more open to radical right appeals (Betz 1994). A variant of this occupational account contends that women are socialized differently than men. This leads them to different occupations, which in turn shape their level of attraction to radical right party platforms (Kitschelt, with McGann, 1995).

The second set of gendered explanations emphasizes the role of values and broad political orientations. Some scholars argue that women and men are driven by distinct value priorities which push men toward radical right parties and pull women away from them (Gindengil et al. 2005). Evidence suggests that political tolerance is typically higher among women than among men (Golebiowska 1999) and that the confrontational nature of these parties appeals less to women who value consensus politics (Fish 2002). Recent research also shows that men are more drawn to populist rhetoric than women (Spierings and Zaslove 2017).

Others argue that women in advanced democracies are ideologically farther to the left on average than men (Inglehart and Norris 2000). Psychologically men exhibit higher levels of authoritarianism and social dominance, both of which benefit the radical right (Lipset 1981, Van Hiel and Mervielde 2002). More broadly, research suggests that women in general are less inclined to vote for new parties (Immerzeel et al. 2015) and are likely to evaluate parties according to different criteria than men (Kolinsky 1993). Along similar lines, another set of studies highlights the confrontational, anti-feminist dimensions of radical right parties that turn women off (Kitschelt, with

McGann, 1995, Mayer 1999) and the policy goals that conflict with those of many women (Akkerman 2015, de Lange and Mügge 2015).[1]

Efforts to explain the difference between men's and women's levels of interest in these parties have yielded useful insights. However, there remains a residual difference between the sexes for which existing theories cannot account. Givens describes the persistence of the gender gap:

[T]his analysis indicates that the gender gap in the radical right vote does vary across countries. However, I was unable to find any variables that reduced the gender gap in these countries ... I find that there is a persistent gender gap when controlling for social, economic, and political variables. Although the gender gap in the vote for mainstream parties may have complex underpinnings, it would appear that in the case of the radical right, simply being female may make one less likely to vote for these parties. (2017: 304)

In similar terms, recent studies show that the gender gap cannot be fully accounted for by factors such as socio-economic traits, anti-immigrant sentiment, and authoritarian orientations (Immerzeel et al. 2015, Spierings and Zaslove 2015a, Spierings and Zaslove 2015b).

Observations that the radical right is not female-friendly, and the difficulty of existing theories to fully account for the gender gap, prompt reversal of the typical gender gap question. Rather than asking why women are less supportive of the radical right than men, perhaps we should ask why women support the radical right at all. In the spirit of this revision, I argue that the radical right literature does not adequately consider the ways that women and men differ politically. Existing accounts have not sufficiently explored the likelihood that women and men – on average – approach politics from different starting points. Perhaps women and men travel different pathways to find the radical right appealing. Indeed, a study of SVP voters in Switzerland confirms the gender gap and shows that existing models are much better able to explain radical right voting among men than among women (Fontana et al. 2006).

An explanation for the persistent male-female gap in radical right support may stem from the gendered ways in which people relate to their local communities. Geographer Doreen Massey explains, "Particular ways of thinking about space and place are tied up with, both directly and indirectly, particular social constructions of gender relations" (1994: 2). The nexus of gender and place is further explored in the feminist geography literature, notably by Carolin Schurr's development of the concept of emotional geography (see Schurr 2013).

Furthermore, community sociology research finds that gender is intimately intertwined with different kinds of local ties (Beggs et al. 1996), while social

---

[1] This explanation finds support in the shrinking gender gap among FN voters in France as Marine Le Pen softens the messaging somewhat (Mayer 2014).

psychology contributes an understanding that men and women relate to and identify with places differently as a function (at least in part) of socialized gender roles and expectations (Proshansky et al. 1983).[2] These observations are reinforced from an environmental psychology perspective; past work finds that when describing the positive aspects of their homes women tend to emphasize the overall atmosphere and positive social relationships with others (including with pets) while men are more likely to describe physical features. Women also emphasize the sense of security they derive from their homes while men do not (Smith 1994).

Local attachments, I suggest, may hold the key to women's radical right support. Consider the following collection of discoveries on gendered political behavior. Socialization of gender roles during formative years produces distinct orientations to politics in established democratic settings (Jennings 1983, Kitschelt, with McGann, 1995), while evidence also suggests that in newer democracies men and women experience democratic citizenship differently (Heinen 1997). Other gendered findings signal that women and men are differently oriented to their local political arenas. For example, women's political knowledge is greater with respect to local facts, men's with respect to national facts (Verba et al. 1997). Women tend to trust local governments more than men do, and they have more favorable views of local as compared to national government (Fitzgerald and Wolak 2016).[3] Findings such as these underpin the notion that local attachments may be pivotal in accounting for gendered paths to radical right support. Motivated by the many differences in the ways women relate to their communities and to politics in general, I test this notion that localism is an effective vehicle for the female radical right vote.

SOCIAL ENGAGEMENT

How, exactly, does social engagement – or the absence of it – relate to radical right support? The finding from Chapter 3 that local attachment is on balance positively associated with extremist voting supports a "dark side" account of social capital's political implications. Yet the companion finding that organizational memberships are negatively associated with support for radical right parties enriches the narrative. These results serve as a reminder to distinguish between or among the different dimensions of a person's links to society. I do

---

[2] They argue that social class, age, and certain features of personality are also relevant characteristics that influence the nature and experience of place identities (Proshansky et al. 1983). See also Manzo (2003) on the politics of place identity and the role of emotion in people's connections with particular places.

[3] This raises the point that men and women relate differently to their national political arenas, as well. This would fit with the observation that nationalism is deeply connected to notions of masculinity (Nagel 1998).

this in Chapter 2 by conceptually and theoretically distinguishing feelings from behaviors. A sense of local attachment represents a psychological dimension; participation in associational life implies an active, behavioral link to society that is more sociologically and structurally oriented.

Moving beyond the recognition that feelings about one's community and formal participation in it have opposing implications for radical right support, this chapter considers whether these factors interact in meaningful ways. One directional expectation is that associational memberships counteract local attachments, muting their radicalizing effect. This is the relationship implied by the models in Chapter 3 that include the local attachment and organizational membership variables side-by-side. As outlined in Chapter 2, mass society theory and mainstream social capital theories predict that organizational participation should minimize the attraction of radical right parties. This line of reasoning further suggests that such engagement would diminish the local attachment-radical right link. If individuals who feel strongly tied to their localities are also engaged in associational life, then perhaps these factors cancel each other out. By engaging in civil society, any extremist impulses spurred by feeling close to the locality may be quashed or perhaps reversed. Participation in societal organizations may preclude altogether any interest in the appeal of right-wing radicals. More broadly, engagement in associational life may channel locally rooted feelings in a more politically moderate direction.

While a growing set of studies consider the way that associational participation at individual and aggregate levels connects to political radicalism (Norris 2005, Coffé et al. 2007, Rydgren 2009, Cutts et al. 2011), examinations of conditional effects are quite rare. One exception finds that social capital erodes the positive connection between unemployment in a particular area and radical right electoral success (Jesuit et al. 2009). This suggests that associational engagement can undermine or "block" proven pathways to radical right support.

Alternatively, it might be the case that community engagement boosts the positive effect of local ties on extremist voting. Perhaps the radical implications of feeling close to a locality are enhanced when participation in associational life is high. In other words, engagement in civic life may deepen psychological attachments and boost the link between local attachment and radical right voting propensity. Research in fields such as anthropology and sociology shows that place attachment and organizational participation are positively correlated and mutually reinforcing in a range of countries (Boulianne and Brailey 2014, Vidal et al. 2013, Lewicka 2005, Dekker 2007). If this is the case, it implies that whatever pro-democratic effects associational participation might have on political choices can be undermined when they enhance local in-group sentiments.

A complicating aspect of the survey items on associational memberships in the EVS and Selects surveys is that they do not differentiate between organizational participation within and outside the local community. Furthermore they only represent formal participation in organizations, while research tells us that informal relations can also generate social capital (Newton 1997, Forrest and Kearns 2001, Pichler and Wallace 2007). One way to get at the more locally defined, informal aspects of a person's routines is to consider their relationships with neighbors. Neighbors, by definition, share a local space. Therefore, by establishing how links to neighbors interact with local attachments, we gain purchase on the mechanisms at work. To this end, I consider the conditioning effects of associational memberships, frequency of helping neighbors, and feeling of preparedness to help neighbors on the relationship between local attachments and radical right party support.

ATTITUDES

One of the strongest predictors of radical right support across Europe is a person's views on the subject of immigration. This is demonstrated in the previous chapter and in scores of other studies. But it is a stronger predictor in some cases than in others (Ivarsflaten 2008), and indeed it is a more robust factor in Western Europe as compared to Eastern Europe (Allen 2017). Given the potency but also variability in the strength of such attitudes' effects, it makes sense to investigate whether they might interact with local attachments to predict radical right support. One interpretation of the localist impulse might be that it is rooted in a desire to protect one's community from the effects of immigration. Research pointing to a not-in-my-backyard aspect to immigration attitudes supports this expectation (Goodwin 2008, Hopkins 2011, Astor 2016). If this is valid, then localists who are also against immigration should be especially likely to support radical right parties.

Alternatively it is also possible that while national attachments and anti-immigration attitudes are complementary and mutually reinforcing, localism as a predictor of radical right support is not strengthened by anti-immigrant views. Once national attachments are controlled for, a negative interaction between local attachments and anti-immigrant views may be present. Drawing on aggregate-level studies strengthens this expectation. Plenty of communities with little-to-no diversity host high levels of radical right support (Bréchon and Mitra 1992, Mayer and Perrineau 1996, Bowyer 2008, Dancygier 2010), and indeed diversity is a factor that weakens the link between community solidarity and radical right support at the municipal level (Fitzgerald and Lawrence 2011). To the extent that immigration to the local area undermines the potency of positive feelings about community for politics, this would imply a non-complementary relationship between local attachment and anti-immigrant views. As such, one might predict that local attachment's correlation with radical right party support would be weakened among those who are most concerned about immigration.

DATA AND METHODS

I use the EVS data and the Swiss Selects data described in Chapter 3. These surveys contain the most comparable local attachment measures among the datasets I draw on in that chapter. The EVS provides a general view of patterns across many countries while the Swiss data facilitate a more focused look at radical right support in one national context. A benefit of the Swiss data is that the local attachment item does not ask respondents to rank order their geo-spatial attachments (like the EVS does). Another is that it contains a higher percentage of radical right voters than does the EVS. As such, these two datasets complement each other well.

To examine the interactive relationships of interest, I run a series of models that contain the full battery of controls presented in Chapter 3. For the EVS models these are: Local attachment, National attachment, Distrust parliament, Distrust EU, Anti-immigrant, Memberships, Education low, Education middle, Full-/part-time, Self-employed, Retired, Homemaker, Student, Unemployed, Male, and Age, plus fixed effects for country and year. In the Selects models they are: Local attachment, National attachment, Anti-EU, Anti-immigrant, Education low, Education middle, Full-/part-time, Family business, Housewife/ househusband, Pensioner, Unemployed, In school, Male, and Age. In this chapter I make three additions to this set of variables. First, each model includes one interaction term in addition to all the other variables. The other change is the introduction of *Left-right ideology* and *Community size* to the models. This helps to further clarify the nature of the localist pathway by controlling for basic political and community factors that might confound the analysis.[4]

RESULTS

To illustrate the results, I present a series of figures that plot the coefficients and confidence intervals for Local attachment at different levels of the condi-tioning variables.[5] Each panel of each figure represents the key interactive result of interest from a single model. For the EVS these are logit coefficients because

---

[4] One might suspect community size to exert an influence on local attachments and voting behavior, driving a spurious relationship. Similarly, one might consider conservatism to be a feature of small town life and also a predictor of vote choice, confounding the observed relationships. Left-right ideology is measured in the EVS as follows: "In political matters, people talk of 'the left' and 'the right.' How would you place your views on this scale, generally speaking?" Responses run from 1 (farthest left) to 10 (farthest right). In the SVP the item reads, "In politics, one sometimes speaks of the 'left' and the 'right.' Can you tell me where you would place yourself on a scale from 0 to 10, where 0 signifies 'left' and 10 signifies 'right'?" (author's translation). Community size in both cases is a generated variable with eight categories in EVS and nine cat-egories in Selects.

[5] These are calculated via lincom in Stata 14. All variables are coded to range from 0 at their min-imums to 1 at their maximums.

the radical right support variable is dichotomous; for the Swiss data they are regression coefficients because the SVP support variables I utilize here are the probability of support in upcoming election and (only in Figure 4.1, Panel B) sympathy for the party leader (both of which are 11-point scales).[6] Not all of the figures depict statistically significant interactive relationships, but most are either significant at .95 or close to that cutoff. Therefore, plots of marginal effects supply important information. I also report significance levels below each figure so that it is clear which results are the most statistically robust. I provide odds ratios in footnotes as relevant to interpret the logit model results. I do not provide each of the models in table form but instead graphically present the relevant findings.[7]

Gender

Women demonstrate the strongest propensity to combine strong local attachments with radical right party (RRP) support. Figure 4.1, Panel A presents results from the EVS models. It shows that local attachment is only a statistically significant predictor of radical right party support for women; the coefficient for men is not distinguishable from zero at the .95 confidence level.[8] This lack of significance is indicated by the confidence interval crossing the zero line as well as the empty dot representing the coefficient.[9] Filled-in dots indicate statistically significant point estimates. Although the interaction term, itself, is not significant at conventional levels, this does suggest that locally oriented radicals in Europe tend to be women.[10]

In the Swiss data, the interaction between gender and local attachment is not statistically significant when the probability of voting for the SVP is the dependent variable. (Though the regression coefficient for women (.03) is about three times the size of that for men (.01).) But when the dependent variable is level of sympathy for the SVP, the interaction is significant and favors women.[11]

---

[6] Ordered logit specification for these Swiss models does not substantively alter the results.

[7] Foundational tables as well as figures depicting all ancillary findings described herein are readily available from the author.

[8] In simple descriptive terms per the EVS data, women are significantly more likely than men to feel strongly attached to their communities.

[9] These logit coefficients are useful for displaying conditional effects in the EVS data. Their direction and significance level can tell us a great deal about how a particular independent variable of interest relates to the dependent variable as a conditioning variable is manipulated. However, the substantive meaning of these coefficients is not evident from the figures. Using Clarify (Tomz et al. 2003) to calculate predicted values associated with these interactions reveals modest substantive effects on par with those presented in the previous chapter. The Swiss Selects regression models yield more readily interpretable coefficients.

[10] Per the odds ratios from the EVS model, the impact of local attachment on radical right support is 20 percent higher for women than for men.

[11] The coefficient for men is -.01 (not significant) and .07 for women (significant at .023). Because the interaction variable, itself, is not statistically significant in the EVS model, this effect across European countries should be treated carefully. But the Swiss result is quite robust.

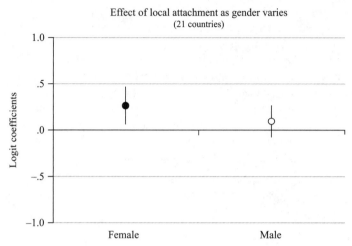

FIGURE 4.1 PANEL A Dependent variable: Would/would not support RRP if election were tomorrow. Interaction term p-value is .112, full battery of controls, N = 28,282. *Source*: European Values Study

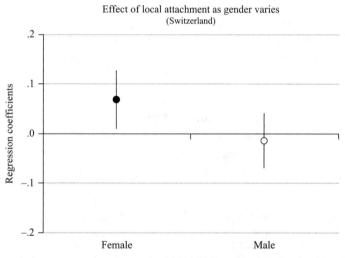

FIGURE 4.1 PANEL B Dependent variable: Level of sympathy for SVP. Interaction term p-value is .041, full battery of controls, N = 1,812.
Source: Swiss Selects

Figure 4.1, Panel B, shows these results. Here, women prove to be 7 percentage points more sympathetic toward the SVP if they are strongly tied to their communities than if they are not. Men are actually slightly less supportive of the SVP if they feel tightly linked to their communities. Using this particular measure of SVP support, these Swiss data corroborate the EVS finding that the localist pathway to radical right support is one most frequently traveled by women.[12]

Social Engagement

How do a person's connections to society condition the link between local attachments and radical right party support? Here, I depict three interactive relationships, drawing on the EVS and Selects data. The first examines associational life. Figure 4.2 demonstrates the interactive effect between number of organizational memberships and local attachment in predicting radical right support.[13] The positive effect of local ties on radical right support loses significance at two memberships. Participation in more than one membership washes out the role of local attachment in motivating a radical right vote. At four or more memberships, the coefficient is essentially zero. This is the case for the logit models from the EVS (Panel A) and regression models from the Swiss Selects (Panel B).[14] The Selects regression coefficient for local attachment drops more than .06 when shifting from zero to four memberships. It should be noted, however, that neither of these interaction terms is a statistically significant predictor of radical right support at conventional levels. So to the extent that there is an interaction effect to speak of, it is rather weak.[15]

As noted above, the data on associational memberships cannot tell us whether they reflect actual participation in community life. Organizations to which people formally belong might be non-participatory or national in nature with little active, local engagement by members, for instance. And while this should not matter when the goal is to test the ways that civil society participation – broadly defined – relates to radical right support, it does matter for questions about the implications of local social engagement. To gain a better view of the ways people connect with their local scenes, I introduce two new variables to the analysis. *Prepared to help neighbors* is in the EVS; the item asks whether a respondent feels prepared to help his or her fellow community

---

[12] There is no SVP support dependent variable for which the gendered interaction favors men.

[13] Memberships per the EVS ranges from zero to sixteen; in the Selects it ranges from zero to seven. It is an additive item indicating the number of organizations of which an individual is a member. I provide point estimates up through four memberships because this represents the bulk of respondents in both samples. Removing outliers at the high end of the scales from the models does not alter the results substantively.

[14] Calculating odds ratios for the EVS marginal effects shows that the odds of supporting a radical right party associated with local attachment is approximately .35 higher for non-members than for those with four memberships.

[15] This might be a function of the combination of different kinds of memberships (union, animal rights, religious, etc.) into a single participation index. Past work shows that the attitudinal implications (for instance, toward immigrants) of organizational memberships and other kinds of social participation patterns can vary widely across contexts (see Fitzgerald 2012, Hooghe and Quintelier 2013).

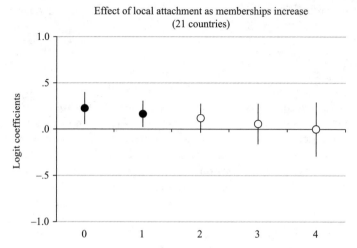

FIGURE 4.2 PANEL A Dependent variable: Would/would not support RRP if election were tomorrow. Interaction term p-value is .221, full battery of controls, N = 28,282. *Source*: European Values Study

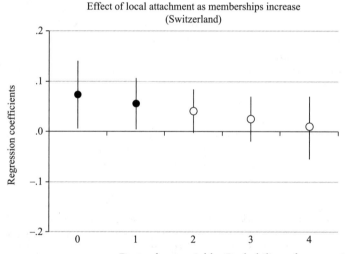

FIGURE 4.2 PANEL B Dependent variable: Probability of supporting SVP. Interaction term p-value is .224, full battery of controls, N = 1,940. *Source*: Swiss Selects

members.[16] This measures an attitude or an orientation toward neighbors since it does not ask whether they *have* provided aid. A behavioral version of this

[16] This question is worded as follows: "would you be prepared to actually do something to improve the conditions of ... people in your neighborhood/community?" The number of observations is

question comes from the Swiss Selects: *Frequently help neighbors.* The item asks how often an individual provides aid to his or her neighbors.[17]

Per Figure 4.3, Panel A, feeling prepared to help neighbors interacts significantly and positively with local attachment to predict radical right support in Europe. The more willing an individual is to assist locals, the stronger the connection between local ties and radical right party support. Local attachment is only a significant predictor of radical right support for individuals who respond "maybe," "yes," or "absolutely yes."[18]

Actually helping neighbors, however, has the opposite conditioning effect. Figure 4.3, Panel B, relates to the behavioral dimension of the neighborly aid concept. When people actively engage with their neighbors, the effect of local attachment diminishes. The coefficient for those Swiss who never help their neighbors is over .10 and statistically significant. For those who help them often, the effect is about zero, leaning negative.

This pair of results signals that actions and feelings send local attachment's effects in different directions. Together, the social engagement evidence suggests that the role of local attachment is undermined by associational participation (weak effects) and routine aid to fellow local residents (relatively robust effects). In contrast, localism is strongest among those who feel positively about their neighbors in that they would hypothetically be inclined to help them out if necessary.[19]

Attitudes

Are localists driven by their anti-immigrant attitudes to support radical right parties? The evidence suggests that this is not the case. Per Figure 4.4, Panel A, the role of local attachment is only significant for those who do not mention

---

significantly lower for this model. The relevant question is only asked in one wave of the survey and only in some countries are there enough radical right supporters to make reliable estimates possible. The countries included in the modeled sample are: Austria, Belgium, Croatia, Czech Republic, Denmark, Finland, France, Italy, Romania, Slovakia, and Slovenia.

[17] The question wording is: "How frequently do you help your neighbors or how often do they help you with practical things? Often, sometimes, rarely or never?" (author's translation). Original text: "A quelle fréquence aidez-vous vos voisines et voisins ou à quelle fréquence vous aident-ils pour des choses pratiques? Diriez-vous … souvent, parfois, rarement, jamais."

[18] Calculating odds ratios reveals that for "absolutely yes" responders, the impact of local attachment is twice that of "absolutely no" responders. The odds ratio is .92 at "absolutely no" and 1.9 at "absolutely yes."

[19] The matter of neighborly relations raises questions about community size. Interactions (not presented) between local attachment and community size (in both linear and non-linear form) in the EVS and Selects data do not prove statistically significant, suggesting that there is no clear role of community size. But in the EVS it is close, with statistically significant coefficients at 10,000–12,000 residents and greater. Taking a non-linear approach to this interaction suggests that in Europe the most hospitable community size for the localist model of radical right support is 100,000 to 500,000 residents.

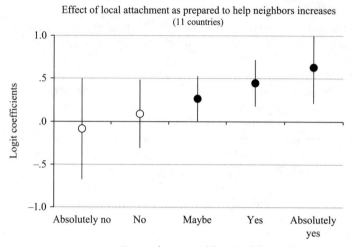

FIGURE 4.3 PANEL A Dependent variable: Would/would not support RRP if election were tomorrow. Interaction term p-value is .102, full battery of controls, N=10,392. *Source*: European Values Study

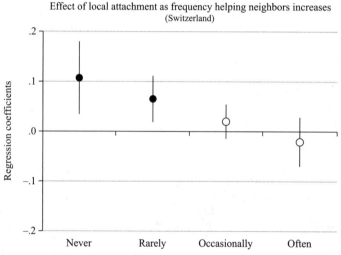

FIGURE 4.3 PANEL B Dependent variable: Probability of supporting SVP. Interaction term p-value is .027, full battery of controls minus memberships due to observation loss, N=3,427.
Source: Swiss Selects

immigrants (labeled "low" on Anti-immigrant sentiment) when answering this question.[20] In Switzerland (see Panel B), a parallel relationship exists. Local

---

[20] Odds ratios associated with this figure are 1.25 for those who do not mention immigrants, and .92 for those who do.

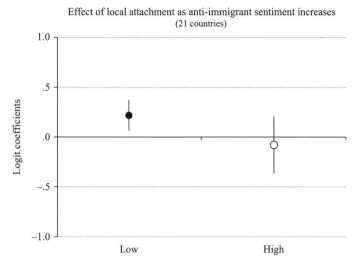

FIGURE 4.4 PANEL A Dependent variable: Would/would not support RRP if election were tomorrow. Interaction term p-value is .057, full battery of controls, N=28,282.
Source: European Values Study

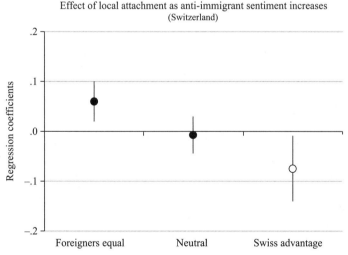

FIGURE 4.4 PANEL B Dependent variable: Probability of supporting SVP. Interaction term p-value is .012, full battery of controls minus memberships due to observation loss, N=3,452.
Source: Swiss Selects

attachment is a significant, positive predictor of radical right party support only for those who think that foreigners should have the same opportunities as Swiss natives. It is a negative (though non-significant) predictor for those who prefer Swiss advantage over foreigners. These interactive results are statistically

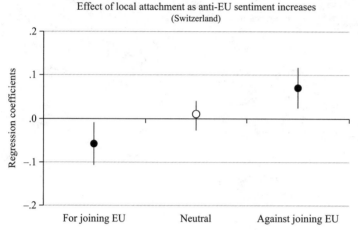

Effect of local attachment as anti-EU sentiment increases
(Switzerland)

FIGURE 4.5 Dependent variable: Probability of supporting SVP. Interaction term p-value is .000, full battery of controls minus memberships due to observation loss, N=3,320.
Source: Swiss Selects

significant in both datasets. They suggest that local attachments provide a parallel, but not an interactive, source of radical right support. While the effects of anti-immigrant sentiments and localism on radical right support are likely additive, they do not rely on each other for influence.

This raises further questions about the political attitudes of localists. In what other ways might a localist differ from or align with the image of far right-wingers assembled by past work? Testing the effects of interactions between Distrust EU and Local attachments as well as Distrust Parliament and Local attachments yields no significant or near-significant results in the EVS. But in the Swiss Selects data, there is a strong, statistically significant interaction between Anti-EU sentiments and Local attachment. I present these interaction effects in Figure 4.5. Local attachment is strongest among those who are against Swiss membership in the EU (the coefficient is .07 with a *p* value of .002). It is actually negative (the coefficient is -.06 with a *p* value of .022) for those who favor Swiss membership.[21] This may connect back to the local authority dimension of radical right support presented in previous chapters and suggested in the above text. I return to this theme below and in the chapters that follow.

These attitudinal considerations point to a complex ideological landscape for localists, prompting the question: how does localism relate to the left-right spectrum? It is in many respects obvious to suggest that voters for the radical right should be far right-leaning in their ideologies. But research that points to the presence of centrist and left-leaning ideologues and working-class members

---

[21] This interactive effect is also statistically significant for the other measures of SVP support contained in Selects.

among radical right voters in Eastern and Western Europe complicates matters in an intriguing way (Andersen and Bjørklund 1990, Oesch 2008, Goodliffe 2012, Allen 2015, and see Kitschelt 2007 for a review).

Thus, Figure 4.6 plots another set of interactions. Panel A shows EVS interaction results that are negative and statistically significant. It is left-leaners who take a localist pathway to the radical right. Localism's effects are only statistically significant among centrist and left-of-center respondents.[22] (Removing control variables strengthens this result.) Similarly, per Panel B, the Swiss localist impulse is strongest among left-leaning respondents. The coefficient for the farthest left respondents is .08 (significant at .027), and it is -.04 (significant at .305) for the farthest right. Removing national attachment as a control boosts the interaction into statistical significance.

Taking these linear interactions at face value, there is a strong suggestion here that the way extreme leftists find their way to the radical right is through localism. But more complex patterns may be obscured by the linearity of the analysis. By modeling this in non-linear form (creating a dichotomous variable for each value on the ideological scale) and calculating predicted changes associated with each new dummy variable yields a slightly more nuanced picture. In the EVS data, the strongest localist effects are at 3, 4, and 5 on the (0 to 10) left-right scale. So slight left-leaners and centrists are the most likely to translate local attachments into radical right support. In Switzerland, the localist coefficient is strongest at the 3 and 5 points on the scale. Localism is primarily a center to center-left phenomenon.[23]

Predicting Local Attachments

In an additional pair of models, presented in Tables A4.3 and A4.4 in the Appendix, I move backward in the causal chain to examine the predictors of local attachment. In this analytical step I ask: what kinds of people feel strongly connected to their localities in the first place? I run these models of local attachment using the EVS and the Swiss Selects data. The expectation is that the results will differ somewhat between the two models because the European survey makes respondents rank order their geo-social attachments while the Selects survey does not.

---

[22] The odds ratio for the farthest left is 1.6 (significant at .004) and .91 (significant at .513) for the farthest right.

[23] In appendix Tables A4.1 and A4.2 I present fully interactive models in which every variable (apart from the dummy variables for each year and country) is interacted with local attachment. In the EVS model, two interaction terms are statistically significant: Anti-immigrant X local attachment and Left-right ideology X local attachment. Both are negatively signed, in line with the results presented above. In the Selects model, both Anti-immigrant X local attachment and Anti-EU X local attachment are statistically significant. In line with the results presented above, the sign for the anti-immigration attitudes interaction is negative while the sign for the anti-EU attitudes interaction is positive.

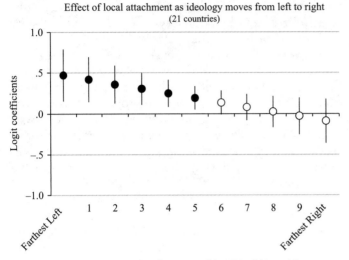

Effect of local attachment as ideology moves from left to right
(21 countries)

FIGURE 4.6 PANEL A Dependent variable: Would/would not support RRP if election were tomorrow. Interaction term p-value is .031, full battery of controls, N=28,282. *Source*: European Values Study

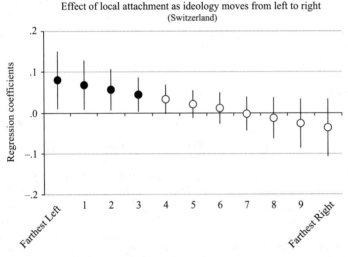

Effect of local attachment as ideology moves from left to right
(Switzerland)

FIGURE 4.6 PANEL B Dependent variable: Probability of supporting SVP. Interaction term p-value is .066, full battery of controls minus memberships due to observation loss, N=3,320. *Source*: Swiss Selects

Per the EVS data, the positive, significant predictors of feeling strongly attached to the local area are: Anti-immigrant, Left-right ideology, Education low, Education medium, Retired, and Age. The negative, significant predictors are: National attachment, Distrust parliament, Memberships, Male, and Community size. In the Swiss Selects, the significant, positive predictors are: National attachment, Memberships, Low education, Age, and Community size. The significant, negative predictor is Student occupational status. The clearest patterns that emerge when combining the results of the Europe-wide and Swiss models are that the most locally attached individuals do not have much education and they are relatively advanced in age.

DISCUSSION

In this chapter, interactive statistical tests provide two kinds of insights. First, they help to clarify certain aspects of a localist model of radical right support. For whom is a localist pathway to these parties most likely? How does such a process operate? It turns out that the localist model is in many ways a conditional model. Certain demographic, social, and political characteristics interact with local attachment in strengthening or weakening the likelihood of radical right support. Women, association avoiders, those who do not routinely help their neighbors,[24] those who feel positive about their neighbors, and individuals who are not so openly anti-immigrant, who are distrustful of the EU, and who place themselves in the center to center-left are the most likely to be motivated by their local attachments to support radical right parties.

The second set of insights relates to existing models of radical right voters. The results presented here establish a relatively independent model in localism. Existing accounts struggle to explain women's support, for instance, while localism is identified here as a potential vehicle for female supporters. And while anti-immigrant attitudes are important dispositions consistently identified by existing work on the behavioral side of the radical right phenomenon,

---

[24] Another potentially useful concept that I do not explore here is efficacy. Social integration and cooperation are known to strengthen people's abilities to work together, which in turn has been found to enhance feelings of efficacy in individuals. A combination of feeling defensive of a particular collectivity and a sense that one cannot take collective action toward affecting change may lead a voter to choose a party or candidate who offers a relatively simple solution to complex societal problems that an individual perceives to be important. This nexus between feeling motivated by local ties to take some kind of action and not having the outlet for collective action among citizens may be an important place to look to predict radical right support. Without ideas or options for alternative strategies, people use their vote to empower forces promising to deliver desired change. It's possible that those individuals who are highly participatory in their communities are the ones most likely to engage in collective action on behalf of the local group. But those who feel tied to the community without such participatory patterns and networks to draw on may not feel the empowerment that comes from engaging in collective, purposive action. It is those voters that may be the most likely to support the radical right: they do not gain the benefits of social capital and thus they feel increasingly frustrated and angry as well as inefficacious. The radical right vote is the only tool they may feel they have. Thus, the combination of politicized local attachments and a dearth of civil society and routine cooperation among neighbors sets the scene for radical right electoral advancement.

they are not a pivotal part of the localist account provided here. Alternatively, it is anti-EU sentiment that operates in tandem with localism, suggesting that matters of authority are important for these radicals.[25]

Furthermore, the role of leftist ideology in localism is interesting. The trend toward left-leaning support for extreme right movements has been explained mainly in terms of economic interests. If modernity threatens workers' livelihoods and status levels, then radical right parties offer the solution in back-ward-looking appeals that vow to restore past economic security and status. But a rival interpretation – that the solidarity and sense of social belonging once supplied by unions and other working-class movements have eroded and left room for new ideas about belonging – better aligns with the localist model. Andersen and Bjørklund (1990) suggest that a "spontaneous working class consciousness" imprints on members an us-them mentality. Based on the results presented above, I argue that this collective mindset is complementary to locally defined in-group feelings.

The findings presented in this chapter provide detail on the localist model of radical right support. Through identification with the local community, many unlikely radical right supporters make their way to these parties. Given the heightened localism across societies emphasized in Chapters 1 and 2, this may be cause for concern among those who wish to weaken radical right parties. This chapter's results may foreshadow how radical right parties will broaden their constituencies in the future. It is to the temporal dimensions of radical right party support that I now turn. Panel data provide important insights into how localism's effects on radical right support operate over time. The next chapter examines individuals from year to year to establish whether people's attachments to their communities can exert a dynamic influence on partisan choices.

[25] To compare the conditionality of local attachments with the role of nationalist sentiments, I replicated all of this chapter's interaction models with national attachment in place of local attachment. Only one interaction term is significant in the EVS models: Nationalism X Left-right ideology. Though the impact is not as significant as the localist version of the interaction (the interaction term is significant at .056), there is still a negative effect. National attachment can motivate leftists to support the radical right. No other interaction term is even close to significant in this configuration. In the Swiss Selects data, none of the interactions is statistically significant. The main point to take from this is that local attachments are more conditionally linked to radical right party support than are national attachments.

5

Neighborly Ties, Local Autonomy, and SVP Support in Switzerland

The ways in which people relate to their communities have important implications for electoral choices. Previous chapters depict a complex attitudinal and social landscape that underpins radical right party support. Local ties, broadly defined, affect the likelihood that an individual will support a radical right party. But not all local ties are alike. The findings in Chapters 3 and 4 suggest that feelings about the community and its inhabitants should be distinguished from social interaction with neighbors and associational participation. Cognitive connections and social networks do not have the same electoral implications; for instance, feeling prepared to help neighbors and *actually* helping them send the effects of local attachment on radical right party support in different directions. The former boosts radical right support while the latter diminishes the appeal of these parties.

This chapter further examines the role of neighborly relations in electoral choice. Neighboring represents a distinct dimension of local engagement. Here I ask four main questions about people's connections with fellow community residents. First, do people's ties to their neighbors influence their likelihood of supporting the radical right, particularly if they have not done so before? Second, if yes, which aspects of neighborly engagement are most relevant? Third, are these effects specific to the far right or do they benefit other parties, as well? And fourth, in what kinds of local contexts are neighborly relations especially relevant for radical right support? Through the use of yearly Swiss panel data, this chapter advances the inquiry beyond contemporaneous correlation models to examine intra-individual shifts in partisan support across twelve years (1999–2010).

This approach is important for understanding the dynamic patterns of support for the radical right. Simply characterizing a person as a radical right supporter through a single-wave survey obscures telling variation. What factors precipitate a choice to support such a party? This question is key to advancing our knowledge about the radical right phenomenon. It will also help to resolve a matter associated with the central argument of this book: that local ties drive far right support. That is, one might consider the possibility of a reverse process through which support for a radical right party engenders or reinforces local ties. The community-friendly rhetoric espoused by these parties might promote enhanced feelings of solidarity with fellow locals. Panel survey data can help to sort this out.[1]

The questions posed above are also important to ask and answer given the debate over whether radical right votes are protest votes (Van der Eijk et al. 1996, Van der Brug et al. 2000, Van der Brug and Fennema 2003). Protest voting, described in the literature as inconsistent over time or non-ideological (or both), should be identifiable as distinct from mainstream or ideological voting. Yearly surveys that tap into partisan support over time stand to provide valuable insight. For instance, if protest theories apply to the radical right, their support should be less consistent in year-to-year terms than support for mainstream parties. The nature of these panel data allow for examination of such dynamic patterns.

This chapter also takes seriously the question of context: under what conditions can we expect a localist impulse to vote radical right to be strongest? Political salience of local identities helps to connect feelings of positivity toward one's community with his or her vote choice in national elections. This chapter develops two measures of political salience that are institutional in nature: the level of authority of the community and the recent decline in authority of the community. These are factors that help to distinguish localities from each other and that help distinguish different regions of Switzerland from each other. Importantly, they are dynamic dimensions of authority structures that can be examined over time to establish their relevance for the localist-radical right link. Furthermore, on the theme of context, this chapter considers whether certain kinds of communities host the strongest localist impulses toward the radical right, further refining the localist account.

To summarize the findings: on balance, neighborly relations are meaningfully predictive of radical right party support over time. Closer ties with neighbors (in the form of a four-item index) are associated with support for the SVP and no other major Swiss party. Yet analyzing different aspects of neighborly relations reveals that those most important for radical right support are: receipt of emotional aid from neighbors and number of neighbors with whom one is on friendly terms. The index components that do not exert independent effects on radical right support are: exchange of practical support and frequency of contact with neighbors. These findings align with the distinction emphasized in previous chapters between psychological ties and social ties in

---

[1] Boonen and Hooghe (2014) ask this question with respect to sub-national identities and radical right support in Belgium. They find stronger evidence that such ideologies motivate radical right support in comparison to the reverse process.

the local arena: attitudinal and behavioral connections to local communities have different implications for politics. I also find that local ties are particularly potent when and where the locality is a salient political unit: specifically, they matter most in parts of the country that hold elections for communal (local) governing parliaments. Neighborly relations also matter most for radical right support in the kinds of communities that are typically characterized by high levels of local cohesion among residents. Preliminary evidence further suggests that the SVP makes electoral gains in parts of the country where and when communities have recently lost local autonomy.

NEIGHBORS AND POLITICS

Political scientists have devoted considerable attention to the nexus of neighborhoods and electoral behavior. The local arena serves as an important locus for the development of people's partisan affinities. The mechanisms come in the form of broad contextual effects (Books and Prysby 1991, Huckfeldt et al. 1993, Burbank 1995, McClurg 2006), organizational influences (Djupe and Gilbert 2008), and interpersonal persuasion (Weatherford 1982, Huckfeldt and Sprague 1995, Pattie and Johnston 2000, Baker et al. 2006). Other work demonstrates that the ways people are connected to their communities shape political attitudes and electoral participation (Knack 1992, Mondak et al. 1996, Timpone 1998, Anderson 2009, Quentin and Van Hamme 2011).

The literature on the forces that hold communities together in the aggregate also identifies several distinct concepts and connects them to political behavior. Local social cohesion, which links local residents cognitively to each other, can have strong electoral effects (Fitzgerald and Lawrence 2011). Social trust at the neighborhood level also shapes people's partisan preferences (Berning and Ziller 2017). Social capital, as it is generally understood today, is rooted in local social networks and the organizations of civil society (Bourdieu 1986) and has been found to influence political behavior (Putnam 1993, La Due Lake and Huckfeldt 1998). Political scientists and sociologists identify the neighborhood as a key arena for social capital's development (Paxton 1999, Putnam 2000). These insights point to the local community as a key arena for developing group bonds and shaping political outcomes.

What we haven't done especially well is separate out the political implications of how people feel about their neighbors as compared to the ways in which they are actively connected to them. As noted in Chapter 2, an early inspiration for this distinction comes from Richard LaPiere's (1934) attitude-behavior gap. The way an individual feels about his or her community should be distinguished conceptually and operationally from the way he or she actively participates in the community. Relevant work differentiates social aspects of neighboring from affective aspects (Unger and Wandersman 1985). Other studies conceptualize "manifest" and "latent" neighboring (Mann 1954). Manifest neighboring involves actual interactions and exchanges among neighbors. Latent neighboring is a mental construct that involves people's positive views of their neighbors and feelings that neighbors would help out if the need were to arise. This latent aspect of the concept does not hinge on past aid from or significant social engagement with neighbors.

Regardless of whether the unit of analysis is the individual or the community, existing work does not sufficiently consider the political implications of different dimensions of people's links to their neighbors. I submit that the literature on neighboring and politics stands to be improved in three main ways. First, it should be more sensitive to the attitude-behavior gap as it relates to the manner(s) in which people are connected to their neighbors. Here, I distinguish different aspects of neighboring to study their effects. Second, it should devote more attention to understanding the conditions under which neighboring is politically salient. In this chapter, I consider contextual factors that may condition the relevance of neighborly ties for vote choice.

Third, this area of research would benefit from a more dynamic approach that considers the effects of neighborhood ties over time. A central consideration about social ties' political implications relates to assertions about causality. Is there justification for making causal claims about the effects of local ties on political behavior? Certain types of people are going to have positive orientations toward their neighbors in the first place, and these may also be the same kinds of people who are drawn to radical right parties. Furthermore, as suggested above, radical right rhetoric might make supporters feel closer to their neighbors. By examining dynamics at the individual level, we can gain clarity with respect to the precise mechanisms at work.

DATA AND MODELS

The Swiss Household Panel (SHP) survey started its annual interviews with respondents in 1999 (Voorpostel et al. 2016).[2] In this chapter I use all waves from 1999 through 2010. This time period covers three federal elections, allowing for a relatively long-term view of partisan support over time. Also during these years, the relevant survey questions associated with party support and neighborly relations are asked in every wave.[3] This uncommonly rich panel provides information about the decision to jump on (and off) the SVP wagon from year to year.[4]

---

[2] For additional information on the SHP, see http://forscenter.ch/en/our-surveys/swiss-household-panel/

[3] Thereafter, the neighborly relations questions are asked every third year.

[4] The SHP is a household panel that surveys all available members of the sampled households. Therefore, the data is structured in clusters by household. In the models I use Stata's cluster command on household identification number to address the effect this is likely to have on the estimates. As a robustness check I also draw a random sample of one person per household and replicate the models. The substantive results remain.

In each wave the SHP records party preference through the question, "If there was an election for the National Council tomorrow, for which party would you vote?" The National Council is the lower house of Swiss parliament. This parallels the party support question from the European Values Study that served as the central dependent variable in Chapters 3 and 4.[5] From this item I create a series of dichotomous variables to indicate support for each of the five main parties in modern Swiss federal elections. These are (roughly from left to right): the Green Party, the Social Democratic Party, the Christian Democratic Party, the Radical Party,[6] and the Swiss People's Party.[7] I provide full models for each of these parties to establish whether neighboring effects apply to the SVP and its electoral competitors as well.

For measuring the role of local engagement on partisan support, the SHP contains four neighborly relations variables: *Number friendly* (number with whom one is close and on good terms), *Frequency of contact* (regularity of interaction: never to daily), *Practical support* (level of support such as helping with errands: none to a great deal), and *Emotional support* (level of support such as showing understanding: none to a great deal).[8] This set of questions taps into the ways in which individuals are socially and emotionally linked to their neighbors. In terms of actual, routine social interaction, the most clear-cut variable is the frequency of contact item, which represents how often people interact with their neighbors. The practical support measure would be a close second although it does not denote any actual rate of engagement. Number

---

[5] This is the same measure used to indicate radical right support in the SHP models presented in Chapter 3. The sample used here includes respondents 18 years old and older who are also Swiss citizens.

[6] In 2009 the Radical party merged with the smaller Liberal party (technically becoming FDP. The Liberals). The SHP provides separate support information for each party even after the merge. I find that combining these parties' followers into one group as of 2009 – as opposed to keeping Radicals supporters separate – does not influence the results of statistical models. Therefore, for the sake of consistency across waves, I do not include in the analysis support for the much smaller Liberal Party or for the combined partisan entity.

[7] See Ladner (2001), Hug and Schultz (2007), and Kriesi and Trechsel (2008) for more details on the Swiss party system.

[8] The questions are worded as follows. Number friendly: "With how many neighbours are you on good terms and enjoy a close relationship?" Frequency of contact: "How frequent are your contacts with these neighbours?" Practical support: "If necessary, in your opinion, to what extent can these neighbours provide you with practical help (this means concrete help or useful advice), if 0 means 'not at all' and 10 'a great deal'? Even people who do not need any help should consider possible ways in which they could get support. If some neighbours can help a great deal and others not at all, indicate 'a great deal'. Practical help = for example doing the shopping for them when sick, taking them to the doctor or giving useful advice in case of problems or when looking for specific information." And Emotional support: "To what extent can these neighbours be available in case of need and show understanding, by talking with you for example, 0 means 'not at all' and 10 'a great deal'? Even the persons who do not need any help should consider possible ways in which they could get support. If some neighbours can help a great deal and others not at all, indicate 'a great deal'." Translations from original survey languages are provided by the SHP.

of neighbors with whom one is friendly reflects how a person feels rather than how actively connected he or she may be. Indeed, there are hundreds of respondents who feel close to at least one neighbor but report seeing neighbors "less than monthly" or "never." The emotional support measure can be characterized as indicating the psychological links to neighbors. Taken together, then, we have two clear social variables (frequency and practical support) and two clear psychological variables (number friendly and emotional support).[9] The tables below present the results of models that test their effects in the form of a combined *Neighbors index* and individually.

Most of the other variables included in these models are the same used in the SHP models displayed in Chapter 3. *Memberships* is operationalized here as an additive index of belonging to the following types of associations: local or parents, sporting, cultural, professional, partisan, environmental, charity, women's, or tenants. The index runs from zero to seven memberships in total. I also add *Religious attendance* to gauge the effects of this kind of organizational involvement. The survey provides nine options ranging from "never" to "several times a week." The attitudinal battery includes the *Anti-EU* and *Anti-immigrant* variables previously described in Chapter 3. It also includes *Distrust government* and *Political interest*.[10] The measures of socio-economic status are also more robust than in the previous models. Education is included, as are occupational variables to better address skill-specific interests and perspectives (Betz 1994, Kitschelt, with McGann, 1995, Oesch 2008). I control for *Election year* and include a time trend variable (*Year*) to capture the temporal contexts of the survey waves.

Additional contextual factors are type of commune in which a person lives and how much political salience the commune has in each canton. *Commune type* is an indicator of the kind of area in which a respondent resides. This stems from a nine-item typology scheme used by the Swiss Federal Statistical office and incorporated into the SHP data. Each commune is classified as one of the following types: city center, suburb, wealthy, peripheral, tourist, industrial, rural, mixed agricultural, and peri-agricultural (see Schuler et al. 2005). Though the public use sample of the SHP does not provide information on which commune a person lives in, it does catalog the kind of community. Dummy variables derived from this typology are interacted with the Neighbors index to establish whether it has stronger or weaker effects depending on the nature of the area in which a respondent lives.

---

[9] These variables all load onto a single factor through primary-components factor analysis. And together they have an alpha over .8. The two dimensions I outline above (one social, one psychological) are not reflected in the factor loadings and so they should be interpreted with some caution as distinct dimensions of neighborly engagement.

[10] This question asks, "Generally, how interested are you in politics, if 0 means 'not at all interested' and 10 'very interested'?"

Finally, this chapter starts to empirically test the idea that community ties are most potent for radical right voting when the locality is a salient political unit. (The theoretical groundwork for this idea appears in Chapter 2 and is further expanded in Chapter 7.) Switzerland's cantons are responsible for deciding how much power the communes (basically municipalities, the lowest level of independent government in the Swiss federal system) have. This kind of authority represents the political salience of the locality. Having meaningful local elections fuses the notion of community to the political realm, I contend, making local considerations politically relevant to residents. To measure local political salience in this chapter I leverage the complex set of authority structures of the Swiss state. A relatively weak central government is balanced by sub-national units – cantons – with significant authority, and cantons vary dramatically with respect to how much power their communes have. To proxy communal autonomy by canton, I record the percentage of communes in a canton that have their own, elected legislative bodies known as communal parliaments. In many Swiss communes, particularly those with fewer than 1,000 residents, the legislative branch takes the shape of a communal assembly. In these assemblies, all citizens of the commune are eligible participants. In contrast, communal parliaments are formally elected, representative bodies that are more professionalized and the positions are typically full-time (Linder 1997).[11] The BADAC project supplies the number of communes in each canton that have their own parliaments.[12]

Not all cantons allow for the communal parliament option – even for their larger communes. In cantons such as Uri, Schwyz, and Glarus, there are no communal parliaments. In Neuchâtel and Genève there are no communes *without* such a body. The average percentage of communes with parliaments across the cantons is eighteen. Below, the prevalence of communal parliaments is interacted with the neighboring index to see if local political salience – measured as the prevalence of elected communal parliaments – is a conditioning factor.

The models presented in this chapter take several forms. The first models are logistic regressions that include a one-year lag of the dependent variable. This makes it possible to establish the factors predicting a particular party support choice net the respondent's partisan selection in the previous year. Functionally, this captures individuals who *adopt* support for a certain party in a particular year. It also captures individuals who move away from a certain party in a particular year. These models provide insight into the factors that distinguish individuals who report SVP support from individuals who do not, net their previous year's choices. They are therefore between-group (or inter-individual)

---

[11] A separate local institution is the communal council, which is the formally elected executive body at the communal level (see Linder 1997: 9, and Bulliard 2005 for details of Swiss communal governance).

[12] Source: IDHEAP-BADAC 2001.

comparisons. They do not assess within-group (or intra-individual) variance, however. Therefore, I provide additional models that accommodate a multilevel data structure in this chapter's appendix. Random effects multilevel logistic regression models estimate the extent to which people's partisan choices correlate with other variables over time and among individuals. Fixed effects multilevel logistic regression models estimate intra-individual shifts. Finally, contextual effects are measured using a multilevel mixed effects specification in which individuals are nested within their cantons of residence.

DESCRIPTIVE DETAILS

Figure 5.1 provides a bird's eye view of the SVP's electoral fortunes relative to the other Swiss parties over the past two decades. The full, black line marks the rise of the SVP across elections. The Greens have also grown in popularity, though more modestly. The remaining main parties weakened across these six elections. As for the SVP's relative popularity, their number of votes has similarly climbed from election to election. From 1999 to 2015 it nearly doubled (rising from approximately 440,000 in 1999 to 740,000 in 2015).[13] Many Swiss citizens have shifted from not supporting to supporting the SVP; this spotlights the importance of examining the factors that would push somebody toward the SVP. It is also not clear whether those who decide to support the SVP at one point ultimately remain supporters over time. Given the relatively low turnout rates across these elections it is quite possible that the SVP vote in any one year is comprised of very different people as compared to another year.[14]

As noted above, protest theories would predict that radical right support is less stable over time than support for mainstream parties. To subject this to a simple test, I calculate year-to-year correlations for the SVP and the other main parties in Swiss electoral politics. Figure 5.2 displays basic cross-tabulation evidence to establish the level of partisan support stability for SVP and other Swiss parties. What percentage of supporters for a particular party (at time t) also supported that same party in the previous year (at time t-1)?[15] How stable

---

[13] Source: Swiss Federal Statistical Office: www.bfs.admin.ch. The SVP's upward march took a pause in 2011 when it was weakened over the previous election in terms of votes, vote percentage, and seats. It rebounded in 2015 to its best showing yet in all three dimensions.

[14] The average turnout rate for federal elections from 1995 to 2015 is approximately 46 percent. Turnout has not surpassed 50 percent in a federal election since 1975. www.idea.int/vt/countryview.cfm?CountryCode=CH

[15] For this descriptive step, all available observations from 1999 to 2011 are used so anyone who answered this question at least two years in a row is included in the analysis. The number of observations is over 66,000. Because person-year is the unit of analysis, many individuals are counted repeatedly. The correlations for those who answer the party support question in every wave (1,671 respondents) of the survey are quite similar: 57 for the Greens, 77 for Social Democrats, 67 for Christian Democrats, 64 for Radicals, and 71 for SVP.

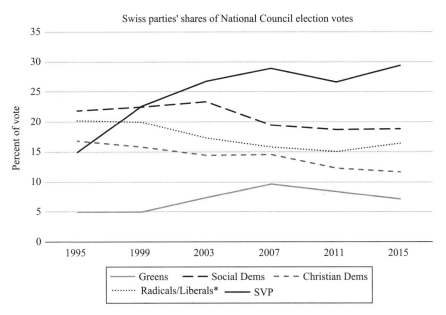

*As of 2011 election, Radicals' (Free Democrats) share of votes includes Liberals: they merged in 2009 into FDP. The Liberals.

FIGURE 5.1
Source: Swiss Federal Statistical Office

is SVP support relative to support for the other parties? The party that receives the most consistent support is the Social Democratic Party: 73 percent of those who support them in a given year also supported them the previous year. The second most stable party is the SVP with 68 percent. The least stable support goes to the Greens. These patterns do not comport with a protest interpretation of SVP support. At least, they do not conform to the notion of a protest party as one that sees fleeting support by individuals.[16]

These numbers show stability and demonstrate that SVP support is similar to support for other parties. Yet while there is significant parity and stability in evidence, these figures also demonstrate change from year to year. This is important in reflecting on our knowledge of radical right support and supporters, which comes mainly from cross-sectional data. In simple terms based on cross-tabulations, of those individuals who support SVP in a particular year, 70 percent of them support this party a year later (at $t + 1$). And in evidence of even greater variation over time, of those who supported the SVP in 1999, only

[16] Tetrachoric correlations between support for each party at time t and support for that same part at t-1 reveal similar patterns across parties: Greens .81, Social Democrats .89, Christian Democrats .87, Radicals .86, SVP .89.

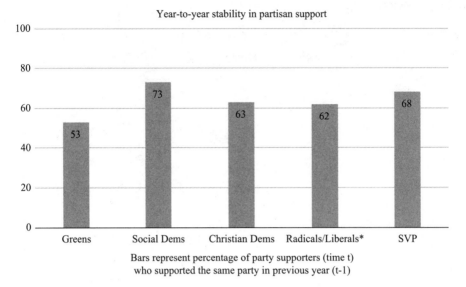

Year-to-year stability in partisan support

Bars represent percentage of party supporters (time t)
who supported the same party in previous year (t-1)

*As of 2011 election, Radicals' (Free Democrats) share of votes includes Liberals: they merged in 2009
into FDP. The Liberals.

FIGURE 5.2

57 percent support them in 2011. Looking backwards through all the waves
of data, of those who support the SVP in 2011, 47 percent supported them
in 1999. (This is in line with stability over these years for the other parties.)[17]
Therefore, it is important to use models that address this rate of change to
understand the radical right vote more fully.

This instability also raises questions about whether survey respondents are
moving from support for one specific party to not supporting any party (and
back again) over time or whether they actually switch parties. Other studies
of party support that examine panel data find evidence of both patterns
(Zuckerman et al. 2007, Kuhn 2009). What is important for understanding
radical right support is knowing whether there is a profile of an SVP supporter
that is distinct from other parties' supporters. If individuals support radical
right parties sometimes and more mainstream parties at other times, then much
of the work on radical right support is missing the complexities of the phenomenon. How common is party switching in general among individuals sur-
veyed in all twelve waves? Of the 1,671 individuals who provide their party

[17] When examining evidence of change across the range of these years (1999–2011), there is further evidence of shifting support for the other parties as well. Of those who support a particular
party in 2011, what percentage supported them in 1999? The figures are: 24 for the Greens, 70
for the Social Democrats, 49 for the Christian Democrats, 48 for the Radicals. To generate these
details only requires that an individual responded to the party support question in 1999 and
2011. The number of observations is 3,271.

preference in every wave, 606 (36 percent) register support for at least two different parties across these twelve years.[18] Of those observations that record support for the SVP in a given year (*t*), about 12 percent supported a different, mainstream party in the previous year (*t*-1). As the distance from *t* increases, the percentage who supported or who in the future will support another party grows. This underscores the difficulty of painting extreme right supporters with a broad brush. Their motivations are diverse and their support is somewhat inconsistent over time.

RESULTS

Table 5.1 displays the results of five logit models of SVP support that contain a lagged dependent variable: support for the SVP in the prior year's survey. The first tests the effect of the Neighbors index composite variable; the remaining four models measure the effects of each index component. The logit coefficients represent the direction of the relationships while the asterisks denote significance levels below .05. Model I contains the index that averages scores for the four neighboring variables. Its effect on SVP support, net last year's SVP support, is positive and significant. Moving to Model II, it becomes clear that emotional support from neighbors is positively and significantly related to SVP choice in this specification. Similarly, Model IV shows that the number of neighbors with whom respondents are on friendly terms is positively and significantly related to the dependent variable. The remaining models, III and V, show that neither high levels of practical support from neighbors nor frequency of contact with neighbors is meaningfully associated with SVP support on its own. The significance of emotional support and number of friendly neighbors in contrast to the insignificance of practical support and frequency of interaction aligns with a finding from Chapter 4. That is, positive *feelings* toward community members (as opposed to frequent and practical interaction with them) tend to be particularly relevant for radical right support.[19]

Many of the other independent variables have predictive power as well. Each of the additional attitudinal variables is significant: Distrust government, Anti-EU, Anti-immigrant, and Political interest positively predict shifts

[18] Five percent supported the Radicals in the previous year (*t*-1), 3 percent the Christian Democrats, 3 percent the Social Democrats, and less than 1 percent the Greens.

[19] What of anomie? Descriptive details make it possible to identify those individuals who are most isolated from others in their communities. Of those who report SVP support in 1999, 33 percent report no chance of practical support from their neighbors. The corresponding figures for the other parties are: Social Democrats 36, Greens 35, Christian Democrats 29, and Radicals 34. For emotional support (no chance), the numbers are: SVP 31, Social Democrats 36, Greens 35, Christian Democrats 29, and Radicals 33. For number of neighbors (none): SVP 28, Social Democrats 32, Greens 33, Christian Democrats 27, and Radicals 30. For frequency of seeing neighbors (never): SVP 28, Social Democrats 33, Greens 33, Christians 27, Radicals 30. Per these numbers, the SVP does not stand out as the party of those fully disconnected from their neighbors.

TABLE 5.1 *Predicting shifts to SVP support*

Logit models with lagged dependent variable

Predictor	I Coeff.	S.E.	II Coeff.	S.E.	III Coeff.	S.E.	IV Coeff.	S.E.	V Coeff.	S.E.
Lagged DV (t-1)	3.38	(.07) *	3.37	(.07) *	3.38	(.06) *	3.38	(.06) *	3.38	(.06) *
Neighboring										
Nbrs: index	.25	(.11) *								
Nbrs: emot. support			.15	(.07) *						
Nbrs: pract. support					.10	(.07)				
Nbrs: num. friendly							.82	(.25) *		
Nbrs: freq. contact									.14	(.11)
Organizations										
Memberships	-.55	(.11) *	-.54	(.11) *	-.53	(.11) *	-.56	(.11) *	-.54	(.11) *
Religious attendance	.03	(.11)	.02	(.11)	.05	(.11)	.02	(.11)	.04	(.11)
Attitudes										
Distrust gov.	.59	(.11) *	.60	(.11) *	.59	(.11) *	.60	(.11) *	.60	(.11) *
Anti-EU	1.15	(.06) *	1.15	(.06) *	1.14	(.06) *	1.15	(.06) *	1.14	(.06) *
Anti-immigrant	.66	(.05) *	.65	(.05) *	.65	(.05) *	.65	(.05) *	.65	(.05) *
Political interest	.76	(.11) *	.78	(.11) *	.76	(.11) *	.76	(.10) *	.75	(.10) *
SES/Modernization losers										
Education low	.62	(.19) *	.64	(.19) *	.63	(.19) *	.61	(.19) *	.58	(.19) *
Education medium	.39	(.07) *	.40	(.07) *	.39	(.07) *	.39	(.07) *	.39	(.07) *
Unemployed	-.22	(.27)	-.22	(.27)	-.22	(.26)	-.23	(.26)	-.24	(.26)
Occupational status:										
Employer	.38	(.29)	.37	(.29)	.44	(.30)	.44	(.30)	.43	(.30)
Petite bourgeoisie	.17	(.08) *	.18	(.08) *	.17	(.08) *	.17	(.08) *	.17	(.08) *
Manager	-.07	(.08)	-.07	(.08)	-.06	(.08)	-.06	(.08)	-.06	(.08)
Professional	-.83	(.19) *	-.84	(.19) *	-.80	(.18) *	-.80	(.18) *	-.80	(.18) *

	(1)	(2)	(3)	(4)	(5)
Semi-professional	.19 (.09) *	.18 (.08) *	.17 (.08) *	.16 (.08)	.16 (.09) *
Worker	.00 (.07)	.00 (.07)	-.01 (.07)	.00 (.07)	-.01 (.07)
Socio-demographics					
Male	.37 (.05) *	.37 (.95) *	.36 (.05) *	.36 (.05) *	.37 (.05) *
Age	.09 (.17)	.08 (.17)	.06 (.17)	.00 (.16)	.04 (.16)
Temporal context					
Election year	.55 (.06) *	.55 (.06) *	.55 (.06) *	.56 (.06) *	.56 (.06) *
Year (trend)	-.08 (.08)	-.08 (.08)	-.08 (.08)	-.08 (.08)	-.08 (.08)
Constant	8.26 (14.03)	9.85 (13.98)	8.78 (13.90)	7.79 (13.75)	6.47 (13.73)
N observations	37,159	37,524	37,962	38,440	38,318
-2Xlog likelihood	15,226	15,396	15,530	15,736	15,696
Wald chi^2	4,642 *	4,677 *	4,342 *	4,733 *	4,736 *

* $p<.05$. Models include a dummy variable for each canton. Standard errors clustered by household.

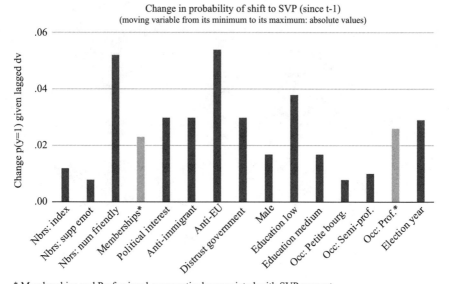

Change in probability of shift to SVP (since t-1)
(moving variable from its minimum to its maximum: absolute values)

* Memberships and Professional are negatively associated with SVP support.
Based on Table 5.1 models.

FIGURE 5.3

to SVP support. Similarly, the education variables, Petite bourgeoisie and Semi-professional are relevant, positive predictors, as are Male and Election year. Memberships and Professional occupation are the only factors with negative coefficients, predicting lack of shift to the SVP or perhaps a year-to-year shift away from SVP support. These patterns support previous research findings on radical right support. The difference is that by modeling SVP party adoption, the influence of these factors is more firmly established.

To assess the relative strength of the statistically significant predictors in these models, Figure 5.3 presents substantive effect estimates (calculated via Clarify (Tomz et al. 2003)). The bars represent the absolute value of the change in probability of shifting to SVP associated with moving each predictor from its minimum to its maximum value. All estimates are based on Model I in Table 5.1 with the exception of Neighbors support emotional and Neighbors number friendly, which come from Model II and Model IV, respectively. The weakest of the significant predictors is Petite bourgeoisie; the strongest is Anti-EU attitudes. An individual with the highest value of the Neighbors index is just over one percentage point more likely to adopt SVP support than is an individual with the lowest value. Moving from the lowest to the highest value of the neighborly emotional support variable is associated with increasing the probability of switching over to SVP by just less than one percentage point. Individuals who feel friendly toward thirty or more neighbors are over five percentage points more likely to support the SVP.[20]

[20] Being friendly with thirty neighbors implies that an individual has at least thirty identifiable neighbors. This may correlate with living in a densely populated community. Controlling for

Given the inconsistent nature of partisan support in Switzerland, an important next step is to consider how these factors relate to support for other parties. Are the identified factors specific to adoption of SVP support or do they help to predict shifts toward other parties as well? Table 5.2 provides answers to this question; it includes five logit models. The fifth model (labeled SVP) is exactly the same as Model I in Table 5.1, placed in this new table for comparative illustration. The remaining models estimate the effects of the full set of predictors for supporting the Greens, Social Democrats, Christian Democrats and Radicals – net respondents' support for these parties in the prior year.

According to these results, only two factors significantly predict *only* SVP support and no other party support. The first is the neighborly index. Neighboring is not associated with a shift toward or away from support for any other party.[21] The second is low education. Those with relatively weak educational backgrounds are linked solely to the SVP in these models. One factor is negative for the SVP and positive for some other parties: Memberships. Broader participation in associations boosts support for the left-leaning parties and minimizes it for the radical right.

Several factors are significant for other parties but are only positive and significant for the SVP: those with negative views of the EU, intermediary levels of education,[22] and petite bourgeoisie or semi-professional occupations are drawn to the SVP and repelled by the Greens and/or the Social Democrats. Notably, anti-immigrant attitudes predict SVP adoption as well as Christian Democrats and Radicals adoption, though the effect for the SVP is strongest in substantive terms. Distrust in the government pushes people toward the SVP as well as the Greens. Two variables are significant predictors of all parties except for the SVP: Religious attendance and Age. To summarize the key observation: those who adopt SVP support from one year to the next are fully distinguishable by their neighborly, educational and occupational features as well as anti-EU attitudes.[23] They are not distinguishable by immigration attitudes or governmental distrust.

type of municipality (via the dummy variables representing nine community types described above: city center, suburb, wealthy, peripheral, tourist, industrial, rural, mixed agricultural and peri-agricultural) does not weaken this substantive effect. But still, only two percent of the sample is friendly with thirty or more neighbors. Those friendly with ten neighbors are about two percentage points more likely to move toward the SVP than those friendly with none.

[21] None of the four components of the Neighbors index matters for any of the other parties with one exception: interacting frequently with neighbors is a negative, significant predictor of support for the Radicals.

[22] The SVP is the only party that draws year-to-year from the low and middle educational categories. This implies that the high education group – as the reference category – is significantly less likely to adopt SVP support. But it is not so clearly related to any of the other parties.

[23] The strongest predictor of each dependent variable in this table is the lagged dependent variable. For the SVP, the probability of supporting this party at time *t* is .46 higher if an individual supported SVP in the previous year. The corresponding figures for the other parties are: .37 for the Greens, .60 for the Social Democrats, .46 for the Christian Democrats and .57 for the Radicals. This comparative view corroborates the point suggested by Figure 5.2 about the relative stability of SVP support over time. This seems contradictory to the protest thesis.

TABLE 5.2 *Predicting shifts to support for party*
Logit models with lagged dependent variable

Predictor	Greens		Social Dems		Christian Dems		Radicals		SVP	
	Coeff.	S.E.	Coeff.	S.E.	Coeff.	S.E.	Coeff.	S.E.	Coeff.	S.E.
Lagged DV (t-1)	3.28	(.08) *	3.43	(.05) *	3.55	(.07) *	3.55	(.06) *	3.38	(.07) *
Neighboring/organizations										
Nbrs: index	-.05	(.14)	.02	(.10)	.09	(.13)	-.11	(.11)	.25	(.11) *
Memberships	.85	(.11) *	.35	(.08) *	.20	(.11)	-.16	(.10)	-.55	(.11) *
Religious attendance	-.75	(.15) *	-.64	(.09) *	1.56	(.12) *	-.32	(.10) *	.03	(.11)
Attitudes										
Distrust gov.	.70	(.15) *	-.26	(.10) *	-1.25	(.14) *	-1.05	(.11)	.59	(.11) *
Anti-EU	-.40	(.07) *	-.82	(.05) *	.06	(.06)	.04	(.05)	1.15	(.06) *
Anti-immigrant	-.46	(.08) *	-.36	(.05) *	.12	(.06) *	.12	(.05) *	.66	(.05) *
Political interest	.24	(.13)	.78	(.09) *	.16	(.12)	.54	(.11) *	.76	(.11) *
SES/Modernization losers										
Education low	-.14	(.25)	-.01	(.18)	-.17	(.24)	.07	(.20)	.62	(.19) *
Education medium	-.37	(.08) *	-.11	(.05) *	.11	(.07)	-.10	(.06)	.39	(.07) *
Unemployed	.32	(.27)	.08	(.20)	-.31	(.38)	-.10	(.23)	-.22	(.27)
Occupational status:										
Employer	-.11	(.34)	-.80	(.30) *	-.71	(.37)	.01	(.26)	.38	(.29)
Petite bourgeoisie	.17	(.11)	-.41	(.08) *	-.03	(.09)	-.05	(.08)	.17	(.08) *
Manager	-.13	(.10)	-.03	(.06)	-.08	(.08)	.10	(.07)	-.07	(.08)
Professional	.31	(.12) *	.06	(.09)	-.23	(.14)	-.25	(.11)	-.83	(.19) *
Semi-professional	-.16	(.11)	.00	(.07)	-.26	(.10) *	-.09	(.08)	.19	(.09) *

	(1)	(2)	(3)	(4)	(5)
Worker	−.05 (.11)	.15 (.06)*	−.23 (.08)*	−.16 (.07)*	.00 (.07)
Socio-demographics					
Male	−.36 (.06)*	−.09 (.04)*	.19 (.05)*	.22 (.04)*	.37 (.05)*
Age	−.92 (.24)*	−.65 (.15)*	−.87 (.20)*	.34 (.17)*	.09 (.17)
Temporal context					
Election year	.07 (.06)*	.07 (.05)*	.22 (.06)*	−.13 (.06)*	.55 (.06)*
Year (trend)	.08 (.01)*	−.10 (.07)*	.73 (.09)*	−.01 (.08)	−.08 (.08)
Constant	−3.43 (.63)*	−1.95 (.13)*	−3.18 (.43)*	−3.50 (1.03)*	8.26 (14.03)*
N observations	37,159	37,119	37,159	37,096	37,159
−2Xlog likelihood	11,466	21,446	12,878	17,198	15,226
Wald chi²	3,066*	5,430*	3,877*	4,364*	4,642*

* p<.05. Models include a dummy variable for each canton. Standard errors clustered by household.

Note: N observations differ slightly from model to model due to certain cantonal dummies predicting failure perfectly. In this situation Stata drops all observations from such cantons.

Alternate model specifications corroborate these findings. In the Appendix I supply additional tables containing between- and within- person analyses per random effects logistic regressions (Tables A5.1 and A5.2) and within-person analyses per fixed effects logistic regressions (Table A5.3). The population average, random intercept models show that SVP support is positively predicted by the neighborly relations index, with emotional support and number of neighbors with whom one is friendly carrying the most weight. These effects are not relevant for other parties except for the Christian Democrats, for whom the Neighbors index is significant but is driven primarily by practical support from neighbors rather than the more attitudinal dimensions that are relevant for SVP support.[24] The cluster specific, fixed intercept models (Table A5.3) demonstrate that within-person patterns of SVP support are strongly associated with receipt of emotional support from neighbors (but not the other neighborly measures); none of the neighborly relations dimensions is associated with any other party in this specification. The only other variable that predicts SVP support when examining only intra-individual factors over time is Anti-immigrant.[25]

CONTEXTUAL CONSIDERATIONS

An exploration of neighborly ties should consider the type of community within which such connections develop. The previous chapter reported some evidence that local attachment is most closely linked to radical right support in large towns or small cities. Yet the nature of such communities was not clear from those population-based results. With the SHP data, it is possible to ask: what *kinds* of communities host the most positive links between neighborly ties and SVP support? Interactive analysis produces two answers to this question. (These models are in Table A5.4 in the appendix.) The areas that host the strongest neighboring-SVP support link are of the "industrial or tertiary" community type. These are communities that produce particularly high levels of industrial goods and services. These communes are often periphery centers where people live and work. The impact of the neighboring index is approximately 4 percentage points stronger in industrial areas as compared to others. The kinds of areas hosting the weakest neighboring-SVP link are rural commuting communities. These are peripheral areas characterized by high percentages of residents who commute out of the locality for work. The effect

---

[24] Detailed results that unpack the neighboring index to model partisan support for other parties are available from the author. For plots of substantive effects from the random effects logit model in Table A5.1, see Figure A5.1. For plots of substantive effects from the fixed effects logit model in Table A5.3, see Figure A5.2.

[25] Replacing party support with each of the attitudinal factors (Distrust EU, Anti-immigrant, Anti-government, and Political interest) as dependent variables reveals that *only Anti-EU sentiment is significantly (and positively) predicted by neighboring.*

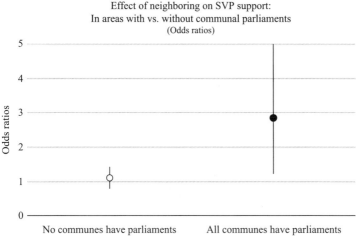

FIGURE 5.4 Based on model in Table A5.5.

of the neighboring index on SVP support is approximately 3 percentage points lower in rural commuting areas than in other kinds of communes.[26]

Another important aspect of context is the level of community politicization. For attachments to neighbors to be relevant for political behavior, one would expect these ties to have their greatest impact in areas where the locality is salient for politics. Individuals should be prompted by some external factor to connect their locally oriented feelings to the political realm. I interact the prevalence of communal parliaments with the neighborly relations index to see where connections to neighbors are most relevant for voting behavior. If this interaction term is significant, it suggests that the political relevance of localities strengthens the role that neighboring plays in the choice to support the SVP.

Table A5.5 in the Appendix supplies the model details and Figure 5.4 displays the predicted effects. The relevant substantive impacts are predicted odds ratios. In cantons with no communal parliaments, the effect of neighboring is positive but cannot be statistically distinguished from a null effect. In areas where all communes elect local parliaments, the effect of shifting from the minimum to the maximum values of neighboring is significant and associated with nearly tripling the odds of supporting SVP. In cantons where the locality is the most electorally politicized, positive neighboring is most closely tied to radical right voting.

---

[26] Predicted change in SVP support is calculated using Clarify. Substantive effects results are available from the author. No other community type significantly conditions the neighboring effect on SVP support.

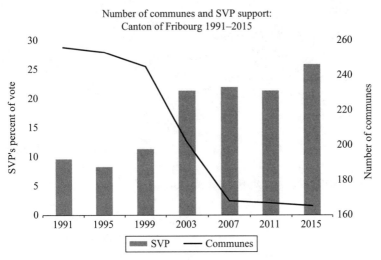

Number of communes and SVP support:
Canton of Fribourg 1991–2015

FIGURE 5.5

While the presence of meaningful elections at the local level is one measure of local political salience, another dimension to consider is the sudden loss of communal autonomy. And while communal parliamentary structures hardly change over time, communal independence is much more variable. In Switzerland the relevant shifts to the authority structure have come mainly in the form of communal amalgamations. As Steiner explains, "When a municipal merger occurs, one or more municipalities cease to exist. The essential trait of a merger is the complete surrendering of independence by one or several municipalities. All municipal tasks are fulfilled by the new municipality" (2003: 554). In many cases these mergers can be contentious, given the high level of local attachment and proud tradition of local independence in Switzerland. They can also have significant economic implications with respect to taxation and they often affect the logistics of service provision (Ladner 2007).

This potentially controversial process has resulted in a reduction in the number of communes from 3,203 in 1848 to 2,408 as of 2013, and the pace of amalgamation has picked up significantly since 1990 (van den Hende 2015). As with most developments at the commune level in Switzerland, there are dramatic differences among cantons. Here, I look at aggregate trends in two Swiss cantons, Fribourg and Valais, across the most recent seven National Council elections. I track the support for the SVP and the pace of communal merging (measured as the number of existing communes in the canton).

Figures 5.5 and 5.6 display these over-time patterns: the bars represent the percentage of the cantonal vote going to the SVP in each National Council election and the lines represent the number of communes in the canton.

These figures suggest that the two trends may be related. In Fribourg, 2003 marks the year when the SVP made a breakthrough and the number of

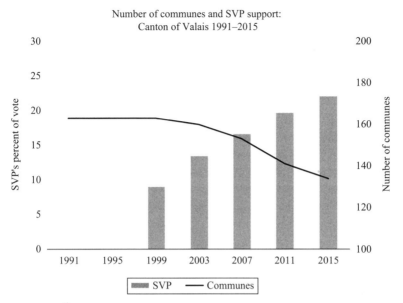

Number of communes and SVP support:
Canton of Valais 1991–2015

FIGURE 5.6

commutes was in the midst of a precipitous drop. In Valais, the more subtle decline in communal numbers over time aligns with a progressive upward march of the SVP across the same years. Other cantons, including Vaud and Jura, display similar patterns (results are available from the author). Though a full examination by commune is beyond the scope of the current analysis, there is reason to think that the radical right is a beneficiary of reductions in communal autonomy.

DISCUSSION

Individual-level Dynamics

This chapter enriches the analysis of radical right support and contributes to our understanding of the political implications of neighborly ties. It examines the phenomenon of neighboring in detail, demonstrating that certain aspects of neighborly ties benefit the radical right. The most influential dimensions of neighboring are feeling like one can receive emotional support from fellow residents and perceiving that one is on friendly terms with many neighbors. This is a new direction for studies of community ties and their links to radical right support, both in the attention to different aspects of neighboring and the consideration of how it might influence partisan choices. Importantly, neighboring patterns do not make any other political party more appealing; the effects are specific to the SVP.

An additional insight that can be taken from the SHP data that is not modeled above is that the neighboring-SVP link is particularly strong among women. A simple pairwise correlation between the neighboring index and SVP support is twice as strong for women as it is for men. The gendered differences are even greater for the components of the neighboring index that are more about feelings than about routine behavior. Most notable is the difference between men and women in terms of the number of neighbors with whom one is on friendly terms. The correlation between this variable and SVP support is nowhere near statistically significant for men, but it is robustly significant for women. This contributes additional support to the notion that women are more motivated than men by their community ties to support the radical right.

The analysis is sensitive to temporal dynamics and distinguishes support for the SVP from support for other parties. Also, the models in this chapter include a range of variables not included in previous chapters' models to provide a fuller account of radical right support. These include more detailed occupational factors as well as political interest and religious attendance. The results show that low- and middle-level educational qualifications are highly predictive of adopting SVP support, as is petit bourgeois occupation. As expected, the radical right gender gap is alive and well in Switzerland as men are more likely than women to move toward the SVP over time, making the relevance of neighboring for women all the more informative. Also, political interest is associated with movement toward the SVP, and SVP preference rises in election years.[27] This last point is likely not surprising, but I do not think I have seen it noted elsewhere. Anti-EU is the most powerful predictor, just ahead of the number of neighbors with whom one is on friendly terms.

The individual-level analysis also provides insight into how SVP support looks over time for people. While there is change from year to year with respondents dropping into and out of the SVP supporter category, these rates of change are on par with other major parties. To the extent that instability is a feature of protest voting, these results challenge a protest thesis as it relates to the radical right. The use of panel data also facilitates a test of the reverse-causation thesis, which would put SVP support in a position to influence people's feelings about their neighbors. By including lagged dependent variables in the models, the analysis indicates a clear direction toward the SVP if an individual has certain neighboring perceptions.

Conditioning Factors

The conditional analysis shows that contextual factors play a role in that they influence the effects of neighborly relations on SVP support. People's ties to neighbors are most predictive of radical right support in the kinds of

---

[27] The effect of an election is stronger for the SVP than for any other party. It is also negative for the Radicals, who enjoy more support in years that do not host National Council elections.

communities where people live and work and where industrial and service outputs are significant. They are weakest in rural areas characterized by high levels of out-commune commuting. That the effect of neighboring is strongest in industrial-tertiary areas and weakest in rural commuting areas is telling. These two sets of Swiss communes are similar on a number of dimensions such as level of foreign born, population growth rate, and household factors such as marriage rates and family structures (Van den Hende 2015).

From a theoretical point of view, the opposing contextual effects of these two types of communes can be explained. Specifically, work on social cohesion demonstrates that high levels of commuting frays the social fabric of local communities (Putnam 2000). When local residents commute in large numbers to other areas for work they are less focused on and engaged in life at home. They spend a good amount of their time in the workplace with people who are not from their home areas. This is significant because the workplace can be an important arena for building and strengthening community ties (Cox and Mair 1988, Wilkinson 1986). So high levels of out-commuting are associated with weak local cohesion; working and living in the same community boosts such cohesion. Rural commuter communes, therefore, will have particularly low levels of social cohesion while industrial-tertiary communes should have especially high levels. The results I present suggest that neighboring at the individual level is intricately tied to the nature of community ties in the locality. The conditioning impact of local commuting patterns on radical right support is further investigated in the following chapter.

The results also suggest that the SVP does best in parts of Switzerland that have the most meaningful local elections and also where communes are losing their autonomy. Though the aggregate patterns associated with autonomy loss should be assessed conservatively, they are provocative. While Switzerland is not the only country to engage in municipal amalgamation, it has been decades since most countries took these steps. Sweden, for instance, merged many communes in the 1950s, while Germany and the UK did so in the 1970s. My analysis suggests that the timing of these changes in Switzerland helped to generate an environment at the local level that fuels the radical right.

Together, this chapter highlights the importance of three contextual themes that vary over space, over time, or both: (1) the nature of community and its level of social cohesion, (2) the electoral relevance of the locality, and (3) the loss of local autonomy. Their temporal variability is important for accounting for shifts in radical right support from year to year, which this chapter demonstrates to be quite common. Furthermore, each of these factors has the potential to make radical right parties more appealing to voters across space and time. The coming chapter further investigates these contextual themes in France.

6

Local Autonomy Shifts, Local Cohesion, and Le Pen Support in France*

Radical right parties attract voters who are fed up with recent societal changes. These parties offer a romanticized vision of a "better" past without so much diversity, economic competition, and supranational control; their programs aim to undo the perceived damage wrought by modernity.[1] Given these parties' anti-modernity themes, there is a certain logic to the fact that much of their support comes from areas affected by trends such as globalization, Europeanization, immigration, and economic liberalism. Natives' perceptions of economic, cultural, and political threats fuel the radical right. Many who share communities with foreign-born residents find the radical right agenda appealing. The same can be said for those who reside in economically declining, post-industrial zones. Numerous studies demonstrate that the locality is a key context in which these dynamics play out and shape voter attitudes and electoral behavior (see, for instance, Mayer 2002, Dancygier 2010, Hopkins 2010, Fitzgerald 2012). So when some people experience unwelcome change in their immediate environments, they increasingly vote radical right.

This narrative of declining, diversifying locales that host significant levels of radical right support makes sense theoretically, and plenty of empirical evidence supports it (Ford and Goodwin 2010). But running counter to this account is the fact that many parts of Europe seemingly untouched by what some might think of as modern strains also host significant support for these parties. In this chapter, I ask: what explains votes for radical right parties from those whose day-to-day lives seem unaffected by these specific kinds of change?

* A version of this chapter was presented at the 74th Annual Meeting of the Midwest Political Science Association, April 7–10, 2016, Palmer House Hilton, Chicago, Illinois.
[1] See Minkenberg 2000 for more on these defining features.

I found answers to this question while conducting fieldwork in south-western France in 2005, 2006, and 2008.[2] I was drawn to this area, in part, by the 2002 presidential elections in which the National Front (FN) attracted new support from rural areas. Jean-Marie Le Pen reached out to corners of France that have little in common with the urban areas that had traditionally endorsed him. This tactic catapulted him to the second round of the election, stunning commentators in France and abroad. In many villages and small towns across France upwards of 20 and 30 percent of voters endorsed Le Pen for president.

I spent most of my time in the Gironde department of the Aquitaine region. Many of the 540 communes in the Gironde displayed the pattern of low unemployment, little immigration-related diversity, and high Le Pen support. Others that hosted high levels of Le Pen support had higher than average unemployment rates (according to the French census, the average unemployment rate across Gironde communes was 12 percent in 1999) but almost no immigration-related diversity (with an average of less than 3 percent across Gironde communes in 1999).

I spent time in many of these communes; in some I interviewed mayors and council members and talked with residents. I observed that many of the communities so supportive of Le Pen are idyllic, beautiful, bucolic, quaint, quiet, homogeneous, and economically secure. One such village in the Gironde is illustrative: Les Billaux. As of 1999 it had an unemployment rate of 7 percent (below the national average of 9.1), a foreign-born population of 1 percent, and 24 percent of votes in favor of Le Pen in 2002.[3] What could motivate such an electoral choice among residents of this community and so many like it?

I came away from my field work with a better understanding of some of the challenges associated with life in rural France. To summarize the findings: change *has* come to these communities, but it comes in different forms in different places.[4] In rural France, a highly visible dimension of change for residents is recent shifts in authority structures and changes in public service delivery. As I detail below, territorial reforms and the resultant intercommunal cooperation have altered the way decisions are made in France's rural areas. Importantly, authority historically vested in individual communes has been granted in recent years to councils that make binding decisions for collections

---

[2] I am grateful to the University of Colorado and the French Fulbright Commission and the Dutch Fulbright Center for financial support of this research. I am also grateful to the Institut d'études politiques de Bordeaux for hosting me and to the town officials who were generous with their time in letting me speak with them.

[3] In the previous presidential election, about 18 percent of the voters of Les Billaux supported Le Pen.

[4] See Hollifield and Ross (1991) on decades of societal change in France.

of formerly autonomous communities. In many places where the locality is a source of pride and identity, these changes have prompted people to alter their electoral behavior. As I will show, the FN is the primary beneficiary of these changes. With respect to timing, it happens that 2001 and 2002 were boom years for rural intercommunality; more rural communes were integrated in those years than in all other years combined since intercommunality was first introduced in the 1960s. As a result, I argue, the 2002 FN platform's defense of communal liberties hit the right note and Le Pen made major gains in rural France in 2002.

In the following pages, I integrate studies on contextual patterns of radical right support, draw attention to local patterns and dynamics in France, introduce the politics of Jean-Marie Le Pen, and describe intercommunality in France. I then test the localist account of radical right voting by comparing French municipalities with a particular focus on the Aquitaine region and the Gironde department for certain aspects of the analysis. I conclude with observations about some specific villages and excerpts from interviews I conducted in this part of the country, grounding the statistical observations in the ways people describe their communities in their own words.

AGGREGATE-LEVEL ACCOUNTS OF RADICAL RIGHT SUPPORT

Studies of radical right electoral fortunes reveal a complex picture of variance over space and time. In regards to space: these parties fare better in some national contexts than in others. Their popularity also varies within countries: by region, municipality, and neighborhood. With respect to time: national-level statistics from many countries show that their support base has grown steadily. In other countries, these parties' fortunes ebb and flow across elections. At the individual level, voters are often inconsistent in their support from year to year.

What explains variation in support for radical right parties? Most contextual explanations emphasize national dimensions of the phenomenon (see Chapters 2, 3, and 7). Yet such work does not address within-country patterns. As noted above, immigration and unemployment have made the radical right more appealing to voters, and some studies connect local characteristics of these kinds with radical right support. The thesis that living in areas characterized by high levels of immigration and/or economic hardship fuels support for the radical right is generally known as the socio-economic context model. In many studies, these factors account for a non-trivial amount of variance in these parties' electoral shares in certain countries. For example, local presence of immigrants and/or ethnic minorities can significantly benefit the radical right (DeVos and Deurloo 1999, Lubbers et al. 2000, Mayer 2002, Coffé et al. 2007, Bowyer 2008, Rink et al. 2009, Rydgren and Ruth 2013, Green et al. 2015). Yet other studies find that diversity in one's own local area is not significant for explaining radical right support, but that immigrants living in *nearby* localities is (Mayer 1992, Valdez 2014).[5] These factors are not consistently correlated with radical right support, and so conditioning factors are likely key to understanding how they operate (see Rydgren 2006).

Still, we are only beginning to understand contextual effects at the local level. This is unfortunate since we know radical right support varies significantly from community to community (see, for instance, Schain et al. 2002 on variation across France). We also know that the local story is more complex than what sweeping accounts of the implications of ethnic diversity and economic decline would suggest. For instance, local cohesion is positively associated with radical right support in modern and historical contexts in Germany and Switzerland (Hamilton 1982, Fitzgerald and Lawrence 2011); areas with high levels of social capital are less supportive of the radical right in Belgium (Coffé et al. 2007).[6] Along similar lines, in certain countries social isolation benefits the radical right (Rydgren 2009). As previous chapters show, feeling attached to one's locality of residence and feeling close to local residents also predicts heightened radical right support (see also Bulli and Tronconi 2012). But as with the factors that comprise the socio-economic contextual model, the effects of these community characteristics are not consistent across cases.

It is clear that many voters use a local lens when voting – even when participating in national elections. Citizens experience the events and strains of modern life from the point of view of their immediate surroundings, and this can have major effects on their partisan choices. Individuals are especially likely to draw on local considerations when and where the locality is highly salient for politics. In the previous chapter I found that certain contextual features – social cohesion, local autonomy levels and losses – can fuse local attachments and vote choice in national contests. Now, I explore these patterns more systematically in France, developing the argument that local political salience is extremely high in communities that have recently lost formal decision-making authority. Autonomy loss is perceived by residents as a threat to community, and it fuels support for the radical right. Through a comparison of French communes in their support rates for Jean-Marie Le Pen in the 2002 presidential election, I find that when and where communes are made politically salient via intercommunal power shifts, the National Front performs better electorally. This account, unlike others, explains variance in radical right support across localities and over time.

---

[5] For instance, radical right support from certain parts of France in the 2002 presidential election has been explained by a locality's proximity to immigration hot-spots such as Sangatte in the north of France (Alidières 2004).

[6] Though Vanhoutte and Hooghe (2013) do not find significant contextual effects in their study of Belgium.

LOCAL DIMENSIONS OF POLITICAL BEHAVIOR IN FRANCE

Local attachments and themes are highly relevant to French politics. The country has long hosted a tension between sub-national territorial devotion and national loyalty. Historically, one can point to the importance of factors such as state interference in local affairs and robustness of communal organizations for sparking the French Revolution (Markoff 1985). Evidence of sub-national defiance, most notably in the Vendée, comes from the histories of regional hold-outs against revolutionary and other nationalizing forces (see Tilly 1961, 1964). Today, the (relatively sclerotic) Corsican and Basque secessionist movements signal that the Republic is not indivisible. On a less explosive scale, powerful local attachments have also been documented in different parts of France. Laurence Wylie's (1957) sociological study of a small town in the Vaucluse reminds us that for many, political life in France is lived at the village level. Wylie's research also reminds us of the suspicion with which some residents of the French countryside view outside forces (including the national government).

The right-wing Poujadist movement of the 1950s mobilized rural France to protest the effects of modernization and encroachment by French central authority (Shields 2007). Pierre Poujade also recognized the role of localities in shaping people's political views. Roger Eatwell explains, "Poujade himself realized this clearly, and his cadre school, set up in 1955, placed considerable emphasis on the need to aim propaganda at local concerns" (1998: 8). Eatwell also observes that Poujadist support was especially high – though quite variable – in small towns and villages in the department of Sarthe. French national politics is in many ways connected to local trends and contexts.

Similarly, the FN's program appeals to locally oriented individuals through support for communal autonomy and regeneration of rural locales (see Chapter 3 for details from the FN's manifesto). The FN also seeks to empower the people vis-à-vis the central state through popular referenda processes based on the Swiss model of direct democracy (Mayer 2005). The party today has a strong local dimension to its rhetoric and to some of its policy proposals as well. This meets with a locally oriented view of politics by many in France to create an opportunity for radical right expansion through local politicization.

TERRITORIAL REFORMS: LES COMMUNAUTÉS DE COMMUNES

When considering the role of sub-national authority shifts in fueling radical right support, the 2002 presidential election in France is a useful case study. The election took place during a period of rapid and significant change in many parts of France. These were usually the areas of France left relatively untouched by other significant societal changes such as heightened diversity and post-industrial economic strain. In many rural communities at the time, the roots of local frustrations could be found in the newly established inter-communal

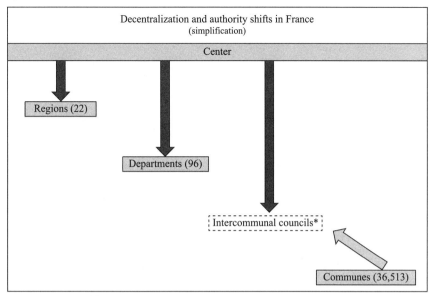

Arrows represent shifts in authority.
*There were 2,581 CDCs as of 2012. Other intercommunal units: urban community (16)
and agglomeration (167). As of January 1, 2016 there are 13 regions.
Number of units noted in parentheses are metropolitan numbers, excluding overseas territories.

FIGURE 6.1

organizations, the communautés de communes (or CDCs). Importantly, the establishment and empowerment of CDCs is part of a larger process of decentralization. But in France, decentralization translates into loss of autonomy for the lowest level of political aggregation, the commune. Figure 6.1 illustrates this process in an abstraction of the power-reallocation process ongoing in France.[7]

As part of a decades-long program of empowering sub-national authorities to develop and implement strategies for economic development, CDCs have been created to manage the affairs of groups of communes.[8] The process to create these institutional bodies across France has been a long and uneven one. Some intercommunal collectivities were established in the 1960s, while others have yet to be created. Figure 6.2 depicts the number of communes

---

[7] Between the communes and the departments are two administrative units. Cantons are collections of communes that chiefly serve as districts for departmental elections. Arrondissements are collections of cantons. Furthermore, the intercommunal system is constantly changing. For instance, through laws passed in 2010 and 2014, 27 métropoles have been established, which are highly integrated units of communes, each anchored by a large city (such as Bordeaux, Dijon, Grenoble, Nice, and Toulouse).

[8] See Kerrouche (2010) for a comprehensive analysis of the politics of communal authority in France.

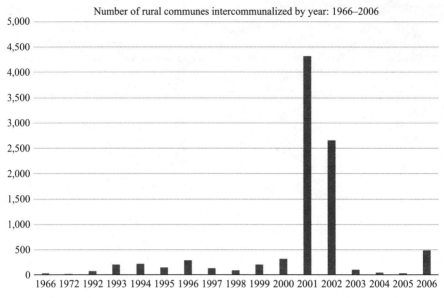

FIGURE 6.2

intercommunalized by year since the process began. Clearly 2001 and 2002 stand out as the top years for communal integration.

The legal foundations of modern CDCs stem from a 1992 Act of Parliament that outlined the structure for rural intercommunality within France. The process of creating these supracommunal collectivities was given a boost by the 1999 Chevènement Law, named after Jean-Pierre Chevènement (incidentally, a candidate for president in 2002), who spearheaded the legislative initiative to move intercommunality forward. There are three classes of groupings defined in terms of the type of communities being integrated: CDC applies to rural communes, Communautés d'Agglomeration (CA) to areas anchored by towns, and Communautés Urbaines (CU) to the larger cities and their suburbs. Since the 1992 legislative initiative, intercommunality has developed quite rapidly. As chronicled by Knapp and Wright (2001) at the beginning of 1993, 5,000 communes had already been grouped into intercommunal cooperatives. By 2000 this number had quadrupled, with over 20,000 communes belonging to these bodies. According to the Assemblée des Communautés de France (AdCF 2009), the number of communes inter-communalized as of 2009 was over 34,000 (or 93 percent of France's communes).[9]

[9] Laws on these territorial collectivities can be accessed directly here: www.legifrance.gouv.fr/affichCodeArticle.do?cidTexte=LEGITEXT000006070633&idArticle=LEGIARTI000003111164 86&dateTexte=20160326. See also Dollery and Robotti's (2008) edited volume on local government reforms across countries.

Here, I focus on the CDCs because they are the dominant form of inter-communal cooperation in rural France. Each CDC is empowered with a specific repertoire of authority spheres, but overall their competencies are divided into a handful of core activity areas: economic development, infrastructure and construction, spatial planning, social space management (for spaces such as parks), transportation, service provision, environmental matters, cultural and sporting life, and schools. Those charged with making decisions in these local policy arenas are appointed by local elected officials – they are not democratically elected to CDC positions, themselves.[10]

Importantly, intercommunality is not without its controversies. I learned from my interviews in the Gironde that some citizens and local officials are concerned that the actions of the CDCs are not legitimate. Some local leaders also explained that communal officials that are democratically elected, such as mayors and council members, often find themselves confused about their roles given the shift in local authority. Another critique of authority structure changes is that the state has devolved authority over certain sectors of public life to the sub-national bodies without assuring that they would have the fiscal capacities to carry out their work. Other interview subjects pointed out that the decreased capacity of the central state translates into a weaker set of mechanisms for redistribution, meaning that the wealthier segments of the country stand to get richer, while the developmental laggards may fall farther behind. More broadly, I learned that these new CDCs have introduced profound changes to local life, and they have in many cases ignited communal protectiveness and resentment among citizens.

LE PEN

Jean-Marie Le Pen is the founder and was the longtime leader of the National Front, which has gained ground in French elections since its early local victories in the 1980s. Considered a proto-type of the modern radical right party, the FN integrates harsh rhetoric on immigrants and the European Union with promises to protect French traditions and a French way of life. Figure 6.3 presents Le Pen's success rates across presidential elections. His most successful year was 2002. He earned 16.9 percent of the vote in the first round and 17.8 percent in the second round. Over 5.5 million people voted for Le Pen for president in 2002.[11]

---

[10] Though oftentimes elected communal officials, such as mayors, appoint themselves to these seats. As of 2010 this changed for CDCs with more than 3,500 residents. Now CDC council members are to be democratically elected in these areas.

[11] Approximately 5.5 million voters supported him in the second round; 4.8 million voters supported him in the first round. His previous best performance at the national level was 4.5 million in the first round of the 1995 presidential election.

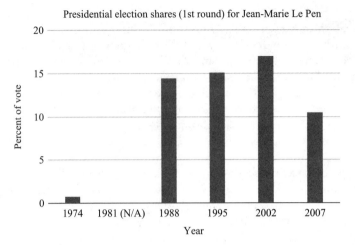

FIGURE 6.3

Examination of support for Le Pen in 2002 stands to advance our under-standing of radical right voting in France and more broadly for two, connected reasons. First, the big news about this particular election (apart from Le Pen's unexpected breakthrough to the second round run-off against the center-right incumbent, Jacques Chirac) was that new parts of the country started supporting Le Pen. Though Le Pen had stood in nearly every presidential election since 1974, 2002 was the year his popularity surged in areas out-side his typical strongholds of north and north-eastern (predominantly urban) France.[12] This caught many off guard because existing accounts of Le Pen support were rooted in theories of economic decline and immigration-related diversity. These were the trends encountered by Le Pen's more traditional supporters in areas that also face post-industrial decline, ethnic diversifica-tion, and in some cases elevated crime rates. So the extension to new regions raised novel questions about the appeal of this party. The second, related aspect of this election that makes it a propitious case study is that it was rural areas that hosted much of the new support for Le Pen. From tiny villages to small to medium-sized towns, Le Pen drew support from many corners of France visibly untouched by unemployment and immigration, trends that many identify as the hallmarks of globalization. Most notably, municipalities

---

[12] Le Pen did not stand in the 1981 elections due to his inability to surmount new legal hurdles for would-be candidates. But he participated in all subsequent elections (1988, 1995, 2002, and 2007) until his daughter Marine Le Pen assumed control of the party in 2011 and ran as the party's presidential candidate in 2012 and 2017.

with fewer than 2,000 residents took an interest in Le Pen like never before (Hainsworth 2004).

Given the prevalence of intercommunal grouping at this time, it makes sense to ask whether these autonomy shifts were connected with Le Pen's rise in rural popularity. But what – beyond FN themes already noted above – would make Le Pen the beneficiary of communally rooted frustrations? Though Le Pen has always favored a strong, central French state, at times he has passionately defended the rights of the commune. According to Comparative Manifestos Project (CMP) party manifesto data from 1988 to 2012 (Lehmann et al. 2015), the National Front attributed more attention to issues of local versus central authority in 2002 than it did in any other year. Among all the parties cataloged, the FN's stance on communal authority stands out for advocating communal rights and criticizing intercommunal measures that undercut local autonomy. For instance, it argues for local referenda on environmental issues and for an end to structures that integrate communes. It also asserts that the "socialist state" has abandoned the rural world which cries for revitalization.[13] The 2002 FN manifesto vows: "Our communes where, according to Tocqueville's expression, lives the force of free people, will be fully preserved and will continue to be the base of local liberty."[14]

Here, I test the idea that the Le Pen vote in 2002 was linked to the introduction of CDCs in particular localites. I also consider the extent to which such a boost for Le Pen hinges on certain local features, such as the level of rootedness felt by residents and the vibrancy of associational life. To address unresolved questions about the role of immigrant presence and unemployment discussed above, I include measures of these local characteristics in the models below. Furthermore, socio-economic accounts of radical right support emphasize the potential effects of living in an area that is home to a large number of economically disadvantaged (and not solely unemployed) residents. Therefore, the models also consider how the occupational breakdown and educational qualifications of local communities may shape vote shares for the FN.

The models below provide insights into shifts toward Le Pen over time, estimating support for Le Pen while controlling for how well he did in the previous presidential election. This provides a more dynamic view of local levels of radical right popularity than exists in studies of these parties and their supporters.

---

[13] See Chapter 3 for more FN programmatic details of relevance.

[14] Author's translation. The original text reads, "Nos communes où, selon l'expression de Tocqueville, reside la force des peoples libres; seront intégralement préservés et continueront à être la base des libertés locales" (2002 FN manifesto, p. 33).

CROSS-COMMUNAL ANALYSIS

Data

The main dependent variable is first round support for Jean-Marie Le Pen in the 2002 presidential election as a percentage of valid votes cast by commune. In many of the models, I also include a lagged dependent variable: first round support for Le Pen in the 1995 presidential election as a percentage of valid votes cast by commune.[15] The unit of analysis is the municipality, known in France as the *commune*. There are over 36,000 of these municipalities in France; approximately 80 percent have fewer than 1,000 residents. The commune is the oldest political unit still in existence in France, and it is the lowest geo-political level of state authority. Instituted in 1789, though with histories dating back to the Middle Ages, these traditional territories have developed their own cultures, stories, and identities over hundreds of years. Because electoral statistics are collected down to the commune level in France, it is possible to compare local areas with respect to their electoral profiles. All models are ordinary least squares regressions.

Data on year of CDC establishment is made available by the Assemblée des Communautés de France (www.adcf.org). The first CDCs began operations in the 1960s and the intercommunal aggregation process continues today. But the largest wave of intercommunality washed across France in 2001 and 2002 when over 4,300 and over 2,600 communes, respectively, were integrated into CDCs. For coding, a dummy variable for each year (i.e. *Est. 1996*) signals whether a particular commune was intercommunalized[16] in that year ($x=1$) or not ($x=0$). And because one consideration in this analysis is to address temporal trends in Le Pen support, another dichotomous variable (*Established 1996–2002*) indicates whether a commune became part of a CDC since the last presidential election. If the CDC establishment year was within the 1996 to 2002 timeframe, this variable has a value of 1. Otherwise it is coded 0. Finally, since the communes entering into intercommunal arrangements may share features not directly related to the causal inquiry at hand, another dummy variable (*Established ever*) represents whether a commune had been intercommunalized at all as of 2002.[17]

---

[15] Including a lagged dependent variable in the model is important for specifying the impact of key contextual predictors. See Poznyak et al. (2011) on dynamism in contextual effects on radical right support in Belgium.

[16] Being intercommunalized means being formally integrated into a CDC. Laying the groundwork can take several years so in most cases the process is triggered earlier.

[17] Factors that might influence when and whether a particular CDC is established and contains a particular commune include geographical proximity among communes and socio-economic factors not captured in my control variables. Excluding this variable (Established ever) from the models does not substantively alter the results. An alternative modeling strategy to address these

To test alternative accounts of radical right support, I rely on data from the 1999 French census (www.insee.fr). This was the most recent census conducted before the 2002 elections, and it was also the last French census to manually count residents in the smallest of communes. I see this as an advantage since the smaller communes are of particular interest in my study. In Table A6.6 in the Appendix I provide original census codes utilized to create the variables.

Two explanations are considered directly using census data. Per the socioeconomic context model, people who live in areas characterized by high levels of immigration and unemployment are expected to be influenced by this environment and support radical right parties. Second, the modernization "losers" model posits that economic vulnerability, represented by education level and occupation type, are predictive of support for these parties (Betz 1994). This thesis is articulated to explain individual-level behavior rather than contextual influences, but areas with many voters that fit the "loser" description may show constitutive effects.

Percent foreign indicates the percentage of local residents who were born abroad. *Unemployment* is the percentage of the local working age population who are officially registered as unemployed. Local education level is divided into two categories: first, *Low education* represents the percentage of the local population aged 15 and over who are not in school and do not have a diploma. Second, *High education* measures the percentage of this same base population that has some baccalaureate training completed. This leaves an intermediary level of education as a reference category. To account for the nature of the local economy, percentages of the working age population employed in different economic activities are also included: *Agriculture* (farmers), *Artisans* (shopkeepers, small business owners), *High skilled professions* (executives, intellectuals, engineers), *Intermediary professions* (such as school teachers, health care workers, and clergy), *White collar workers* (such as government employees), and *Manual laborers*. Additionally, a *Population* measure is included as a control since the sizes of the communes vary widely.[18] The observations are weighted by population to further address the significant disparity in commune sizes.[19]

potential complicating characteristics is a two-stage selection model. Use of this kind of model does not impact the substantive results presented in this chapter.

[18] Controlling for population also addresses an issue that was relevant to rural voters, in particular, in 2002. Many were fearful of funding cuts to the gendarmes (police) at the time, and Le Pen's tough law and order stance hit the right note (see Mayer and Tiberj 2004 on the importance of security themes in 2002).

[19] In alternative versions of the models displayed, additional control variables (such as percentage of population that is retired and official designation of commune as "rural") do not alter the reported results. Neither does the adjustment of eliminating from the analysis the very smallest communes. Requiring a commune to have over 100 residents, 200 residents ... 1,000 residents to be included in the analysis does not substantively change the findings.

To provide further insight into the way the CDC mechanism operates, I supply more in-depth analysis of certain communal subsets. Data collected on CDC details in the Aquitaine region of France include a measure of how many responsibilities each CDC assumes. *CDC power* ranges from the minimum of three to a maximum of twelve. I expect that the implementation of a stronger CDC will elicit a more vigorous pro-Le Pen reaction than implementation of a weaker CDC. To create the variable *Biggest in CDC* I collected information on whether each commune is the largest in terms of population in its CDC (for those communes in CDCs as of 2002). The expectations here are a bit less clear. Because most service provision in CDCs comes out of the largest commune, we might expect that these "anchor" communes would be less frustrated with intercommunality. This would be the case if a negative reaction to CDCs is primarily one based on inconvenience.[20] Alternatively, in contrast to this pragmatic mechanism, it may be that those in the anchor communes are especially frustrated about intercommunality because they are the largest community in the region and they are pooling authority with smaller communities. The hit to communal pride and feelings of lost status may be particularly acute in such areas.[21] If this is the case, we can expect a positive interaction effect between CDC establishment and "biggest" status on Le Pen support.

To enhance the interpretation of CDC establishment's relationship with Le Pen support, I add to the analysis a communal index that signifies how rooted or invested residents are in their localities. Among communes with new CDCs, those with more communally oriented residents should be the ones most likely to object to the loss of autonomy. As a result, an interactive relationship can be expected between recent CDC installation and local rootedness. As Duncan Lawrence and I argue elsewhere, social cohesion at the communal level is positively associated with radical right support in Switzerland (Fitzgerald and Lawrence 2011).

I craft a three-item index to measure the extent to which residents are attached to – or rooted in – their communes. First, in-commune workers, or the percentage of the actively employed population who work in their home commune (as opposed to commuting to another commune), are identified

---

[20] By inconvenience, I mean having to travel a greater distance to secure public assistance as a result of CDC's reorganizational mandates. Specifically, a resident from a small, intercommunalized commune might find that centralization of services into the CDC seat means they have to travel farther for such help than they did before.

[21] One of the mayors I interviewed described the main source of pride in the town – in his view – as stemming from its relatively large size in comparison to nearby communes. As a bigger social center it stands as an essential arena for commerce and is able to provide public and private services to people in the surrounding countryside. The mayor views this as a strength of the commune, a source of local pride, and as something that surrounding communities value. As intercommunality progresses, towns like this might feel increasingly devalued.

as the number of residents who live and work in the same commune as a proportion of the economically active local population. Existing research shows that commuting can erode people's connections to their communities (Putnam 2000). Alternatively, when workplace communities overlap with hometown communities, local ties are strengthened (Wilkinson 1986, Cox and Mair 1988).

Second, owner-occupied housing reflects the prevalence of home ownership in the locality. This is a well-known indicator of social cohesion within a local area since owning one's home is correlated with investment and pride in the area (DiPasquale and Glaeser 1999, Forrest and Kearns 2001). It is measured as the percentage of primary residences that are officially zoned as resident owned (as opposed to rented). Third, residential stability is measured as a percentage of the population that lived in the same commune in 1990, the year of the previous national census. This is a phenomenon that has been linked to improved neighborly relations and positive feelings about one's community (Sampson 1991). I use these three percentages to generate the rootedness variable, labeled *Local attachment index*.

For the Gironde department, I also provide a measure of communal social capital, called *Local activities*. To generate this variable I collected data on activities that can bring local residents together for recreational and civic purposes. This insight into the associational life of the commune captures the actual participatory dimension of social ties considered in previous chapters. High levels of social capital of this type can be expected to minimize Le Pen support levels and perhaps to counteract the pro-Le Pen effects of CDC establishment. The measure of social participation used here comes from the Quid profiles, which contain information on all the towns and villages of France.[22] One aspect of the communes that Quid catalogues is the number and types of activities available. These include such recreational outlets as hunting, tennis, and camping, and the number of sporting associations as well as socio-cultural organizations.[23] Here, the number of such activities and associations for each commune is divided by the size of its population (per the 1999 census) to yield a per capita measure of local activities.

---

[22] See www.quid.fr for the full communal profiles.

[23] These were collected in 2005 and so they are only valid indicators to the extent that these characteristics were stable from 2002 to 2005. Checking these details against those from the Quid 2002 volume (Frémy and Frémy 2001) results, which include much of the same kinds of information as the website, shows that this variable changes little over the few intervening years. I also collected additional variables from the Quid communal portraits to test their applicability to radical right support. These include the existence of different types of local festivals (patrimonial, communal), the presence of a local museum, and the nature of the commune's architecture. The idea was that these factors might offer a sense of the content of communal identities. None, however, proved to be useful in a statistical sense for predicting FN support.

MAIN RESULTS

Effects of CDC Establishment

Table 6.1 contains the results of two OLS regression models. The data for these models include French communes (on the mainland) for which all relevant information is available.[24] The difference between the two models is the inclusion of a lagged dependent variable in the second model. The central finding is that communes intercommunalized since the previous presidential election were particularly supportive of Le Pen in 2002. Looking at the first model, communes that recently lost power to CDCs were 5 percentage points more supportive of Le Pen than those that did not.[25] This is a meaningful impact since support across France was 16.9 percentage points. Once a lagged dependent variable is included, the impact is approximately 2 percentage points. Notably, Le Pen beat out center-left Lionel Jospin by less than 1 percentage point to reach the second round of the election. Thus, the effects of CDC establishment displayed across the models in Table 6.1 could be considered decisive.

Looking at other variables, education generally operates as expected: low education is associated with higher Le Pen support while highly educated communes host less support. Though only high education is a significant educational predictor once past Le Pen vote is controlled for. (Recall that mid-level educational qualifications represent the reference category.) Occupational features of communes also conform to expectations for the most part. Areas highly populated by artisans are the most supportive of Le Pen across both models (see Goodliffe 2012). And communes with many farmers are less likely to host Le Pen support in 2002, but are especially likely to host a rise in Le Pen support across the two elections of interest. This comports with the observation that the 2002 election was one in which Le Pen first won over many voters in rural areas.

---

[24] Appendix Table A6.1 presents the results of a parallel set of models that include only those communes integrated into CDCs as of 2002. The reason for a second set of models is that communes that are appropriate for CDC membership are similar on a number of dimensions, such as population size and density, as well as type of location (rural) and nature of land use. This more defined comparison yields substantively similar results as compared to the all-France models in Table 6.1.

[25] Replication of this model for the (fifteen) other candidates in the first round of the election (available from the author) shows that no other candidate benefitted from CDC implementation as much as Le Pen. Models for two of these candidates (both of the ideological left) yield positive, statistically significant coefficients for CDC establishment between 1996 and 2002. But the substantive impacts are small fractions of 1 percentage point. These candidates are Daniel Gluckstein of Parti des Travailleurs and (ironically) Jean-Pierre Chevènement of Mouvement des Citoyens, for whom the 1999 legislation on intercommunality is named. Overall, Gluckstein received less than 0.5 percent of the vote; Chevènement received just over 5 percent of the votes cast in 2002.

TABLE 6.1 *Predicting 2002 Le Pen support at the commune level*

OLS regression models

Predictor	All communes				All communes			
	No lagged DV				*Lagged DV*			
	Coeff.	S.E.	Sig.	Δ	Coeff.	S.E.	Sig.	Δ
CDC								
Established 1996–2002	.05	(.003)	*	.05	.02	(.002)	*	.02
Established ever (as of 2002)	−.03	(.003)	*	.03	−.01	(.002)	*	.01
Socio-economic model								
Unemployed	.20	(.01)	*	.01	.07	(.01)	*	.004
Foreign population	.12	(.01)	*	.003	−.09	(.01)	*	.002
Modernization losers model								
Low education	.41	(.01)	*	.04	−.01	(.01)		
High education	−.12	(.01)	*	.01	−.10	(.01)	*	.01
Occupational status (% employed as):								
Agriculture	−.38	(.02)	*	.02	.04	(.02)	*	.002
Artisan	.93	(.03)	*	.03	.51	(.02)	*	.01
High-skilled	−.39	(.02)	*	.01	.02	(.02)		
Intermediary	.49	(.02)	*	.03	.02	(.01)		
White collar	−.04	(.00)	*	.01	.00	(.00)	*	.001
Manual labor	−.27	(.01)	*	.02	−.07	(.01)	*	.006
Controls								
Population/100,000	.0006	(.0001)	*		.0001	(.0001)	*	
Le Pen support 1995					.82	(.01)	*	
Constant	.09	(.01)	*		.07	(.01)	*	
R²	.59				.76			
N	35,209				35,194			

* p<.05

Results based on weighted observations by communal population size.

Δ = Est. Δ in % Le Pen based on shift from 0 to 1 in CDC variables, from .25 to .75 quartiles in all others.

To make the effects of different independent variables more comparable, Table 6.1 displays the estimated change (Δ) in Le Pen support associated with each predictor. These are absolute values. To better visualize these effects, Figure 6.4 presents them in a bar graph. Each bar represents the estimated change in Le Pen support when a particular predictor shifts from low to high values. For the CDC variables, which are dichotomous, this shift goes from 0 to 1. For all other variables, which are percentages of communal populations with various features, the shift is from the

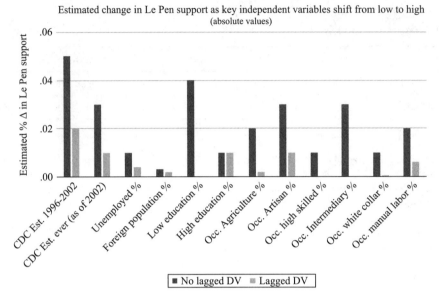

FIGURE 6.4 Estimates based on models in Table 6.1.

.25 quartile to the .75 quartile to eliminate the influence of extreme outliers. The dark bars represent the impacts estimated through the first model in Table 6.1; the light bars represent the effects derived from the lagged dependent variable model.

The strongest predictor in both models is the establishment of a CDC in the years since the previous presidential election. With respect to the socioeconomic context model, unemployment and foreign population predict Le Pen support. Unemployment's effect is decidedly positive across both models, though cut in about half (from 1 percent to 0.5 percent) when past Le Pen support is accounted for. Percent foreign has divergent effects across the two models. The effect is relatively small in both specifications: less than 1 percent change in Le Pen support moving from the lowest to the highest quartile. But it shifts from positive to negative when the lagged dependent variable is introduced. This represents the previously suggested phenomenon of Le Pen's heightened popularity in areas with few immigrants in 2002. The modernization losers thesis also receives support here. Communes populated by those with low levels of education and by artisans and workers in semi-skilled occupations voted for Le Pen in greater numbers. Yet Low education's effect is sensitive to the specification. It is positive in the models that do not control for 1995, and it is non-significant when that control is included. Across the board for both models, it is clear that larger communities are most supportive, and of course prior Le Pen support is a very strong predictor.

Effects of CDC Establishment Timing

These results are consistent with the narrative that 2002 vote shares for Le Pen grew in areas not traditionally supportive of the FN. Where CDCs were established since the 1995 presidential election, Le Pen made the most substantial gains.[26] One way to more precisely link CDC establishment and Le Pen support is to take a detailed look at when, exactly, CDCs were put in place. It stands to reason that the more recent the change, the greater its salience and the stronger the electoral reflex against it. Before people have a chance to settle into new routines, learn the ways in which reconfigured service provision will work, and more generally come to terms with major local changes, they may vent their frustrations in the voting booth.

Figure 6.5 presents the results of "timing" models that disaggregate the variable indicating a commune's inclusion in a CDC. The full set of models appear in Appendix Table A6.2. Seven dichotomous variables are included in these models to determine whether more recent transitions are particularly influential. *Est. 1996*, for instance, is coded 0 if the commune was not intercommunalized in 1996; it is coded 1 if it was intercommunalized in 1996. And so on. There is one of these dummy variables in the model for each year since the previous presidential election (including 2002).[27] The yearly impact for each variable in a baseline model (dark bar) and a lagged dependent variable model (light bar) is presented.

Per these models Le Pen support gets the biggest boost in areas most recently integrated into CDCs. Le Pen received the most support (and the strongest boost over 1995) in communes intercommunalized in 2001, the year leading up to the election. Communes intercommunalized in 2001 were 6 percentage points more supportive of Le Pen in 2002 than were communes not intercommunalized in 2001. Controlling for Le Pen support in 1995, this impact is 2 percentage points. The results for CDC establishment in 2002 are also noteworthy. They are weaker than the 2001 CDC effects in the baseline model, but the 2001 and 2002 CDC establishment variables are very close in

---

[26] These electoral benefits did not fully endure into the subsequent election. Running this same set of models with Le Pen's vote share in the 2007 presidential election is informative. The impact of CDC establishment between 1995 and 2002 is about halved in each model. This implies that while Le Pen received a boost of 2–5 percentage points from recent communal power losses, only half of this effect endured into the next presidential election. This points to a dual mechanism: one that is lasting and one that is a relatively short-term reflex.

[27] For the models in Table A6.2 that include all communes, the reference categories are: communes that never became grouped into CDCs (as of 2002) as well as communes that were already grouped into CDCs as of 1995. For the second set of models that include only communes that were intercommunalized as of 2002, the reference category is those communes subjected to CDC authority before 1996.

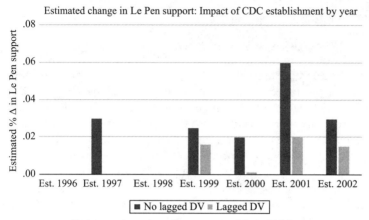

FIGURE 6.5 Estimates based on first two models in Table A6.2.

impact in the lagged dependent variable models.[28] Recent and current CDC establishment boosts Le Pen support.

An alternative way to look at these results is to consider the timing of other elections in France: 1997 hosted French parliamentary elections, 1999 was the year of European elections, and 2001 was the year of French local elections; 1997 and 1999 stand out as years of CDC establishment that fueled 2002 Le Pen support nearly as much as the 2001 and 2002 establishment years. Perhaps the coincidence of CDC implementation and a major election enhance the salience and political impact of intercommunality. I investigate this notion of electoral timing systematically in the next chapter.

To summarize the results presented in Figure 6.5: recent CDC establishment on average is associated with greater and increased Le Pen support in 2002, and where CDCs came into being in the year of a(nother) major election, the correlation with 2002 Le Pen support is especially strong. I interpret these results to mean that the potency of 2001 CDC establishment for Le Pen support stems from its proximity to the 2002 election and the focus on local matters prompted by the municipal elections of 2001.

CONDITIONING FACTORS

CDC Strength, Relative Commune Size

What are the effects of CDC strength (in terms of the range of authority areas) and being the largest commune in a particular CDC (in terms of

---

[28] Est. 2002's relative weakness as compared to Est. 2001's impact may be due to the timing of the election early that year (round 1 in April, round 2 in May). Intercommunal transitions that went into effect in 2002 may have not yet had an impact on residents.

population)? Table A6.3 in the Appendix provides answers to these detailed questions. All else equal, Aquitaine communes that are integrated into relatively powerful CDCs that have control of many aspects of local life, are especially supportive of Le Pen in 2002. And being the biggest in the commune has a negative coefficient. These are the direct effect estimates. Once these variables are interacted with the establishment of a CDC in the years since the last presidential election, a different, more informative pattern emerges. The second and third models in Table A6.3 provide the interactive results. Both interaction terms are significant, positive predictors of Le Pen support in 2002.

Figures A6.1 and A6.2 in the Appendix display the substantive effects of these interactions. Per Figure A6.1 Le Pen received 8 percent more votes in areas with the strongest CDCs and around 1 percent fewer votes in communes that are members of the weakest CDCs. In communes that are part of especially powerful CDCs, the establishment of these bodies in recent years boosts Le Pen support considerably. In the weakest CDC areas, the impact is not distinguishable from zero. This means that where CDCs have the most power, the effect of CDC establishment (since the 1995 presidential election) on Le Pen support is greatest.

Per Figure A6.2 Le Pen did nearly 1 percent better in communes that anchor their CDCs as compared to those that did not. This tells us that the connection between CDC establishment in recent years and Le Pen support is strongest in communes that are the largest in their intercommunal groupings. It gave Le Pen an advantage of well over 2 percentage points in the largest communes and 1.5 percentage points in all others. This difference, although statistically significant, is not so large in substantive terms. Yet these findings provide additional insight into how CDC establishment connects to local residents' Le Pen vote choice. They also serve as robustness checks on the thesis that loss of status and authority enhanced the appeal of Le Pen in 2002. CDC establishment benefitted Le Pen most in communes that lost the most power and in communes that are large (highly populated) as compared to their communal partners. Again, the results are consistent with an account that places negative views of recently implemented CDC arrangements within the calculus of an individual who decides to support Le Pen.

Local Cohesion

Given the findings presented in previous chapters, it is important to consider whether intercommunality interacts with the nature of community to boost radical right support. Are the areas with the most cohesion also the ones that respond most strongly to lost autonomy? Per the logic of my localist argument, autonomy loss should condition the effects of local attachments and vice versa. Local cohesion in the aggregate should also, on its own, have a positive effect on Le Pen support.

I test this using the Local attachment/Rootedness index described above. This is an aggregate version of the local attachment concept examined in previous chapters. Here, I consider it a contextual feature of communes: where substantial shares of a communal population are home owners, are longtime residents, and live and work within the commune, local solidarity should be at its peak. Stable, inward-looking communes should host the most communal pride. And where and when a commune's political authority is lost, this should boost the political salience of their connections to the commune and ultimately benefit Le Pen. On the flip side, a more transient, less invested population would not logically have the same negative reflex against intercommunality as one that is stable and focused on the locality.

Table 6.2 presents the OLS rootedness models. The first two models establish the direct effects of the Rootedness index on Le Pen support. The first is a baseline model; the second includes a lagged dependent variable. Per both specifications, communes that rank highest on the rootedness scale are most supportive of Le Pen in 2002; those with low levels of rootedness are the least supportive. The direct impact of rootedness on Le Pen support (from the least rooted commune to the most rooted commune) ranges from 15 percentage points in the baseline specification to 3 percentage points in the lagged dependent variable model.[29]

The third and fourth models include the interaction between CDC establishment and rootedness; one is a baseline model and the other is a lagged dependent variable model. These models show that there is an interactive effect between the rootedness index and CDC establishment. Two things stand out here. First, the interaction effect is statistically significant with a positive coefficient. Second, from one model to the next, the magnitude of the interaction effect is not much diminished. This tells us that the conditional impact of these two factors is primarily contemporaneous. The effect is nearly as significant in the lagged dependent variable model as in the baseline model.

Figure 6.6 plots these interactive effects. Panel A shows that communes intercommunalized since the last presidential election host a stronger effect of rootedness on Le Pen support than those that were not. Varying CDC establishment 1996–2002 from 0 to 1 is associated with boosting the effect of rootedness (when it's shifted from its lowest to highest quartiles) from less than 2 percent to 9 percent. Panel B shows that this same magnitude of effect is present when accounting for Le Pen support in 1995. Le Pen support *grew* the most (by a product of nearly six) in communes with high levels of rootedness that recently lost authority to CDCs.

The interactive findings boost confidence that the proposed mechanism, reflex against CDC establishment by voters, meaningfully reflects citizens'

---

[29] This is the impact as rootedness ranges from its minimum to maximum. Using .25 to .75 percentiles of rootedness instead, the impact in the first model is 3 percent and in the second model it is approximately 1 percentage point.

TABLE 6.2 Predicting 2002 Le Pen support at the commune level: rootedness

OLS regression models

Predictor	Rootedness						Interaction					
	No lagged DV			Lagged DV			No lagged DV			Lagged DV		
	Coeff.	S.E.	Sig.	Coeff.	S.E.	Sig.	Coeff.	S.E.	Sig.	Coeff.	S.E.	Sig.
CDC												
Established 1996–2002	.04	(.003)	*	.02	(.002)	*	.00	(.01)	*	-.01	(.004)	*
Established ever (as of 2002)	-.02	(.003)	*	-.01	(.002)	*	-.03	(.003)	*	-.01	(.002)	*
Rootedness												
Local attachment index	.15	(.004)	*	.03	(.003)	*	.14	(.00)	*	.02	(.01)	*
Interaction												
CDC 96-02 X Local attachment							.08	(.01)	*	.06	(.01)	*
Socio-economic model												
Unemployed	.21	(.01)	*	.08	(.01)	*	.23	(.01)	*	.09	(.01)	*
Foreign population	.22	(.01)	*	-.07	(.01)	*	.20	(.01)	*	-.08	(.01)	*
Modernization losers model												
Low education	.40	(.01)	*	-.001	(.01)		.41	(.01)	*	.01	(.01)	
High education	-.10	(.01)	*	-.10	(.01)	*	-.11	(.01)	*	-.10	(.01)	*
Occupational status (% employed as):												
Agriculture	-.36	(.02)	*	.030	(.02)	*	-.35	(.02)	*	.04	(.02)	*
Artisan	.91	(.03)	*	.51	(.02)	*	.90	(.03)	*	.50	(.02)	*

(continued)

TABLE 6.2 (continued)

Predictor	Rootedness						Interaction					
	No lagged DV			Lagged DV			No lagged DV			Lagged DV		
	Coeff.	S.E.	Sig.	Coeff.	S.E.	Sig.	Coeff.	S.E.	Sig.	Coeff.	S.E.	Sig.
High-skilled	-.09	(.02)	*	.07	(.02)	*	-.07	(.02)	*	.09	(.02)	*
Intermediary	.61	(.02)	*	.05	(.01)	*	.62	(.001)	*	.06	(.01)	*
White collar	-.04	(.001)	*	-.003	(.001)	*	-.04	(.01)	*	-.004	(.001)	*
Manual labor	-.11	(.02)	*	-.05	(.01)	*	-.10	(.0001)	*	-.04	(.01)	*
Controls												
Population/100,000	-.002	(.0001)	*	-.0004	(.005)	*	-.002	(.0001)	*	-.0001	(.0001)	
Le Pen support 1995				.81	(.01)	*				.81	(.01)	*
Constant	-.04	(.01)	*	.04	(.01)	*	-.04	(.01)	*	.04	(.01)	*
R²	.61			.76			.61			.76		
N	35,209			35,194			35,209			35,194		

* p<.05
Results based on weighted observations by communal population size.

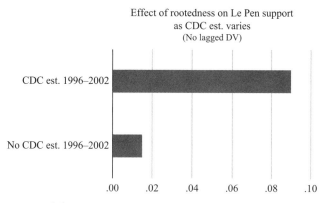

FIGURE 6.6 PANEL A

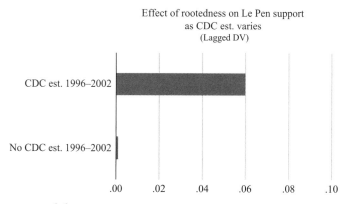

FIGURE 6.6 PANEL B

Results based on interaction models in Table 6.2 as Rootedness shifts from lowest quartile (p25) to highest quartile (p75).

decisions to support Le Pen. When and where local attachments are strong and politically salient, the radical right can make significant gains, particularly where local autonomy has recently been diminished. The fact that the magnitude of this interaction is not undercut by the inclusion of a lagged dependent variable shows that the effect is contemporaneous. This also means that the impact of CDC establishment is strongest in communities with high levels of local cohesion. These interaction effects represent the crux of this book's argument, linking local attachments with radical right support most vigorously where the locality is threatened and thereby politically salient.

Immigration, Unemployment, and Associational Density

To examine the ways that CDC establishment may relate to other contextual features, Table A6.4 in the Appendix contains additional models. These show

how CDC effects on Le Pen support are shaped by the prevalence of unemployment and the presence of foreign-born residents (as a percentage of all residents). I find that establishment of a CDC since the last presidential election is at its strongest as a predictor of Le Pen support where there are relatively significant numbers of foreign-born residents in the community. This is the case in both the baseline model and the dynamic model that controls for communal support of Le Pen in 1995. Reversing the interpretation of this interaction tells us that the influence of immigrant presence on Le Pen support is strongest in communes that have recently lost autonomy. This suggests that these two factors are complementary, perhaps rooted in a similar, sentimental reflex against unprecedented change in the communal environment.

Unemployment rate, on the other hand, weakens the effects of CDC establishment on Le Pen's popularity; losing autonomy is not so politically motivational for community residents where unemployment is relatively high.[30] Flipping the interpretation of these interaction effects around tells us that the effects of local unemployment are contingent on other community-level considerations in both the baseline and lagged dependent variable configurations. I interpret these findings to signify that economic calculations represent an alternative route through which people arrive at a radical right vote. This evidence of conditionality for both immigration and unemployment helps to account for the contradictory findings of studies that find local diversity and local unemployment to matter for vote choice and those studies that do not.

Finally, the role of social capital is also a consideration when examining where the implementation of CDCs has the greatest impact on Le Pen support. Table A6.5's models in the Appendix establish that the presence of a large number of local activities weakens the impact of CDC establishment. Based on the analysis of the Gironde's communes, it becomes clear that where civil society is well developed, as evidenced by the rate of associational opportunities available to residents, Le Pen does worst. This is the direct effect of the social capital variable: areas with the highest levels of associationalism are on average 12 percentage points less supportive of Le Pen in 2002 than areas with the densest civil societies. In interactive terms, where civil society is well developed the impact of CDC establishment is considerably diminished. The political salience of the locality is less predictive of radical right support where people are integrated via community associational life.

---

[30] One interpretation of this result is that areas with high unemployment are also low on local cohesion as removal from the workforce can have isolating and atomizing effects on a community (see Fitzgerald and Lawrence 2011 on the ways these community traits relate to each other in the Swiss context).

SUMMARY OF RESULTS

The question of why voters in rural France became interested in Le Pen in 2002 guides the analysis in this chapter. It derives from the broader question: what explains voter support for radical right parties? The focus on certain areas of France at this particular time point allows for an expanded understanding of radical right support. The evidence points to a localist reflex against the removal of authority from individual communes and bestowing it on inter-communal councils. This institutional change boosted Le Pen support in 2002.

I also consider which kinds of communes would host the most Le Pen support upon losing communal powers. The answer is that where residents are most rooted in their localities, the more their loss of autonomy predicts enlarged Le Pen vote shares over time. When and where local authority is diminished, the flames of local pride are stoked. Across French communes, the local becomes politically salient when its integrity as a meaningful unit of government is under threat. When communal authority is relocated to a CDC in the year of a major political event (such as municipal, legislative, or European elections) there are lasting electoral implications. Shifts in state structures (and the political salience of those shifts) and voters' attachments to their local communities are important predictors of voter behavior – independently and in interaction with each other. The central finding is that where people are most rooted and where newly established CDCs have the most supra-communal power, the boost for Le Pen is strongest.

INSIGHTS FROM FIELDWORK

The lessons of fieldwork undergird these statistical findings: many residents and elected officials of communes that do not fit the socio-economic contextual profile for radical right support described their frustrations with intercommunality.[31] Returning to my example commune of Les Billaux: it was grouped into a CDC in 2001 which was a municipal election year and one year before the presidential election. This commune is also above average on the rootedness measure and below average on the social capital measure. As such,

---

[31] CDC headquarters are typically located in the largest village or town in the collectivity. Alternatively, in many cases the CDC grouping aligns with cantonal boundaries (cantons are the administrative unit that exists between the commune and the department). The commune that sits at the head of the CDC tends to also be the traditional head of the canton. And this cantonal chief may or may not be the largest commune in the CDC. As a CDC begins to do its job, the center for services tends to grow up around the headquarters. This means that those who do not live in the commune with the CDC offices now find themselves traveling to another village to accomplish administrative tasks and to seek services that previously did not require travel out of their commune. One local councilor I interviewed described the entire process of shifting authority away from his commune as an "affront."

this commune is a nice fit with my localist account of radical right support, given its high level of support for Le Pen in 2002.

Other communes help to further illustrate the real-world applicability of the statistical models. The comparison of Ambès and Castillon-la-Bataille, two Gironde communes, helps to ground the narrative. Le Pen support in Ambès went from 12 percent in 1995 down to 11 percent in 2002. In Castillon-la-Bataille it rose from 13 to 23 percent. These two villages are similar on several dimensions: population approximately 3,000, unemployment around 16 percent, foreign-born under 5 percent, rootedness index within .06 from each other (on a 0 to 1 scale), and similarly empowered CDCs at the time of the 2002 election.

The key difference, from my point of view, is that Ambès became part of a CDC in 1966; Castillon-la-Bataille was intercommunalized in 2002.[32] Furthermore, social capital is significantly higher in Ambès per the activities index described above.[33] Foreigners are more prevalent in Castillon-la-Bataille: 5 percent of the population versus just over 1 percent in Ambès. When spending time in both places, I noticed that social diversity is significantly more visible in Castillon-la-Bataille. The center of town is more commercially vibrant, and all kinds of people find themselves sharing common spaces such as small courtyards and plazas. The overall ambiance of Castillon-la-Bataille is one of heightened energy with a hint of agitation. In central Ambès it is one of tranquility.

Taken together, Ambès and Castillon-la-Bataille tell the story of a rural landscape in which local communities are adjusting to modern changes and strains at different times. Each village has its own character, history, sense of pride, and social norms. But there are systematic patterns associated with their voting behavior from election to election that – when aggregated – have major national-level consequences.[34]

---

[32] In 2002 Castillon-la-Bataille became intercommunalized with twenty other communes. Since then two more communes have joined, bringing the total to 23. The CDC seat is in Pujols, which is about 3 miles away. The intercommunal situation in Ambès is a bit different in that it is more urban (Ambès and Castillon-la-Bataille are about 30 miles apart). Ambès became part of the newly formed Bordeaux Métropole in recent years along with 27 other communes. The Métropoles are the most integrated version of intercommunality to date.

[33] Castillon-la-Bataille also has a proud history as the site of the final battle of the Hundred Years' War which led to the expulsion of the English from the area.

[34] The 2017 presidential electoral returns show that things have changed significantly in Ambès. In the second round Marine Le Pen received over 46 percent of the vote (in Castillon-la-Bataille she received 42.6 percent; nationally Marine Le Pen received about 34 percent). A slow transition has moved Ambès from its traditionally leftist voting patterns toward the radical right. In 2007 Jean-Marie Le Pen's first round vote share was less than 11 percent (around the national average); in 2012 Marine Le Pen's was approximately 22 percent in the first round (the national figure was about 18 percent). Then in the first round of 2017 she received about 27 percent of the Ambès vote. While many things have surely changed in Ambès over the years, a few specific developments align with a localist understanding of radical right support. First, in 2014 the

In interviews with village and town mayors and council members conducted in the spring of 2008, a number of the themes raised in this chapter came up. In fact, it was through these interviews that they first came to my attention. The excerpts below substantiate many of the cross-communal findings presented above, and they offer further insight into rural life in modern France. I provide some of these insights in interviewees' own words, anonymizing the speakers and the towns out of respect for their privacy. These quotations all come from villages and small towns that voted in large numbers – above the national average – for Le Pen in 2002. They all have very low levels of ethnic diversity (almost none) and they were all intercommunalized in either 1999, 2001, or 2002. To be clear: **to the best of my knowledge these interview subjects were not, themselves, FN supporters.**

The CDCs are a source of frustration that some people feel on a very personal, sentimental level in many villages. From a small village where intercommunalization took effect in 2001 comes a description of the feelings evoked by these changes and how people relate to their communes. The setting was a group of five village council members sitting at a table in the town hall.

JF: Please comment on the changes [in commune A] in the past ten, twenty, thirty years? When did you observe the most significant changes?

RESPONDENT: Oh yes, in the last ten years … We try to unite … [takes a breath to start over]. Because the problem is that France, of the European community, it's the country that has the most municipalities. We have 36,000 distinct communities in France. This is huge! We like our little communities. And we love our steeples.[35] You know that we are a little regionally biased and we love our home. For us it's always a bit difficult to just accept these mergings of communes, because we are all very attached to our commune. Yes, a great deal. That's quite typical. In general, the French, it's "my steeple." There you have it … Not necessarily out of temperate convictions. Because a community, for the French, that is something familial: a nest. It is not like this [in the United States (implied)]? Less? Perhaps you move a lot

commune voted for a new mayor (of the right), replacing the longtime mayor of the left (he had been mayor since the 1980s). Things changed quite a bit in town in terms of communications in the wake of this change in leadership. The communal website is now a wealth of local information, including the refurbished communal newsletter (previously called *Ambès Actualités*, which translates to Ambès News), now entitled *L'Ambésien*. Through this well-appointed and user-friendly site, local residents can learn a great deal about the goings-on in town and they can be reminded of their common identity as Ambésiens. The website links to statistics on communal demographics and other details about the local population. Also around the same time as the mayoral transition, Ambès became more fully integrated than before into the newly formed Bordeaux Métropole, boosting the level of authority transferred to higher order units of governance. Finally, a rash of break-ins was taking place in the spring of 2017 just as the presidential campaign season was heating up. Per the local newsletter, the perpetrators were apprehended in March thanks to the vigilance of the community. The mayor, at the time, said that the village was considering video surveillance measures to prevent a recurrence. This connects with law and order themes that the FN leverages and that are well received in many rural areas.

35 Alternative translation: bell tower.

more. The French tend to not want to move much ... We are attached to our roots. (commune A, quotation 1)[36]

This local resident describes strong feelings of attachment to the locality and the difficulty of accepting the agglomeration of communes into larger units. I followed up by asking others in the room what they like about their commune.

JF: What is it that you like here?
RESPONDENT: That is *my* community.
JF: You are at home.[37]
RESPONDENT: There you have it. That is all. After all, it is one whole isn't it? The church, the town hall, it is all one. It is our community. It's important. One finds that in the traditional families but a lot less in the contemporary ones. Maybe that will happen one day again. (commune A, quotation 2)

This respondent went on to explain that this is a feeling among the longtime families of the commune.

Yet in spite of these statements of strong affections for the commune, these same residents lament the relatively inactive population with respect to social engagement. One resident describes another part of the country where people are very socially oriented. He depicts a locale where residents are always outside their homes talking to each other, saying his son lives in a community close to the Mediterranean with a similar social vibrancy. In this other part of France, he explains, local residents stay outside socializing until midnight: young and old alike. He considers the possibility that the weather makes this possible. I followed up by asking:

JF: Would you say that [commune A] is less social than the other community you were describing? One does not see the people in the street ...?
RESPONDENT: Yes. Because [commune A] perhaps is not representative of the villages of France, we don't really have a village center. We're very dispersed: many little hamlets, little neighborhoods ... there you go ... so, we don't meet up with each other. People don't drop in, 84 percent of the community has no reason to come by the city hall. One doesn't see many people. They are dispersed. There are villages like that in France, but [commune A] is not representative of the villages of France. (commune A, quotation 3)

The conversation turned to changes in the town's population over the past several years: people moving in from nearby Bordeaux or Libourne or (more rarely) from other parts of France.

JF: Are the newcomers integrated?
RESPONDENT: Some, but there are those if you will, it's like a dormitory town.[38] They work outside [the town], and they come back later on: the weekend or in the evening.

---

[36] See Table A6.7 for original wording of the quotations presented in this chapter.
[37] The original wording in French is: "Vous êtes chez vous." This also happens to be the second person plural version of the FN's slogan (coined years after these interviews): "Nous sommes chez nous" or "We are at home."
[38] Alternative translation: bedroom community.

They arrive, it's 6 or 7 pm, they stay at home. They come to sleep here, but they don't have time [to participate in social life]. (commune A, quotation 4)

These last four statements signal a strong sense of connection to the community, yet from a social perspective one does not see a great deal of interaction among neighbors. As the conversation turns back to what people appreciate about the village, one resident helps to make sense of this apparent tension between the feelings people have for their community and the relative lack of participation in it:

RESPONDENT: And I find this more and more. My town is my steeple. That's it – we're back to the steeple. People need a communal identity, even if they don't participate. (commune A, quotation 5)

Other villages and towns in the region experience similar social strains. With local economic shifts, new residents moving from the Bordeaux area, and people working two jobs, things changed a great deal in the early 2000s.[39] The mayor of another village describes the weakening of interpersonal ties in his town:

JF: Would you say that this village has changed a lot in the last ten years? ... Are these changes difficult for the residents?
RESPONDENT: That's life, isn't it? But regarding communal identity, there are fewer interpersonal relationships between residents than there used to be. Before, there was support when someone had difficulties. There was a neighbor, friends, who would come to help them. (commune B, quotation 1)

He explains that there is a strong sense of pride in the town – with some parts of its built environment dating back to the Romans – and its beautiful local church. But he notices the profound changes in the ways people relate to each other. This village was intercommunalized in 1999; in 2002 over 20 percent of voters chose Le Pen in the first round and over 30 percent voted for him in the second round. In this village unemployment (at the time) was relatively high at 22 percent.

In a larger commune in the Médoc part of the region, the challenges of integrating new residents are described by the mayor. This theme arose in response to my question about what it means to be from this town, what the sources of local pride might be.

JF: What are the sources of pride in this town? What does it mean to be [commune C] ais?
RESPONDENT: It means that you are Médocaine and Médocain[40] ... It's a tradition ... there's a history ... There you go ... We are here; we exist. In fact, we say that a lot ... I often compare the Médocains, and I am one of them, a bit to the Corsicans. We are on a peninsula, so we are not an island, but we exist. That's all. It is very difficult to get into a Médocaine family. It is very difficult. The average Médocain is rather

---

[39] "A few" Moroccan families are the only ethnic minorities in town, according to interviewees.
[40] This term refers to inhabitants of the region of the Médoc.

timorous. There you go. When I say timorous, that means that he will not welcome you with open arms. He will want to know. He will create distance between himself and you … and entering into a Médocaine family is very difficult. That being said, the day you are accepted, you are truly a part of the family. But you must make yourself part of it. It is very difficult. (commune C, quotation 1)

This speaks to the character of the residents and their relatively closed nature when it comes to newcomers and change more generally.

The matter of newcomers came up quite often in my discussions with residents of small communities in the Gironde. Oftentimes, more firmly rooted residents noted that "les nouveaux" had different values and priorities as compared to longtime community members. In one relatively large town the mayor commissioned a local survey to elicit feedback on various issues from the townspeople. He learned that more established residents prioritized economic development and (re)industrialization while newer arrivals emphasized quality of life, environmental protection, and better public services. People moving into these areas often come from larger nearby towns and cities – where they often still work – and choose these more rural areas for the affordable land and tranquility. Another mayor observed that in addition to demands for more public services, which are not typically available in very small communes, they clamor for better internet connections.

Given the results displayed above on the role of rootedness in boosting Le Pen's popularity, the challenges of integrating newcomers merit further consideration. It seems that this kind of dynamic in which new people move into rural or semi-rural localities can have implications for community life. My sense from spending time in these areas is that the presence of relatively new residents (in contrast to families with deep roots in the soil of a town or village) both erodes interpersonal ties among residents and fuels people's feelings of attachment to their localities. Here again is the duality in the nature of community ties – the feelings are often disconnected from the routine social activities. Many of these communities of the Gironde where Le Pen is popular, even the larger communes, do not participate in large numbers in civic life. Residents also do not participate much in local politics, and church attendance is low and declining. When I asked the mayor of a relatively large town about associational life in the commune, he explained:

RESPONDENT: There is strong associational activity in [commune D], but that essentially rests on a core of volunteers that is rather small and that takes care of several associations. So there is not strong volunteer or associative or civic engagement. Overall, it is rather weak, really. (commune D, quotation 1)

To bring this content back to its original intention – understanding the decision to vote radical right – it seems important to connect themes of community attachment to FN support. One mayor I spoke with (whose personal politics lean to the left) identified for me the three pathways he sees people in his village taking to arrive at a vote for Le Pen.

RESPONDENT: If you wish, there are the seniors who vote Le Pen whom I know. Those are the rural folks who have their thing, new things scare them. There are those who vote Le Pen because they have been disappointed by everyone from the right and the left, so they will vote Le Pen. Therefore, there are very few pure racists, but there are more people unhappy with the system. And then they say to themselves, there it is, the right told us this but they don't do it, the left told us that but they don't do it, is it Le Pen who …? … There are those who have a very fixed mentality, very specific, that it is their land, it is their thing … for many it is a protectionist reflex. And then there are the people who are fed up with politics, who go to the extreme right or the extreme left. (commune E, quotation 1)

This statement describes the different motivations behind a radical right vote. First, there is a protectionist reflex that is rooted and territorial and aimed at those who are outsiders from a localist perspective. Second, there is also a racist or anti-foreigner mentality among some. The mayor acknowledged in our conversation that some people have negative views of Arabs. But he also described suspicion of other "outsiders" (who are not of foreign derivation) who move from Bordeaux to buy land in the commune. Third, he identifies a motivation among those who are frustrated by and disappointed with mainstream left and right politics.

All of these interviews provided insight into the ways that people relate to and understand their communities, how change has shaped life in these localities, and what kinds of motivations are relevant for understanding vote choice in times and places characterized by change.[41]

DISCUSSION

The establishment of the CDCs introduces a new dimension to the radical right narrative. It offers a novel answer to the "when-where nexus" question of partisan support. Many European countries are in the midst of reforming subnational authority structures. This case study suggests that seemingly benign changes at the local level may have major implications for radical right politics. Certainly there has been increasing attention in the years since 2002 to the continued "ruralization" of the FN constituency (Ivaldi and Gombin 2015). Yet

---

[41] Aligning with these insights from rural interviews, a popular account of recent social developments in France reminds us of how important space and place can be for drawing lines within society. Christophe Guilluy's (2015) thesis posits that a major, growing fault line within France pits a periphery that feels left-behind against cosmopolitan centers that dominate politics and society. He argues that this frustration energizes the radical right. Notably, he draws attention to the popular idealization of culturally homogeneous, small-scale social groups that are worlds away from urban life characterized by diversity. While the intimate local dimension is borne out by my research, Guilluy's controversial emphasis on the role of immigration-related diversity as a main source of the periphery's frustration is not. I find that while immigration does play a role in some of the defensiveness people feel about their local areas, it is not in all places the pivotal matter that Guilluy makes of it.

the full force of these effects may not be long-lasting. Le Pen's gains from CDC establishment in 2002 were nearly halved by 2007. This implies that some aspect of the autonomy loss impulse weakens over time. These results, therefore, stand to help us understand the building over time of radical right support as well as spasms or peaks in support that do not endure across elections.

In France, a new set of such challenges to community autonomy is just around the corner. So far, intercommunality has been the main form of local authority reform. As I show, the local-level frustration and dislocation associated with this power loss fueled local ties and helped Jean-Marie Le Pen in 2002. Now, a new phase of communal reform is beginning in France. The central government is starting to implement a process of communal fusions on the order of what the Swiss have been doing since the 1990s. This may help the FN to get a greater share of the vote than ever before. In particular, Marine Le Pen stands to expand her popularity among French voters if she makes appeals rooted in the notion of local autonomy, local tradition, and the value of local communities.

This examination of French voting patterns also addresses the larger question of when and where certain social identities become relevant for vote choice. Earlier chapters emphasize the influence of feelings of local attachment on electoral decisions. This chapter, in tandem with Chapter 5, enriches the narrative by introducing a clear-cut example of an institutional factor that influences the relevance of such attachments for political behavior. Structural changes in the form of authority shifts can fuel the politicization of certain territorial attachments. Democratic countries vary significantly in terms of their authority structures across different levels of governance. They also adjust these structures in response to various pressures over time (Baldersheim and Rose 2010). Although much research addresses the implications of these patterns for government performance, their effects on public opinion are perhaps more important in the long run and are certainly less understood.

To pursue these themes further, the next chapter investigates two additional institutional factors as they relate to radical right party support. Building on the analysis of CDC timing presented above, it considers the impact of holding local and national elections in the same year. It also tests whether the levels of autonomy enjoyed by localities in different countries are associated with radical right support. Taking advantage of differences across countries and over time, Chapter 7 casts light on the importance of local institutional factors on the successes of radical right parties.

7

Local Political Salience and Radical Right Party Success in OECD Countries*

In this chapter I ask whether the political salience of countries' local units influences the success rates of radical right parties in national elections. Evidence presented in previous chapters highlights the importance of local attachments as motivations for radical right voting. Further analysis also points to a strong conditioning role of local political salience in enhancing the impact of the localist impulse on radical right support. In Chapters 5 and 6 I demonstrate that local political salience factors such as having meaningful local elections and forfeiting local authority (in France and Switzerland) render local attachments particularly potent for electoral behavior in favor of radical right parties and candidates.

Here, I investigate the concept of local political salience and its implications further, asking what conditions allow radical right parties to flourish and what conditions make them fail to thrive or fail to even emerge? I examine the role of the political relevance of localities across Organisation for Economic Co-operation and Development (OECD) member countries and over time within these countries. The analysis draws on a novel dataset combining parliamentary election results, local autonomy measures, electoral timing, and socio-economic contexts – all at the national level. It covers three decades (1980–2010) and over thirty countries. I disaggregate the concept of local political salience into three dimensions: level of tax authority, level of policy control over areas such as primary education and policing, and electoral institutional features. I use measures associated with each aspect of local salience to predict radical right support levels in legislative elections. The central finding

---

* A version of this chapter was presented at the 72nd Annual Meeting of the Midwest Political Science Association, Chicago, Illinois, April 2–5, 2014.

is that radical right parties are more successful where and when localities are particularly salient units for politics.

INSTITUTIONAL/STRUCTURAL ACCOUNTS OF RADICAL RIGHT SUPPORT

To account for the fact that radical right parties thrive more in some countries than in others, scholars have put forth a host of institutional theories. National factors such as citizenship and nationhood regimes (Koopmans and Statham 1999), party systems (Bale 2003, Givens 2005, Bustikova 2014), welfare systems (Swank and Betz 2003, Arzheimer 2009) socio-economic structures (Betz 1994, Kitschelt, with McGann, 1995), and internal party features (Art 2011, Widfeldt 2015) headline various accounts. Certain electoral institutions also feature prominently in several studies. Proportionality of the system and the related electoral threshold for gaining seats, for instance, are key predictors of radical right success rates (Carter 2005, Norris 2005, Veugelers and Magnan 2005, Skenderovic 2009). I address many of these in Chapter 3.

While we have learned a great deal from institutional studies, these kinds of factors tend to be relatively stable over time. As such, they are not well suited to addressing the dynamic nature of radical right party success rates. National institutional factors that change significantly over time and that differentiate countries have not yet surfaced in the literature to address both dimensions of variation. Furthermore, existing institutional theories of radical right support are not equipped to predict which *kinds* of parties will rise in popularity and maintain electoral relevance. They tend to be value-neutral in that these are features that theoretically could facilitate the rise of any kind of party. As a result, they do not help us to understand the advent of radical right parties in particular.

A major aspect of national institutions that has shifted significantly over time and across countries is the structure of state authority. Chapter 5 examines key aspects of this process in Switzerland; Chapter 6 explores its electoral implications in France. Reorganization of powers across various levels of government has been a major trend in many democracies over the past three decades. The main direction of authority shifts have been downward: central states are devolving formal authority to regional parliaments and lower units. Existing research details processes of devolution of authority over time in democratic systems (e.g. Rodriguez-Pose and Gill 2003, Hooghe et al. 2010, Schakel 2011). The dominant version of the narrative is state-centric: it relates to central governments handing down responsibilities to a range of subnational units. A locally centered version, which I develop here, emphasizes trends through which municipalities – in particular – gain powers.

Despite the prevalence of large-scale authority changes in many democratic societies, their attitudinal and electoral implications have not attracted much scholarly attention. In particular, we do not yet understand how these shifting institutional factors may relate to radical right success rates. Some work considers the impact of "federalism" generally on the radical right phenomenon. Swyngedouw (2001) stands out for connecting individual voters' support for federalism to Vlaams Blok support in Belgium.

Others have considered the role of authority structures in influencing how radical right parties do at the national level. For instance, Arzheimer and Carter (2006) broke ground by presenting and testing hypotheses on the role of federalism in their study of radical right support across countries over time. These authors outline competing propositions for the relationship between devolved authority structures and radical right electoral success levels. Using a political opportunity framework to understand how these parties can rise to relevance on the national stage, they reason that *either* decentralized authority helps parties develop because they can get a foot in the door via lower-level elections *or* that decentralized authority undermines these parties at the national level when voters are satisfied to vent their frustrations only in lower-level elections. The first mechanism they put forth is primarily mechanical in nature. Party development may be more possible in national contexts where new parties can gain a foot-hold in governing units below the national arena. Others have made this argument with respect to the nature of party organizations (i.e. Lubbers et al. 2002).[1] The alternative hypothesis Arzheimer and Carter posit can be described as expressive; where citizens have lower order opportunities to register their dissatisfaction with politics-as-usual, political development is less likely at the national level. In their study, the authors do not find evidence in support of either hypothesis linking federalism to radical right support. But their intuitions about authority structures hold significant potential.[2]

To the extent, then, that federalism has been advanced as a possible explanation for variation in radical right electoral success rates, the existing approach is limited. First, the ideas advanced so far involve a circumscribed view of federalism with the central state as the point of departure (how much power does it share with lower units?) rather than focusing directly on lower levels of authority, namely the municipality, that are closer to people's daily experiences.[3] Second, by evaluating static authority structures rather than dynamic ones, a

---

[1] This logic may be more useful for understanding radical right parties' national breakthroughs rather than their electoral returns once they have established a national presence.

[2] Schain (2006) provides a different logic connecting authority structures that is more dynamic in nature. He observes in France: "decentralized structures – regions and municipalities – are reinforced by strong local party units and local notables to give these structures important policy-making roles. These structures, then, can be used as leverage to magnify the influence of the extreme right in national politics" (287). The proposed mechanism is similar to the first outlined by Arzheimer and Carter in that it explains how sub-national structures may enhance a party's status at the national level.

[3] Arzheimer and Carter, for instance, use the Lijphart index of territorial decentralization as their measure of authority structures. This approach aligns with the classic conceptualization of federal versus unitary structures (Lijphart 1999).

traditional federalism approach forfeits an opportunity to trace patterns of radical right support as these structures shift over time. Third, an authority structure approach has great potential to generate novel insights if it is theoretically linked to what we know about public opinion. Here, I redirect this line of inquiry to gain leverage on aspects of radical right support that are thus far under-theorized and under-studied. I take a different viewpoint of devolution and federalism. Per the theoretical framework built in the preceding chapters, I consider whether the level of authority attributed to localities relates to radical right support. I predict that greater local political salience boosts radical right support. This approach is a novel way to consider the role of a country's institutions in structuring local political salience.

In addition to authority structures, I propose that electoral institutions represent another aspect of political salience. As I posit in Chapter 2, the presence of *meaningful* local elections links people's notions about their communities to the political realm in a powerful way. Impactful local elections politicize the community sphere. In Chapter 5 I show that when Swiss citizens feel close to their neighbors, they are particularly likely to support the Swiss People's Party. This impulse is especially strong in parts of the country that elect local parliaments. I argue that these elections fuse the local and the political in people's minds. In this chapter I further test this idea that meaningful local elections benefit the radical right – this time directly rather than in interactive fashion. The greater the implications (or "stakes") of local elections in a country, the more support the radical right will receive in national contexts as local considerations and attachments become politicized.

The notion that electoral timing matters for radical right vote shares also merits additional attention. In Chapter 6 I supply descriptive evidence suggesting that Jean-Marie Le Pen benefitted in the 2002 presidential election from the combination in 2001 of communal authority losses *and* local elections. Losing communal power in 2001 was a significant predictor of Le Pen support (boosts) at the communal level in 2002. Generalizing from these French patterns yields an expectation that when local elections – which politicize local ties – are held in close proximity to national elections, the radical right benefits in these latter contests. Chapter 2's development of the concept of local political salience underpins this expectation. This chapter furthers the exploration of this theme.

DATA AND METHODS

I subject the local salience thesis to a cross-national test in which national success rate of radical right parties in legislative elections is the dependent variable. The data include several cases where no viable radical right party competes in national elections. Examples include Ireland and Portugal within Europe and the United States and Japan outside of Europe. There are also years since 1980 (the starting point for the data employed here) during which countries – even those that have since hosted radical right party development – did not exhibit any support for such parties. Accounting for these variations across countries and over time is essential to ensure that selection bias does not interfere with statistical analysis of the radical right phenomenon. This is a critique leveled at much of the radical right literature. For discussion of selection bias inherent in models that exclude countries because they do not have radical right parties that compete in national elections, see Jackman and Volpert (1996) and Golder (2003a). Yet simply coding as zero those cases where and when no radical right party exists can also threaten the validity of estimates. Both of these matters should be dealt with in modeling radical right support across countries.

To address this issue of selection bias, I use tobit models for this chapter's primary analyses (per Golder 2003b: 434–435).[4] Tobit models distinguish between level of support for the radical right where it actually competes and the zeros that represent no support due to the non-existence of such a party. Tobit's maximum likelihood estimator accommodates what in this case can be called "left-censored" data, providing more valid inferences than other estimators.[5] Another advantage of this modeling strategy is that as a censored regression model, tobit coefficients can be interpreted in a relatively straightforward manner.

The cases are OECD members for which there is standardized OECD data available to measure concepts such as the level of authority granted to municipalities, immigration levels, and unemployment rates. The countries are: Australia, Austria, Belgium, Canada, Czech Republic, Denmark, Estonia, Finland, France, Germany, Greece, Hungary, Iceland, Ireland, Israel, Italy, Japan, Luxembourg, Netherlands, New Zealand, Norway, Poland, Portugal, Slovakia, Slovenia, Spain, Sweden, Switzerland, the UK, the US. Years covered are 1980–2010. The unit of analysis is the country-year (i.e. Austria 1980, Austria 1981, Austria 1982 …). This data structure allows for a country's values on key variables to vary over time, capturing shifts in the fortunes of radical right parties across years. Also, only country-years in which there is a national legislative election are included in the models. Including intermediary years would be problematic as radical right vote shares could not change while other variables could.[6]

---

[4] I also run all models as time series regressions (using xtreg in Stata 11) to address the panel nature of the data and the results are substantively consistent.

[5] Hiro (2012) takes on this topic as well, advocating Cragg's model instead of tobit to model successes of radical right (and other "new challenger") parties across countries. He argues that the *presence* of a radical right party should be modeled in a separate step from the *level* of support for an existing one. And while he makes a strong case for a "double hurdle" model given his dependent variable (number of seats won by the party), it is less applicable for the modeling of vote percentage.

[6] Though including non-election years, as well, produces the same substantive results.

Because the data come from a range of continents, it makes sense to address the implications of extending the analysis beyond Europe, which is the focus of most radical right studies. Numerous cross-national comparative analyses as well as single-country case studies of the radical right phenomenon consider non-European cases. Norris (2005), for instance, includes Canada, Australia, Japan, and other non-European countries in her study. Mughan and Paxton (2006) study support for Australia's One Nation party,[7] and Mondon (2013) compares the rise of Australia's radical right with parallel electoral developments in France. It is reasonable to include non-European cases that are also advanced industrialized democracies since they share important characteristics (such as basic institutional structures, similar economic strains, etc.) found to be relevant to the phenomenon of interest.

The data come from a variety of sources. The dependent variable, *Radical right vote*, represents the percentage of the valid vote won by a country's radical right party (or, in the case of more than one, the combined electoral percentage) in national elections.[8] This information is drawn from various electoral sources on the web: Psephos (Adam Carr's Election Archive),[9] Extreme Right Electorates and Party Success (Evans and Ivaldi 2000–2002),[10] and numerous national statistical agencies. Approximately 41 percent of country-years in the data have no radical right support. The maximum value is 31.1, which is the combined vote share for all of Switzerland's radical right parties in 2007.[11]

The key independent variables in the models represent the political salience of localities.[12] I use a number of these measures to gain a broad perspective on the role of local unit salience for radical right support. The central measure of local salience at the national level is the *OECD-DPI Local authority index* that I created by combining three distinct indicators of powers held by municipalities. The first is local tax authority, which denotes the percentage of a country's tax revenue that the locality spends (OECD 2010b). The second component of this index measures the level and kind of discretion localities have in establishing taxation rates and tax policies (OECD 2011). It indicates the percentage of local tax revenues that are primarily controlled by localities.[13] The

---

[7] This party peaked electorally in 1998 with 8.4 percent of the national vote in Australia.

[8] This raises (again) the important matter of identifying a party as Radical right. See Chapter 3 and Norris (2005) for extreme right party identification rationale. And see Table A7.1 in the Appendix for the full list of parties classified as radical right in this selection of OECD countries.

[9] http://psephos.adam-carr.net/

[10] www.politik.uni-mainz.de/ereps/electoral_results.htm

[11] Smaller radical right parties (in addition to the Swiss People's Party) are: Lega dei Ticinesi, Swiss Democrats, and Freedom/Automobile Party. See Helms (1997), Norris (2005), and Skenderovic (2009). For this analysis the vote shares of all four parties are summed.

[12] For methodical examination of various measures of decentralization and federalism, see Blume and Voigt (2008).

[13] This percentage is calculated by adding up the portions of collected taxes over which localities have the power to set rates. The categories that I include to pull together this total figure are described as: "(a.1) The [locality] can set the tax rate and any tax reliefs without needing to

basis for this OECD tax autonomy measure is described as "the proportion of the revenues of … local governments that fall into each of the autonomy categories" (Blöchliger and Petzold 2009: 7). The third component of the OECD-DPI Local authority index is the level of electoral control citizens have over their municipal leadership. Are local legislatures (or city or town councils) publicly elected or appointed from a higher power? Are local executives (typically mayors) publicly elected or appointed from a higher power? The Database of Political Institutions (DPI) supplies this information for numerous countries over time (Keefer 2010, Beck et al. 2001). Their "muni" variable is coded so that higher values mean more local choice in these leadership positions. These three items – local tax authority, local tax discretion, and local leadership choice – are combined into an index to represent how much power local leaders and residents have to shape their own fortunes. By integrating these three components of local salience, this index represents key dimensions of interest (spending authority, policy autonomy, and electoral relevance). According to my theory, the greater this power, the greater the political salience of the locality.

For some context, the highest case on this scale is Sweden in 2010.[14] Thirty-five percent of total tax revenues were spent by localities, the rates of nearly 98 percent of local taxes were controlled substantially by the localities, and municipal legislators and executives at that time were publicly elected. The lowest values are for Ireland in 2002. Two percent of revenues were spent by localities, none of the tax rates for such revenues were established by the localities and both local legislators and local executives were popularly elected. I predict that higher levels of local authority are associated with greater radical right support.

I also ran a robustness check using a separate local salience index. The *Kearney local authority index* was created using data collected by Kearney (1999), who coded a range of sub-national powers across countries and over time. Kearney compiles data on the division of authority across local, regional, and central governments in fifty countries, including numerous developing

---

consult a higher level government; (a.2) the [locality] can set the rate and any reliefs after consulting a higher level government; (b.1) the [locality] can set the tax rate, and a higher level government does not set upper or lower limits on the rate chosen; and (b.2) the [locality] can set the tax rate, and a higher level government does set upper and/or lower limits on the rate chosen." Taxes that are not controlled in one of the ways just described, fall into the following alternate categories: "(c) The [locality] can set some tax reliefs (tax allowances and/or tax credits) but not tax rates; (d4) there is a tax-sharing arrangement in which the revenue split is determined annually by a higher level government; and (e) other cases in which the central government sets the rate and base of the [localities'] tax[es]" (OECD 2011). All of the associated percentages (a–e) sum to 100 percent. Only the (a) and (b) categories are combined to create this local tax rate autonomy measure.

[14] This is the year the Sweden Democrats made their electoral breakthrough with nearly 6 percent of the vote and twenty seats.

ones, at five year intervals from 1960 to 1995. The four items that provide insight into the autonomy of local governments are combined to create an index: (1) autonomous selection of local executive, as well as levels of local authority over (2) primary education, (3) infrastructure, and (4) policing. The present analysis uses data from 1980, 1985, 1990, and 1995 (imputed forward through 2010).[15] Though there is much stickiness to these institutional features, some change does occur over time. Notably, many Central and Eastern European countries devolved powers to the local level in the course of the 1990s; these shifts are reflected in the data. Hungary is the country with one of the lowest scores: in 1990 residents could elect local executive(s) but local authorities had no policy control in any of the three areas under investigation. Hungary's score then shifts to the highest score in the dataset as of 1995, with local power in all three policy areas and continued electoral choice over local executives. The expectation here, again, is that more local authority is associated with greater shares of votes for radical right parties at the national level.[16]

A third measure of local political salience denotes whether each national election studied takes place in what is also a *Local election year* for the country as a whole.[17] While some countries leave the scheduling of local elections up to the municipalities, themselves, or an intermediary regional authority, other countries hold all of their local elections simultaneously. Where and when this occurs, this Local election year variable is coded 1. Where and when this is not the case (either it's an off-year in countries that do coordinate their local elections or it's a country in which local elections are held at varying times), the variable is coded 0. The expectation is that when local attachments and contexts are prevalent and politicized in people's minds, as they would be at the time of municipal elections, the radical right will benefit electorally at the national level.

Several controls are also included in the models. *Immigration level* and *Unemployment rate*,[18] collected from the OECD's International Migration Database,[19] Annual Labor Force Statistics,[20] and national statistical offices, represent socio-economic context at the national level.[21] *Electoral threshold*

---

[15] Running these models only through 1995 and through 2000 generates the same substantive results as those presented below. The effect sizes are slightly larger when analyzing this more limited subset of the data.

[16] The pairwise correlation between the OECD-DPI authority index and the Kearney authority index is .40 (significant to .0001).

[17] I pieced this variable (as well as a dummy variable for regional elections) together using a host of national statistical agencies. This measure is a combination of "vertical" and "horizontal" simultaneity (Schakel 2011).

[18] These have been found to be relevant predictors across national contexts, whether independently or in conjunction with each other (Anderson 1996, Jackman and Volpert 1996, Golder 2003b, Lubbers et al. 2002).

[19] http://stats.oecd.org/Index.aspx?DataSetCode=MIG

[20] http://stats.oecd.org/Index.aspx?DatasetCode=STLABOUR

[21] An interaction variable of immigration and unemployment rates was introduced into each of the models shown below as a further robustness check per Golder (2003b). In no configuration did it approach statistical significance. These models are not included in the presentation.

and partisan *Polarization* represent political opportunity structures; these are drawn from the DPI database (Keefer 2010, Beck et al. 2001). Electoral threshold ("thresh" in the DPI data) is defined as "the minimum vote share that a party must obtain in order to take at least one seat in PR [Proportional Representation] systems. If there are more than one threshold, [we] record the one that governs the most seats" (Keefer 2012: 17). And polarization ("polariz" in the DPI data) is defined as "the maximum difference between the chief executive's party's value … and the values of the three largest government parties and the largest opposition party" (Keefer 2012: 19).

The analysis also considers the general role of federalism as a separate phenomenon. To ensure that local salience measures do not simply reflect this broader, decentralization phenomenon, a standard *Federalism* control is also incorporated into the statistical models. This, too, comes from the DPI database (labeled as "state"). It is coded highest if regional legislative bodies and executives are publicly elected and lowest if neither is publicly elected. The DPI measures whether public elections are in place for selecting both regional legislators and regional executives, whether only regional legislators are elected but not executives, or neither electoral procedure is in place. Per these data, countries in which there are no regional elections include Finland, Hungary, Lithuania, and Portugal. Countries with only legislative (and not executive) elections at the regional level are Belgium, Croatia, Netherlands, and Poland. And though most countries do not alter these arrangements during the course of the time period covered by this study, some do. Countries in flux include Belgium, Portugal, Romania, and Finland. Country dummy variables are included in all models to account for national-level factors, such as citizenship regimes, that are not specifically measured by these variables.

In models that estimate the Local election year impact, *Regional election year* is introduced as a control to rule out the possibility that the effect is associated with sub-national elections in general rather than local ones in particular. The local election variable also raises questions about the mechanism(s) at work here. The thesis is that there is something specific to the presence of a local election during a national election year that benefits radical right parties at the national level. Yet it is important to consider the possibility that scheduling various levels of elections to occur simultaneously can raise turnout rates (Lijphart 1997, Geys 2006). It could therefore be argued that the effect of combined local and national elections operates through influencing participation levels. To test for this possibility, *Turnout* in the national election is utilized. The turnout rate comes from the Comparative Political Data Set (CPDS) database (Armingeon et al. 2012).

A final variable, *Decentralization platform*, comes from the Comparative Manifestos Project (CMP) database (Lehmann et al. 2015). The CMP codes parties' manifestos to facilitate comparison of their attention to various themes. For the parties of interest in this chapter, the variable derived from the CMP represents the percentage of statements in the party's most recent manifesto at the time of each election that positively emphasizes decentralization.[22] Though this is not so precise as to directly connect to municipal themes alone, the overall interest in delimiting central authority in favor of sub-national units complements the local salience theme. While most radical right manifestoes coded by CMP do not bring up this issue at all, some of the high scorers are the Slovak National Party and Italy's Lega Nord in the early 1990s as well as Belgium's Vlaams Belang/Vlaams Blok since 1995. For each of these countries during those years, the radical right parties' platforms included double-digit statement percentages of decentralization content.

Due to the diverse sources of data, these predictor variables detailed in the pages above provide substantial but inconsistent coverage for the set of countries identified above. This means that by including certain independent variables, the set of countries represented in the models shifts somewhat. Table A7.2 in the Appendix reports the countries and years included in each model's sample. To ease interpretation of model results, all predictors are coded to run from 0 to 1. This means that each coefficient represents the percentage change in radical right support associated with moving the relevant predictor from its minimum to maximum value. I also present substantive effects of key independent variables as they shift from their lowest to highest quartiles. This makes for a more conservative set of estimates.

DESCRIPTIVE PATTERNS

Here, aggregate patterns in radical right support and shifts in local authority levels are investigated in relation to each other. Figure 7.1 displays shifts in the OECD-DPI local authority index and shifts in support for the radical right parties over fifteen years in fourteen countries.[23] Local authority, which ranges from values of 0 to 1 in the data, trends upward from .62 to .73 during this period for this set of countries. Average radical right support nearly doubles during this period, ranging from 3.9 percent in 1995 to 7.7 percent in 2010. Recall that these are somewhat conservative numbers for the radical right since countries without meaningful radical right parties competing in elections (such as Ireland and Japan) are included in these data.

Figure 7.2 presents these same trends using the Kearney authority index. Because this index is comprised of four snapshots (1980, 1985, 1990, and

---

[22] Per the CMP codebook, this variable is described as "Support for federalism or decentralisation of political and/or economic power. May include: Favourable mentions of the territorial subsidiary principle; More autonomy for any sub-national level in policy making and/or economics, including municipalities; Support for the continuation and importance of local and regional customs and symbols and/or deference to local expertise; Favourable mentions of special consideration for sub-national areas." See https://manifestoproject.wzb.eu/coding_schemes/mp_v5

[23] The countries chronicled annually in Figure 7.1 are: Denmark, Germany, Hungary, Iceland, Japan, Netherlands, New Zealand, Norway, Poland, Portugal, Spain, Sweden, Switzerland, and the UK. These are all the countries for which both variables are available over this timeframe.

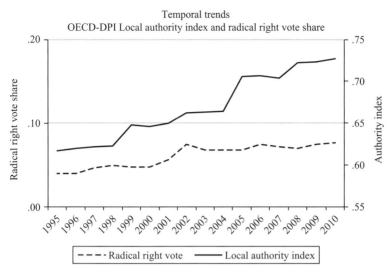

FIGURE 7.1

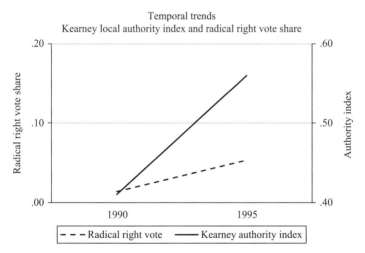

FIGURE 7.2

1995) and elections were not democratic in Central and Eastern Europe in the 1980s, I only plot the figures from 1990 and 1995 data. This provides full data for twelve countries.[24] The authority index, which ranges from 0 to 1, rises

---

[24] These countries included in the data displayed in Figure 7.2 are: Australia, Canada, Czech Republic, France, Germany, Greece, Hungary, Italy, Netherlands, Poland, Romania, and the UK. As in Figure 7.1, this is the full set of countries for which I have relevant data.

during this period from .41 to .56 for these countries. And the radical right share of the vote in the most recent national parliamentary election rises from 1.4 percent to 5.3 percent across these years.

The prevalence of concurrent local and national elections (or at least the prevalence of these elections occurring in the same year) has also risen slightly over time. The variation across countries in election timing makes for a strange figure, but there is efficiency in taking large time segments and reporting average occurrences. For the full set of thirty OECD countries included in this study, approximately 22 percent of national election years were also local election years from 1990 to 1999. The corresponding figure for the years 2000–2010 is over thirty percent. Radical right vote shares also increased modestly between these two decades for this set of countries: 5.3 percent average over 1990–1999 and 6.2 percent average for 2000–2010.[25]

The purpose of presenting data on these trends is to illustrate the upward trajectory in both local political salience and radical right support. To date, no research has considered these specific patterns in relation to each other. Surely, many things have changed in these countries over the past few decades that could fuel the radical right. But the trajectories displayed provide initial empirical support for the proposition that there is a meaningful, aggregate-level relationship between local political salience and support for radical right parties in advanced democracies.

RESULTS

Table 7.1 tests the relationship between the compiled OECD-DPI Local authority index and radical right electoral share. The first model contains only the index (made up of tax revenue expenditure, tax rate control, and public election of local officials) and a dichotomous control variable for each country. Per the baseline model, where and when local authority is at its highest, the radical right receives approximately 10 percentage points more electoral support than it does in cases in which the local authority is lowest. Shifting from the more moderate .25 quartile to the .75 quartile is associated with just over a 4 percentage point boost in radical right support. (Unpacking this index reveals that none of its components is statistically significant on its own, though public election of local officials is very close.) The full model in Table 7.1 contains additional independent variables but includes fewer cases due to issues of data availability. Unemployment rate, Immigration level, Electoral threshold, and Polarization account for the contextual and institutional environment. The federalism variable is also included to test whether the local salience impact is simply an echo of broader, federal authority structures. Per this specification,

---

[25] Figure A7.1 in the Appendix provides a contrast by plotting the change in average percentage of tax revenue controlled by the central government over time alongside the radical right electoral rise.

TABLE 7.1 *OECD-DPI local authority index and radical right vote in legislative elections across countries and over time*

Tobit models

Predictor	Baseline			Full		
	Coeff.	S.E.		Coeff.	S.E.	
Local authority index	.10	(.04)	*	.09	(.04)	*
Unemployment rate				.21	(.24)	
Immigration level				.03	(.12)	
Electoral threshhold				.51	(.41)	
Polarization				−.002	(.02)	
Federalism				.02	(.06)	
Constant	−.14	(.25)		−.17	(.10)	
N (country-years)	90			53		
-2Xlog likelihood	236			198		
LR chi²	184			95		

* p<.05. All models contain country fixed effects.

the Local authority index's effects persist independent of these controls. None of these other predictors achieves statistical significance.

As noted above, Sweden and Ireland stand out as having the highest and lowest levels of communal authority in this collection of country-years. Sweden's peak of local autonomy aligns chronologically with the electoral breakthrough of the Sweden Democrats in 2010. To date, no radical right party has emerged to compete in Irish elections. Norway is a country that exemplifies the temporal trend here. Local tax rate control has risen considerably since the 1990s, shifting from approximately 4 percent to over 98 percent. And during these same years the Progress Party has grown its share of voters from about 7 percent to 23 percent.

Table 7.2 contains models that test the effect of the *Kearney local authority index* on radical right vote share. The models in this table corroborate the story told by previous models. Moving values on the Kearney index from the minimum value to the maximum value is associated with increasing radical right support by nearly 14 percentage points in the baseline specification, while shifting it by nearly 7 percentage points when comparing the lowest and highest quartile cutoff points. The corresponding figures for the full model are 9 percent and 5 percent. No other predictor is statistically significant. See Figure A7.2 in Appendix for comparative substantive effects of the three different local salience measures.

Unpacking this index allows for a closer examination of the most relevant aspects of local authority for radical right voting. The results of these models are presented in Table A7.3 in the Appendix. As detailed above, the Kearney index combines autonomous selection of local executives with municipal authority over primary education, infrastructure, and policing.

TABLE 7.2 *Kearney local authority index and radical right vote across countries and over time*

Tobit models

Predictor	Baseline			Full		
	Coeff.	S.E.		Coeff.	S.E.	
Kearney authority index	.14	(.05)	*	.09	(.04)	*
Unemployment rate				−.18	(.51)	
Immigration level				−.16	(.22)	
Electoral threshhold				.10	(.06)	
Polarization				−.01	(.03)	
Federalism				.04	(.04)	
Constant	−.04	(.52)		−.10	(.06)	
N (country-years)	102			66		
-2Xlog likelihood	105			84		
LR chi^2	36			35		

* $p<.05$. All models contain country fixed effects.

Disaggregating the index and running the above models with each component reveals which components of this index have the greatest impact. In the baseline model, local executive choice, educational control, and policing authority are all statistically significant predictors. The strongest of these is local electoral choice. When controls are added and the number of observations drops (not displayed), only educational policy control and policing authority remain significant. Both of these have a substantive impact on radical right vote share of approximately 7 to 8 percent across these specifications (moving each from its minimum to maximum, which is also the cutoff for the top and bottom quartiles due to the distribution of values within these data).[26]

A subset of countries that represents these general findings is composed of France, Italy, and Germany. France and Italy rank high on this authority index, with democratic elections for communal executives and some level of policy authority over education, infrastructure, and policing. Germany, in comparison, has similarly autonomous elections for local executives, but did not have policy control in any of these areas in the years examined. France and Italy have had relatively successful radical right parties in the past three decades. France's National Front's top legislative electoral share was over 17 percent in 1997; Italy's combined share of radical right votes was over 26 percent in 1996. In contrast, Germany's radical right does not make much progress over

[26] Alternate versions of the models in Tables 7.1, 7.2, and 7.3 include additional independent variables investigated by other scholars. These include: changes in unemployment and immigration levels, the use of proportional rules for legislative elections, mean district magnitude for legislative elections, and GDP and GDP change. None affects the substantive findings.

TABLE 7.3 *Local election timing and radical right vote in legislative elections across countries and over time*

Tobit models

Predictor	Baseline			Full		
	Coeff.	S.E.		Coeff.	S.E.	
Local election year	.06	(.02)	*	.07	(.02)	*
Regional election year				.002	(.02)	
Unemployment rate				−.19	(.22)	
Immigration level				.02	(.16)	
Electoral threshhold				−.21	(.16)	
Polarization				.01	(.02)	
Federalism				.15	(.08)	
Turnout				−.21	(.09)	*
Constant	−.29	(.06)		.10	(.12)	
N (country-years)	296			128		
-2Xlog likelihood	416			250		
LR chi²	304			162		

* p<.05. All models contain country fixed effects.

these years, maxing out around 3 percent. Over time, Hungary's significant boost in local policy control in all areas (especially infrastructure) in the 1990s correlates temporally with the subtle but noticeable rise of the Hungarian Justice and Life Party (MIEP) from under 2 percent of the vote in the 1994 elections to over 5 percent in 1998.

Table 7.3's models display the relationship between the presence of local elections and radical right support at the national level. The first simply estimates the link between Local election year and radical right support with country dummy variables as controls. The presence of local elections is associated with nearly 6 percentage points greater returns for radical right parties in national elections, and the effect is statistically significant. Stepwise addition of other variables into the model does not influence the effect of proximal local elections, but it does reduce the number of usable observations. The second model in Table 7.3 contains the full set of predictors. In addition to the controls for unemployment, immigration, threshold, polarization, and federalism, this model includes two additional independent variables. The first is Regional election year, which shows no significant impact. Its inclusion boosts confidence that the identified impact of electoral timing is specific to local elections and not other sub-national elections.[27] This model also controls for turnout at the national level, which proves to be a strong, negative influence on radical

[27] Regional election has no effect in any version of this model, even in a bivariate configuration.

right support. This implies that if the presence of local elections does raise turnout levels, then it actually does so at the expense of radical parties. So an indirect effect of local elections on radical right successes via raised turnout is not identified here.[28] In this model, the substantive impact of holding local elections in the same year as national elections is about a seven point jump in electoral support for radical right parties. A country that exemplifies this pattern is Denmark. In my sampled timeframe over three decades, only once were Danish local and national elections held at the same time: November 20, 2001.[29] This was also the election that elevated the Danish People's Party from the margins to a more meaningful position in Danish politics (Andersen 2004).

One consistent finding in the analyses presented above is that local electoral factors – be they in the form of meaningful elections for local officials or proximity of local elections to national elections – influence radical right success rates in national legislative contests. Where and when the locality is electorally salient, the radical right does best. One last analytical step serves as a robustness check. If the correct interpretation of this finding is that certain aspects of electoral timing and municipal authority heighten the salience of the local community for national elections, then this effect should be strongest when and where radical right parties campaign on locally relevant themes. In particular, radical right parties that emphasize decentralization of authority from the political center to peripheral units in their platforms should be the most likely to benefit from the heightened salience of the locality.

The Comparative Manifesto Project data makes it possible to test this interactive proposition. I interact Local election year with the Decentralization platform variable to predict radical right support in legislative elections. The baseline and full models are presented in Table A7.4 in the Appendix. Figure 7.3 depicts the conditional relationship of interest. The bars represent the substantive impact of Local election year on radical right vote share when the party's level of attention to decentralization shifts from its lowest (.25) to highest (.75) quartile cutoffs. A proximal local election is only influential on radical right success in legislative elections when there is some attention in the party's platform to devolving authority. The impact of Local election year on radical right vote share is nearly 8 percent for a hypothetical party that devotes over 2 percent of its manifesto statements to decentralization.[30] These results further illustrate a strong local dimension of radical right voting that includes

---

[28] One might also suspect that the presence of coordinated local elections at all in a country represents low local or sub-national authority just by virtue of the fact that these sub-national units do not make their own election schedules. To address this possibility, an alternate version of these models (not presented) includes a control for coordinated local elections. This variable is not statistically significant and does not influence the observed relationship between Local election year and radical right vote share.

[29] In 1981 and in 2005 they were held in the same year but not on the same day.

[30] Replicating this interaction with the authority indices is not feasible due to insufficient observations once the various datasets are merged together.

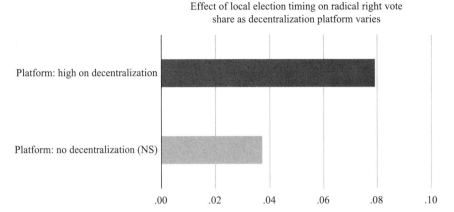

FIGURE 7.3 Results based on model in Table A7.4. Substantive impacts as Decentralization platform shifts from lowest to highest quartile (0 to 2.4 percent of manifesto sentences). Coefficient for "no decentralization" not statistically significant. Control variables in tobit model: Election regional, Unemployment, Immigration, Threshold, Polarization, Turnout, Federalism.

a preference for authority that is not solely divested in the federal government but that instead resides closer to home.

DISCUSSION

Local political salience benefits radical right parties in national elections. In particular, it positively influences the success rates of radical right parties that campaign in favor of devolution. These findings underscore the importance of factors that make the locality politically relevant for electoral outcomes. The concept of local political salience is complex. In this chapter I highlight the importance of three key dimensions: tax authority, policy control, and electoral institutions (which is further divided into meaningful elections of local government officials and the timing of local elections relative to national ones). I pulled measures of these salience dimensions into two authority indices and a simple measure of election timing. Each positively predicts radical right support: where and when the locality is especially salient for politics, the radical right benefits electorally.

In sum, the results presented in this chapter have implications for our understanding of the rise of radical right parties and for knowledge of how certain territorial attachments become relevant for electoral choice. Furthermore, this chapter illuminates some implications of devolved authority and the scheduling of elections in advanced democracies. It is not uncommon for governments to reconfigure state authority structures. Just as centralization of national state structures has been used historically to systematize and unify citizens' socio-political identifications, the reverse process of devolution prompts disaggregation and modern versions of parochialism. These sentiments provide opportunities for parties that criticize national elites and their policies and for platforms that cue local themes. Yet scholarship on how such changes may influence attitudes, shape politically relevant identifications, and motivate different forms of political behavior has not kept up. While this chapter connects authority patterns to far right voting, changes in power structures may have much broader effects that we do not yet observe.

8

Place, Change, Status, and Politics: Concluding Considerations

The ascent of radical right parties is the most significant electoral development in post-war Europe. Millions of citizens across the continent cast votes in favor of policy platforms that are anti-immigrant, anti-European Union, and anti-mainstream politics. These nostalgia parties have attracted significant vote shares across a range of countries, and their popularity is rapidly rising in others. What explains this phenomenon? My investigation into the motivations of radical right voters yields a straightforward answer – politicized local attachments – but a rather detailed narrative. In this concluding chapter I summarize the key findings and consider some areas for future research. In doing so, I provide insights into the UK's 2016 Brexit vote and the 2016 presidential election in the US. I also step back to consider people's conceptualizations of what "us" and "them" looks like in these times of social and political flux. In focusing on these and other developments, I draw attention to societal trends that stand to shape democratic politics for years to come.

KEY FINDINGS

When a person decides how to vote in an election, she approaches the choice from one or more particular social positions. Per my account, a consequential point of departure is membership in one's local community. To greater and lesser extents, people feel connected to their localities, rooted in their communities, supportive of their neighbors, and proud of their villages, towns, or cities. Many people also crave the empowerment that comes with autonomous decision making at the local level. I call this attachment to one's community "localism" and assert that it parallels the concept of nationalism, resting on positive feelings toward fellow members, a profound sense of belonging, a source of identity and pride, and a preference for political autonomy. The main distinction between localism and nationalism is a matter of scale: localism by definition is a concept that relates to people's in-group communities that are closer to home than nationalism.

In Chapters 1 and 2 I note many benefits of strong local ties identified by other studies. These positive externalities have proved to be physical, psychological, social, and economic in nature; socially integrated communities can promote employment growth, boost mental and physical health, reduce crime, and support environmental sustainability (Hirschfield and Bowers 1997, Cotterill and Taylor 2001, Kawachi and Berkman 2001, Uzzell et al., 2002, Callois and Aubert 2007). Theories of social capital and mass society assert that connections among community members can be very good for society as community engagement and organizational participation reinforce democratic norms and inoculate citizens against radical appeals. Indeed, this is what I find. Individuals who participate in civil society are disinclined to vote for radical right parties, and areas rich in such participatory opportunities are similarly resistant to these parties' appeals.

Yet more centrally my study shows that feeling strongly tied to one's community can predispose people to be supportive of far right, extremist movements. Public opinion data from many advanced industrial democracies and case studies of France and Switzerland show that affective ties to one's local community motivate radical right party support. Because the focus here is on local communities, the notion of neighboring is another important part of the story. The radical right makes gains among those with positive affect towards their neighbors.

I also identify corresponding community-level patterns. In localities characterized by high levels of social cohesion the radical right is particularly popular when national elections come around. This is exemplified by France's growing enthusiasm for the National Front. Per my aggregate-level analysis across French municipalities, Jean-Marie Le Pen gained the most votes in 2002 in areas with particularly high levels of local cohesion. This implies that voters, more broadly, who live in high-solidarity communities are especially supportive of the radical right. In contrast, I also find that French localities that are rich in associational life fend off radical appeals.

In bringing these connections to light, I supply evidence to corroborate "dark side" social capital theories and social psychological approaches that emphasize the exclusionary, illiberal implications of strong feelings of belonging. This relationship between powerful local attachments and radical right vote choice is not a simple one, however; it applies best to certain kinds of people and it is conditional on a range of contextual factors. It is these interactive findings that help to refine the localist account.

For instance, participation in civic life and social networks can weaken the link between localism and radical right voting. This highlights the complex nature of social engagement, broadly defined. The far right voter I identify feels attached to her community but does not engage in it routinely; the radical right does not tend to draw support from those individuals who are members of organizations and who engage in mutual aid with fellow community residents. This highlights an important difference between attitudinal attachment to the locality and actual participation in its institutions and networks. Furthermore, it helps to make sense of findings from the vast literature on radical right voting that identifies positive *and* negative effects of social engagement. I also find that the localist mechanism is strongest among women and center-leftists. These are groups that increasingly support the radical right, though prevailing theories are not well equipped to explain this development.

Localism is also closely linked to attitudes on specific issues that are of great political interest these days. Most notably, the anti-EU resentment that's smoldering throughout European societies is connected to local attachments. Localists who vote radical right are especially frustrated with the European Union – even more than they are bothered by immigration. The combination of strong local attachments and anti-EU sentiment leads to particularly favorable assessments of the radical right on the part of voters. There seems to be a complementarity between localism and anti-EU views; themes of sovereignty, autonomy, and home rule that typify anti-EU rhetoric strike a chord in those with strong local identities and those committed to locally devolved power structures. For supporters of an integrated Europe, it is important to understand that local attachments are a key part of the anti-EU and extreme right stories.

These aspects of the analysis provide a novel understanding of radical right voting – a certain constellation of local ties, social contexts, and political attitudes motivates this electoral choice. Yet there is also an important role for institutions in this account. Not all local attachments are relevant for politics; this develops when such sentiments become politicized. I identify three channels through which local attachments can become relevant for national elections and can benefit the radical right. The first relates to the timing of different elections. When local and national elections are held in close proximity to each other, the radical right benefits. This is so across communities and countries and over time. When people are thinking locally and voting nationally, radical right parties reap the electoral rewards. Second, where communities have considerable authority and where their local elections are particularly consequential, the local is similarly politicized in a way that benefits the radical right. Thinking in political terms about local choices and local changes elevates the appeal of radical right programs for citizens. Third, where and when local autonomy is pulled away from communities, a backlash of local defensiveness and stoked pride can also heighten support for the radical right. Processes of agglomeration that are taking place in a number of European countries reduce the authority that many local communities cherish, evoking a strong reaction. Notably, this reaction is particularly feverish in communities that are high on scales of local cohesion. It is also strongest in areas with more immigrant residents who are perceived by some to pose a threat.

Integrating each aspect of the analysis – local ties, community social features, and formal institutional design – the Swiss analysis in Chapter 5 shows that persons with positive feelings toward their neighbors are particularly likely to support the radical right if they live in certain types of communities associated with low levels of social interaction among residents. They are also most likely to do so if they live in areas with either high levels of local autonomy or areas that recently lost such autonomy. This collection of insights summarizes this book's argument. Together, they paint a picture of radical right supporters who are locally rooted, who feel tied to their neighbors, and who care about the status and autonomy of their communities. With their localities in mind and their sense of self at stake, they support radical, backward-looking parties that appeal to them as localists and that evoke themes of identity and belonging. This account is situated at the nexus of identity and institutions. The localist identity interacts with and is shaped by institutional arrangements: state structures that govern electoral timing and electoral stakes and that establish patterns of formal governing authority. When the institutional conditions are just so, localism acts as an especially powerful motivator for a radical right vote.

MAJOR EVENTS, ONGOING TRENDS, AND OUTSTANDING PUZZLES

The localist narrative integrates insights from political psychology and institutionalist studies to explain the radical right phenomenon. It also raises broad questions about public opinion and voter behavior. Here I sketch out a set of developments associated with countries' institutions and people's political attitudes and orientations that are ongoing and that call for future analysis of their implications for politics.

On Brexit: Localism and Electoral Timing

The UK referendum on EU membership provides an opportunity to see politicized localism in action. On June 23, 2016, over seventeen million British citizens voted to leave the EU, winning the referendum by nearly 4 percentage points. This was considered a significant victory for the United Kingdom Independence Party, which has campaigned passionately on anti-EU themes for decades. What explains this historic electoral outcome? Many point to the role of the Syrian refugee crisis as decisive: Britons are anxious about overcrowding, strapped social services, and safety issues. They see the influx of new residents as a significant social and economic threat. Many are also frustrated with the lack of action on the part of mainstream parties to counteract these developments. This, according to the dominant commentary, explains the vote to Leave.

There is no doubt that fear of immigrants and immigration fueled support for the Leave campaign. But at least one large-scale poll shows that issues of sovereignty and self-determination trumped immigration concerns. A survey conducted on the day of the referendum shows that most of those who voted for leaving the EU cited concerns about lost autonomy and lack of independent control over public policy.[1] This aligns with my thematic emphasis on self-determination as a key aspect of radical right support: anti-EU sentiment combined with defensiveness of local autonomy promote extremist vote choice.

Several additional facts of the Brexit case align with the localist theory developed in this book. First, some basic demographics characterizing communities and individuals supportive of Brexit suggest that social solidarity relates to the vote to leave. The Brexit vote was strongest in areas with very few immigrants (Travis 2016), and much research tells us that areas with the least diversity tend to have the most social cohesion (see, for instance, Wilson and Baldassare 1996, Livingston et al. 2008). Thus, communities with high levels of anti-EU sentiment likely host high levels of cohesion. Furthermore, the significant generational and educational gaps in the Brexit vote – with older, less educated citizens especially game to vote to leave – align with the tendency of more advanced generations and those with less education to feel particularly tied to their communities.

Second, many British citizens feel connected to their localities and clamor for more local political control at the same time as they demand less EU control. One study reveals that in every part of England (where the Leave vote was strongest among UK regions) residents feel more tied to their localities than they do to England, Britain, or the EU. The weakest local identities are in London, where the majority of voters opted to remain in the EU. English respondents also feel twice as empowered to influence local decisions as opposed to national ones. As for confidence in institutions, they have the most trust in the local police, then in the local councils; the Parliament in Westminster comes in a distant third place as a domestic body that inspires trust. On average, the English think their local councils should have much more power than they do to influence "the way England is run" and that the EU should have markedly less power. The national parliament, according to respondents, has about the right amount of power. Seventeen percent say that local councils should be the governmental unit with the most political authority. Approximately 1 percent say this about the European Union. Nearly 40 percent of respondents say that "Local authorities in England should have more power" than they currently do (Cox and Jeffery 2014).

Third, the European Values Study provides additional insights on the importance of local ties in the UK. Britons are becoming increasingly connected to their communities over time: feeling more closely attached to one's local area (as compared to other territorial units: region, nation, continent) was much more common in the early 2000s (over 50 percent) than in the early 1980s

[1] www.usnews.com/opinion/articles/2016-06-30/poll-shows-brexit-vote-was-about-british-sovereignty-not-anti-immigration

(36 percent). Also, support for the EU and feeling tied to one's local community are on balance negatively correlated. There is significant support for local autonomy in the UK, as well: over 38 percent of British respondents state that they want local authorities to have more power. Together, these survey findings speak to powerful, deepening local affinities and a widespread desire for governmental power that is close to home. This trend toward feeling more locally connected is also noteworthy since organizational participation has been declining in the UK since the 1970s.

Fourth, it is especially important to note the timing of the referendum on EU membership: it came just weeks after local council elections in England. On May 5, 2016, voters decided who should hold seats in 124 local councils (of approximately four hundred total). Four cities held mayoral elections (Bristol, Liverpool, London, and Salford). Across England and Wales – even in areas that were not choosing any new council members or mayors – police commissioner elections were scheduled for the same day. Altogether, 40 of 43 territorial policing districts in England and Wales held police commissioner elections on May 5.[2]

In my view, these four factors influenced the result of the EU referendum in the UK, though perhaps the most obvious and avoidable miscalculation on the part of the government had to do with the vote's timing. Local elections raise the political salience of local ties, which we see are connected thematically and empirically to anti-EU sentiments. Moreover, to introduce via police commissioner elections the specific issue of local crime, which by definition is a threat to local communities, is to further boost the local fear factor. Local identities can be forged and strengthened when a community is perceived to be under threat (Cherni 2001). To the extent that local campaigns fuel feelings of "we" throughout communities, they heighten sentiments of local attachment and prime voters for a negative vote on the EU.

A quick look at the voting statistics from various areas reveals a picture that is consistent with the localist model. For instance, comparing localities across England shows that communities that held local council elections voted 2 percentage points more strongly in favor of Brexit than did communities that did not hold such contests. Comparing England and Wales, which held police commissioner elections, to Scotland and Northern Ireland, which did not, is also illustrative. England and Wales both voted approximately 53 percent to leave the EU; Scotland and Northern Ireland voted 38 percent and 44 percent, respectively, to leave. Clearly, many other factors separate the English and Welsh from the Scottish and Northern Irish on the matter of the EU. However, there is good reason to think that the police commission elections had an impact. Between the commissioner contests and local council elections, it is not difficult to believe that a 4 percent swing might be attributed to these local

---

[2] Police commissioner elections are a novel introduction to the British electoral landscape. They were first held in 2012 to make police officials more accountable to their communities.

elections. Alternative explanations of the high level of support for "Brexit" in England and Wales do not give enough attention to the local lens through which many make judgments about high-level politics.[3]

The timing of different kinds of elections has heretofore unexpected attitudinal consequences that ultimately influence electoral outcomes. The prevalence of holding proximal local and national elections is increasing over time, and this book begins to identify some important consequences of this trend. While many have argued that electoral simultaneity is good for turnout rates (Lijphart 1997, Schakel and Dandoy 2014) and that it can influence electoral outcomes (Hix and Marsh 2011), my study underlines the importance of the ways that different electoral configurations and their attendant resultant campaigns can shape public attitudes and cue certain social orientations. To understand modern electoral developments, it is important to ask: what kinds of elections are taking place and when?

On Devolution and Amalgamation

As summarized above, there are several specific institutional conditions that help the radical right in its quest for voter support. In addition to the importance of electoral timing and simultaneity, this study highlights the significance of local authority structures and shifts for politicizing local ties and opening the door to radical politics. Living in contexts where municipalities are meaningful political units – with elected executives and devolved powers such as taxation and law enforcement – translates to a stronger link between local attachment and radical right support. Looking at Switzerland we see that positive feelings toward neighbors make individuals more supportive of the Swiss People's Party (and no other major Swiss party) over time – particularly in parts of the country where the locality is especially salient for politics. This draws the eye toward authority structures as they are designed and as they change over time in different countries.

A significant trend in European governance is toward greater decentralization of power to sub-national units such as administrative regions and municipalities. An example of a country that is undergoing such shifts is the UK, where there is significant potential for politicized localism to grow in the coming years. The government has made significant commitments to devolve greater authority to local councils (Sandford 2016). Future plans entail new policy-making powers, fiscal autonomy, tax policy control, and more independent mayoral elections across England per the Cities and Local Government Devolution Act of 2016 for England and Wales.[4] Increasing local authority

---

[3] Instead, the dominant interpretation of the ways local and national matters relate to each other is that the national drives and informs the way people vote in local (or "second-order") elections. My study demonstrates the reverse process in action.

[4] Local governance does not have a linear history in the UK. Notably, in 1972 the British government swept away the existing system of small-scale governance and instituted a fresh set

may solve a number of public policy problems, and it may be the right thing to do in the UK. But these shifts will likely have significant effects on political behavior that have not yet been considered.

Thinking in normative terms, the rise of radical right parties is understood by many to be a critical problem for democratic politics. In contrast, the devolution of democratic power to sub-national administrative units is generally viewed in a positive light. My research raises questions about the long-term democratic benefits of devolving authority to local communities, particularly if they are not equipped with vibrant civil societies to buttress decentralized governing structures. Sellers and Lidström (2012) find that local attachments are strongest where municipalities have been empowered in recent decades. To this identification of a positive connection between local authority and local attachments, I add in this book evidence that local authority and local attachments benefit far right parties. These results suggest that the anticipated benefits devolution processes (greater public satisfaction with governance, heightened trust in public authorities, enhanced governmental input by citizens) should be weighed against potential support for extremist political movements.

In numerous advanced democracies, just as powers of sub-national units are increasing, restructuring processes that take powers away from localities are also underway. In my case studies of Switzerland and France I describe two processes through which authority is removed from local communities: amalgamation (municipal consolidation) and intercommunality (institutionalization of bodies that make decisions for collections of municipalities). I find that both processes can have politicizing effects that influence voter behavior: threats to the independence of localities raise the political salience of the locality in the minds of residents. As a result, localists support radical right parties in locally rooted protest. Anecdotal evidence suggests that diminished local authority (in Australia in the 1990s, France in the late 1990s and early 2000s, Greece in 2010, and Denmark in 2007) is in key cases accompanied by increases in radical right electoral successes.

Weaving together these various evidentiary threads yields fresh insight into the appeal of radical right parties. Whether these parties' leaders laud the virtues of the local community or criticize overreach on the part of the central state, the strategy of fanning the flames of localism is a winning one. Yet there is some tension within this collection of findings about the institutional factors that serve as indicators and motivators of local political salience. Devolving authority to localities *and* taking authority away can heighten the appeal of radical right parties. Such is the nature of salience – it can be enhanced in a number of ways. One way to think about this pair of mechanisms is that they

of administrative layers across the country. (The fact that this obliteration of local governing institutions occurred on the eve of the radical right British National Front's ascent may or may not be a coincidence.) Since then the structural details have changed significantly and unevenly.

are asymmetrical in terms of how rapidly they operate and how lasting their effects may be. Per my analysis of French communes, the public reaction to losing local autonomy is quite rapid. And though I do not test this systematically, I provide evidence in Chapter 6 that such an impact may be fleeting.[5] As local residents become accustomed to the new local normal, the local political salience that received a jolt from authority shifts may diminish. This autonomy loss mechanism perhaps best explains spikes or spasms in radical right support that do not last. Alternatively, devolving power to localities likely has a more slow-moving, lagged effect. It may become normalized over time to think of one's locality in politicized terms.

These two factors operating together – enjoying significant communal autonomy and then having it taken away – may have a particularly strong effect on salience, giving the radical right its greatest boost. Chapter 5 devotes attention to the process of communal agglomeration and its link to increased support for the SVP in Switzerland. This radicalizing effect may be especially powerful in Switzerland because this autonomy loss is taking place in one of the most locally devolved democratic systems in the world. The SVP's status as the most successful radical right party in post-war Europe is by this logic attributable to the multifaceted political salience of local communities.

Given the ongoing processes in European and other democracies toward devolution and local autonomy erosion, it is imperative that researchers take the implications of these institutional trends seriously as they relate to citizen behavior. What effects does local salience have on people's social identities, their links to fellow community members, their definitions of community, their political opinions, and their electoral choices?

On Patterns of Social Engagement and the 2016 Presidential Election

To revisit behavioral themes of local ties among democratic citizens, the analysis raises questions about the benefits of tight-knit communities and people's positive views of their localities and neighbors. As I note at several points in this book, when people invest in local life, a host of social goods can result. Many potential solutions to modern challenges such as financial crisis, democratic deficit, and climate change have been developed in local communities. People operating at a local level are able to address these issues on a small scale, ultimately contributing to large-scale change (Lowndes and Pratchett 2012). Moreover, a valuable aspect of an energized community is that it draws residents into civil society and encourages collective action. A host of local challenges are most effectively addressed by well-meaning collaboration among neighbors.

---

[5] Given that the pervasive, politicized localism that benefitted Le Pen in 2002 didn't seem to give him much of a boost in 2007.

Importantly, I find here that participation in associational and neighborhood life – doing things such as volunteering, joining clubs, and routinely cooperating with neighbors – staves off extremism. The inoculating effect against the appeals of radicals is robust and shows up in cross-sectional as well as over-time analyses. This demonstrates that community engagement reinforces moderate democratic politics. When people are effectively networked within their local communities, they are unlikely to support radicals.

Yet it is positive feelings about the community that relate to radical right support, and in many societies these sentiments are strengthening while social network integration and organizational participation are declining. This leaves individuals with feelings about one or more groups in society that are unaccompanied and unsupported by interpersonal engagement and face-to-face interactions. These are trends that have been found to characterize a wide range of democratic societies, notably in the United States, raising questions about radicalism in the US context. I therefore propose in preliminary fashion that these aspects of the localist theory of radical right support apply to the election of Donald Trump in the US presidential election of 2016. At the same time, this election also raises additional, related questions that merit attention in future research.

The Trump campaign platform was in large part complementary to those of most radical right parties in Europe. The rhetoric contains similar themes such as anti-immigration, tough law and order, and anti-globalism. Furthermore, the fiery populism of the Trump campaign certainly fits the definition of radical right politics (see Inglehart and Norris 2016). Thus, from a supply-side perspective (which focuses on the system-level and party-level features that allow the radical right to grow and thrive in elections) there is some parity. However, the radicalism of Trump was fused in the election with the established Republican Party, so the parallel is not without its complications.[6]

Still, looking at voter data, there is a circumstantial case to be made that localism had a role in shaping the election's outcome. For instance, small towns and rural areas were highly supportive of Donald Trump in the election (Scala and Johnson 2017). As I point out in previous chapters, these are just the kinds of communities where local cohesion and rootedness tend to be strongest. Looking more broadly at localism in the United States, two major studies of Americans' political behavior point to a powerful role of place-based

---

[6] The dealignment aspect of radical right party rise in Europe is not directly relevant to the US case given that Trump was the presidential nominee for the Republican Party. This absence of a distinct, "radical right" party opens an opportunity to consider how the United States may host partisan patterns that do not fit the dealignment thesis. For instance, there is compelling evidence that the US electorate is characterized by the heightened importance of the Republican and Democratic parties for mass behavior (Hetherington 2001). In the US there is also evidence that partisanship as a social identification has strengthened over time for many, perhaps as a result of the decline of alternative, meaningful social groupings discussed in the opening pages of this book.

community identifications for shaping people's political attitudes (see Wong 2010, Cramer 2016).⁷ Pair this with data on large-scale declines in associational membership and neighborly relationships in the United States (Putnam 2000) and the potential for radicalized local attachments becomes evident.

There is also evidence of a detachment in the United States between social and psychological dimensions of community engagement, mirroring the patterns identified in previous chapters. Some of these key insights have only come to light in the wake of the Trump nomination and election, which prompted many observers to reflect on basic facts of American life that typically do not make the headlines. Recent commentary on the social patterns of white members of the American working class point to increasing levels of alienation from societal institutions such as the church, family, and local community. At the same time there are deeply *felt* connections to these very objects (see Dougherty 2016).

In considering the relevance of local ties for the political popularity of Donald Trump, one can also draw on survey data that tells a complex story about how Americans relate to each other and to politics at the local level. A 2016 Pew poll reveals that among those Americans who know all of their neighbors' names, only about 40 percent feel very close to their communities. This suggests a disconnect in the US between social engagement in and emotional connections to local communities. The Pew survey also reports that feelings of community attachment and active engagement in local activities and organizations are differentially linked to local news attention: strength of community attachment feelings is positively associated with following local news very closely; level of local activity is not related to local news consumption patterns (Barthel et al. 2016). These survey results provide additional support for the proposal that localism boosted Trump's vote share, as they suggest a clear demarcation between feeling close to one's community and actively being part of it.

This survey research by Pew raises important points about the social characteristics of highly pro-Trump communities. It also sheds light on the potential for local ties to influence different kinds of behavior such as news consumption habits and information-seeking processes more generally. Zooming out a bit, the 2016 election underscores the importance of several different aspects of social interactions and information environments. Much attention, for instance, has been devoted to the ways that social media influenced people's vote choices, particularly focusing on the social media environment's role as a host for proliferation of inaccurate information and the interference of trolls in shaping public discourse surrounding the election.

---

⁷ While we might suspect that "rootedness" is less prevalent in the US as compared to Europe given that Americans tend to be more geographically mobile on average, Wong (2010) finds that in the US people derive benefits from their communities relatively quickly in the event of relocation.

Yet my findings suggest that social media's effects may be more founda-tional. Per my analysis, the ways people relate to each other in cognitive and face-to-face terms have significant implications for self-identification and for electoral behavior. Thus we can learn a great deal about citizen politics by ana-lyzing the ways that social media and internet use shape people's feelings of belonging, influence their sense of group threat, and politicize those feelings. This would be particularly relevant for social and political orientations if web use and social media interaction take the place of routine engagements with neighbors and associational participation (as some work suggests happens).[8] The configuration of stronger in-group feelings but weaker group interaction, which set the stage for the radical right, may be reinforced by social media use. In reference to local ties in particular, the presence and use of community websites and local news outlets may be particularly consequential. But exami-nation of social media engagement and internet use more broadly as they relate to social identifications and electoral choices is beyond the scope of this book. The complex social and psychological processes associated with social engage-ment through different online forums are themes that require further investiga-tion as they relate to politics.

On Immigration and Social Cleavages

Immigration is another major trend that fuels radical right movements. As much other work shows and as I display in my models, anti-immigrant sentiment is a primary motivator for those who vote radical right. This truism is reflected in the choice by some experts to use the term "anti-immigrant parties" in refer-encing these electoral competitors. Indeed, it is very difficult if not impossible to envision a radical right voter who is tolerant of immigrants and views immi-gration favorably or even in neutral terms. A few examples of statements by leaders of these parties as reported in media accounts drives this point home. The leader of the Slovakian People's Party, Marian Kotleba, is reported to have said that "even one immigrant is one too many" (*New York Times* 2016). Frauke Petry, leader of the Alternative for Germany party, maintains that "Islam does not belong in Germany" (Meaney 2016). The Golden Dawn in Greece refers to immigrants as "the Stench" and the party has been connected to a rash of violent attacks against migrants. There are also reports that the party has set up a "pure" blood bank that only welcomes donors who are eth-nically Greek (Faiola 2012). The stance on immigration and immigrants that these parties take is unambiguous and beyond the boundaries of democratic societal norms.

---

[8] See, for instance, Nie et al. (2002), on the decline in face-to-face interactions associated with internet use. Yet other studies identify no such implications or even heightened sociability by internet and social media users (Baym et al. 2004, Boulianne 2015).

But more broadly the relationship between immigration attitudes and voter behavior is not so simple. For example, radical right parties do not fully capture the anti-immigrant vote. As a case in point, I find that anti-immigrant sentiment benefits mainstream right parties in Switzerland – the Radicals and the Christian Democrats – in addition to the extremist SVP. Moreover, public opinion surveys consistently reveal that a greater number of people oppose immigration and immigrants than vote for radical right parties across a range of countries. The immigration-vote nexus is complex terrain that requires particularly careful analysis.[9]

The phenomenon of localism may be motivationally complementary to the anti-immigrant position. Plenty of qualitative studies and statistical analyses from political science and adjacent disciplines illustrate that some people feel defensive of their towns and neighborhoods in the face of newcomers or potential newcomers. When influxes of people who are considered to be different from a typical local "native" arrive, there is often an acute, negative reflex against their presence. Even the specter of an influx can compel feelings of defensiveness at the local level.

Still, when exploring the interaction between localism and immigration or immigration attitudes I find inconsistent results. First, localism acts as a conditioning factor for the impact of immigrant presence. In areas of France with more immigrants, the role of local threat in the form of autonomy loss as a motivator for radical right voting is strongest. Yet for *individuals* across European countries the interactive effect between localism and anti-immigrant sentiments is not so clear: it appears that those who are motivated by local attachments to support the radical right are not doing so based primarily on their views of immigrants. It may be that these two impulses – localism and anti-immigrant sentiment – operate independently in additive terms: those who feel both tied to their localities and frustrated by immigration or intolerant of immigrants are especially likely to vote radical right. Alternatively, it may be that the aggregate-level results and the individual-level results do not match up due to the social desirability bias that shapes people's survey responses on certain themes and topics such as immigration. The ways immigration and localism relate to each other represent a knot that remains to be untangled.

But the fact that localism's effects do not operate solely through anti-immigrant sentiments is an important observation. This opens the door to an appreciation of the different ways in which social identifications and societal cleavages are formed and politicized in the modern era. For instance, an "outgroup" that is often targeted by the radical right is not immigrants broadly

---

[9] Others have drawn attention to this complexity of the link between immigration attitudes and radical right support. For instance, Rydgren (2008) argues that the more precise motivational concept is immigration skepticism rather than outright xenophobia for most radical right supporters. Furthermore, Mudde (1999) argues that the immigration issue benefits these parties in certain conditions and is not essential for the success of the radical right in future elections.

defined but Muslim immigrants. Furthermore, the anti-Semitic rhetoric of these parties has been pervasive but the subject of relatively little recent work. Clear examples of anti-Semitism include Jorg Haider of Austria praising Nazis, Jean-Marie Le Pen's holocaust denials, and the clear roots of Italy's National Alliance in inter-war fascism (Eatwell 2000).

In addition to the nativist and religious wedges driven into society by radical right parties, some alternative conceptualizations of new, powerful social cleavages appear to invigorate radical right movements. One societal rift that academics have identified separates winners and losers of globalization (Kriesi et al. 2008, Téney et al. 2014). This emerging cleavage has stratified national populations in terms of objective measures such as economic strains and subjective dimensions that are a function of identifying with different societal in-groups. The identification aspect, in particular, is a close companion to the sub-national attachments that I find to matter for people's vote choices. As Roger Eatwell summarizes along these lines, "Globalization encourages the politics of identity, an attempt to find a harbor of calm in a turbulent sea of hyper-change" (2000: 416).

A popular account of modern rifts can be found in David Goodhart's distinction between "anywheres" and "somewheres" (2017). Goodhart argues that a major cultural schism separates those who feel rooted to a particular locality from those who are not so connected to a particular place. In some ways this argument is reminiscent of the cosmopolitan-parochial/local divide that defined people and politics decades ago (Merton 1957, Inglehart 1997). There seems to be something increasingly vital about the spaces to which people feel they belong and the communities of which they consider themselves members. The emergence of globalization enhances the importance and also threatens the status of those corners of the world to which people feel attached.

Place-based attachments are varied and complex. The meaning of place may also be narrower than the rather abstract definition of community that I have used in this book. A distinct neighborhood, housing estate, or street corner may conjure significant meaning for people depending on how they conceptualize the ways they belong. The places that shape some people and keep them feeling grounded may also be larger, more encompassing units such as sub-national regions. High-profile cases of Catalonia in Spain and Scotland in the United Kingdom are among the most politicized and vibrant regionalisms. Many people feel closely tied to their regions; per the European Values Study data drawn upon in this study, over 16 percent of respondents claim that the geographical region they belong to "first" is their region. And it, too, is positively correlated with radical right support. It may be that regionalism operates differently than localism; this is an area for future research. Academic work demonstrates the potency of feelings people have toward their regions (Brancati 2006, De Winter and Türsan 2003) and their neighborhoods (Haeberle 1987) for their self-definitions and the ways they behave in the political realm.

Threats to Belonging: The "Us" of Modern Politics

Clearly, modern electoral politics in advanced democratic systems is heavily influenced by the politics of identity, broadly defined. Debates over economic priorities and policies have to a large extent given way, and symbolic considerations have gained significant ground. It is reasonable to describe this shift as one from the instrumental politics of "I" and "me" to the status-centric politics of "we" and "us." Yet we are only beginning to see the different versions that "we" can take; opening the door to identity politics allows for a proliferation of group memberships to become relevant in the political arena. Scholars of social identity have shown how fluid different identifications can be, and they have called attention to the shifting political salience of different self-conceptions. Feeling connected with a national community is clearly one central form of belonging with significant political implications, as is feeling tied to a local community. But there are many others that we should better understand. This is an area of research that merits further development.

Another point to make with respect to the "I" versus "we" debate over how people approach politics is that there is also a growing politics of "they." As noted above, in today's radical discourse "they" are foreigners or immigrants or, in many contexts, religious minorities. Throughout this book I have demonstrated the importance of attitudes toward immigrants and their presence in society for radical right party support. But this aspect of radical politics has not been the central focus of my analysis. In part this is because scholarship on the radical right is rich with studies of how the presence, characteristics, and perceptions of immigrants influence the choice of "native" citizens to support a far right party. Another reason that I do not more fully examine the role of immigration is that I think in our scholarship we focus too much on the "they" and not enough on the "we." From a theoretical perspective, our understanding of in-group attachments' implications for politics lags behind what we know about how people respond to out-groups. Furthermore, immigration and the diversity that comes with it are only one aspect of change that people in advanced democracies experience. Though in many contexts this diversity is the most visible outcome of globalization, so many other things have changed. By focusing on a particular "other" we do not notice these less obvious, smaller signs of the times. Indeed, in many communities the less headline-worthy topics have more personal importance to people. An example from southwestern France is illustrative.

During the time I spent in the Gironde region, one of my routine activities was to examine the reader posts on the *Sud Ouest* newspaper's online discussion forum. The website contains links to various discussion pages for different public topics. Participants can post anonymously or they can display their "handles" when contributing to various threads. Discussions on two issues in particular caught my eye in 2008. The first regarded a proposal to no longer display department numbers on vehicles' license plates; the second was about local voting rights for non-citizen residents. What struck me was the vibrancy of the former topic discussion and the bland nature of the latter discussion.

The first topic related to the government's proposal to remove departmental identifiers from French license plates (this ultimately became the law of the land in 2009).[10] *Sud Ouest*'s online prompt read, "Registration: for or against the suppression of the department number on license plates? In several months, the new license plates will be introduced in France. The Charente-Maritime department has already voted to retain the number 17. Are you for or against the suppression of the department number on vehicle license plates? For what reasons?"[11] The ensuing debate was lively. The most consistent line of response presented feelings of local/regional identity, tradition, rootedness, and also some nostalgia. Here are two examples (posted May, 2008). First: "I am against, the cultural identity of each person begins with his local identity."[12] Second: "I am against the suppression of the department number. It is necessary to protect the respect of the regions of our country."[13] In total, from the time that this topic was introduced in January 2008 to early August, hundreds of comments had been posted. In May alone, 139 new posts appeared.

In comparison, the issue of non-citizen voting rights for local elections appeared on the same forum site in mid-May. The topic as proposed was: "Local elections: is it necessary to give the right to vote to foreigners from outside the EU? For now, only the citizens of an EU member state have the right to vote in local elections. Should this right be extended to all foreigners?"[14] One might expect this to be a hot topic; since the early 2000s immigration-related issues have been particularly salient in national politics and in the national media. Yet in the following two weeks, there were only thirteen posts. By early June, the discussion had been removed due to lack of activity. Of the few posts, only one read as obviously negative: "No. To allow it for local elections is the mouse hole for later passage to other elections."[15] This lame "debate" on the immigrant issue demonstrated that immigration-related issues do not catch fire

---

[10] Departments are the units between communes and regions in France. See Figure 6.1.

[11] The original text reads: "Immatriculation: pour ou contre la suppression du numéro du département sur les plaques d'immatriculation? Dans quelques mois, les nouvelles plaques d'immatriculation seront mises en place en France. Le département de Charente-Maritime a déjà voté une motion pour le maintien du numéro 17. Etes-vous pour ou contre la suppression du numéro du département sur les plaques d'immatriculation des voitures ? Pour quelles raisons?"

[12] The original text reads: "Je suis contre, l'identité culturelle de chacun commence par son identité locale ..." These are the author's translations.

[13] The original text reads: "Je suis contre la suppression du n° du département. Il faut garder le respect des coins de notre pays."

[14] The original text reads: "Elections locales: faut-il donner le droit de vote aux étrangers non-communautaires? Pour l'heure, seuls les membres d'un pays de l'Union européene ont le droit de vote aux élections locales., Faut-il étendre ce droit à l'ensemble des étrangers?"

[15] The original text reads: "Non. Le permettre pour les élections locales est le trou de souris pour après passer aux autres élections."

in certain corners of Europe in the way topics that might be considered mundane from an outside point of view do. Other dynamic discussions involving hundreds of posts centered around the construction of a local autoroute, bridge construction over the Gironde River, and the creation of a TGV (rapid train) line linking Bordeaux to Spain. In relief, the non-citizen voting issue was not so interesting to residents.

We can think about the license plate issue as one that relates to "us" while the immigration vote matter is primarily about "them." Although it would be incorrect to suggest that the politics of "them" is not highly relevant to public opinion and elections, particularly as they benefit the far right, it would be similarly wrong to underestimate the power of "us" politics. In the case of the license plate issue, the "us" is a departmental, sub-national one. The Gironde department number is 72; this no longer appears on new license plates in the area. At the time of the online discussion, departmental pride, distinctiveness, and status were all on the line. This, to me, encapsulates a major part of my argument. Place attachments can be powerful motivators for people's attitudes about public policy, and their relevance can be enhanced by existing rules that heighten status (having department numbers on license plates in the first place, for instance). Their public salience can be further fueled by the threat of reduced status (by removing the identifiers from license plates). What may seem like small decisions in the larger scheme of things can add up to equal a strong sense of loss over time. Certainly, change in Europe can come in the form of hallal butchers and hijabs,[16] but it also comes as a series of small perceived slights to different kinds of groups in society. A quiet, persistent erosion of status can ultimately have major political implications.

The meaning of community has changed significantly over the past fifty years. People are less socially connected to each other than they were in past eras, less reliant on each other, and less likely to spend time together in organizational settings. But they are also more likely to hold onto a sense of local belonging. If people feel that their local community membership represents an integral part of their sense of self, then when it loses status the hit is personal and psychological. Just as the weakening of the state by intergovernmental organizations and the supranational authority of the EU fans the flames of nationalism, so too do municipal reforms heighten the political relevance of local communities.

Social identities provide reference points for people. In the instance of electoral choice, citizens use their social memberships as points of departure and then find their way to electoral choice from there. As such, vote choice is at once an individualistic process that is also grounded in the social groups to which a person belongs. Local communities are an important instance of social

[16] See Body-Gendrot (2007) on the hijab in France.

grouping that serves this grounding function and that tends to benefit radical right parties. Many votes for extremists come from those who see themselves as members of their communities, who identify with their local areas, and who feel the need to defend local tradition and local autonomy.

BIG-PICTURE THEMES

This chapter calls attention to a number of important trends such as immigration, which has been well studied, and shifts in local authority structures, which represent a new area for behavioral research. And while I focus in this book on the ways local ties influence radical right vote shares, they also likely have more encompassing effects on phenomena such as electoral participation, mass protest, attitudes about system legitimacy, support for democracy, political alienation, political efficacy, and political polarization.

A bird's eye view of politicized localism and its implications reveals three abstract concepts that intersect to disrupt politics as usual. The first of these trends is *place*. People who feel rooted, who feel that they are defined by a particular physical or social location in the world, who feel that they belong to a bounded community, can be inspired by such sentiments to participate in politics in distinct, often exclusionary ways. The twentieth century in Europe was in large measure shaped by nationalism, and for good reason this phenomenon has been carefully studied. This book focuses on localism, about which we know less because it represents waters that have been largely uncharted – in part because it acts as an undercurrent that is less unified and less visible. In this book, I show how much influence localism can have on politics. We stand to learn a great deal about what to expect from other forms of (geo-)social belonging.

The second concept, which heightens the importance and vulnerability of defined places that people think of as home, is *change*. At various points in this book I have relied on terms such as modernization, globalization, and Europeanization to denote ongoing trends that have altered our world. In this concluding chapter I have spotlighted trends associated with electoral configurations, state authority structures, and ethnic diversification. I also call attention to the more defined issues related to license plates and the occurrence of elections for police commissioners. Whether these changes are sweeping or more place-specific, their impact can be acute. As a result, change of a great many varieties can transform people's participation in social and political life.

Place and change interact to heighten the importance people attach to defined social groupings and locations. Yet at the same time these two concepts put the third notion at the heart of this story at risk: *status*. How is one to carve out a place in this world, identify herself in social terms, and derive self-esteem? What personal benefits can people draw from the ways in which they belong, from the groups to which they feel attached? As the groups and places that supply stability, meaning, and autonomy to people's lives face eroding status, new political perspectives and motivations can emerge. It is this intersection of place, change, and status that calls for further exploration because our democracies as we know them may depend on it.

Appendices

APPENDIX TO CHAPTER 3

Country	*Party/Parties*			
Austria	FPÖ	BZÖ		
Belgium	FN	VB		
Bulgaria	Attack			
Croatia	HSP			
Czech Rep.	Republicans			
Denmark	DPP			
Finland	True Finns			
France	FN	MNR		
Germany	Republikaner	NPD	DVU	
Greece	LAOS			
Hungary	Jobbik/MIEP			
Italy	Lega Nord	National Alliance	Tricolor	Forza Nuova
Latvia	LNNK			
Netherlands	PVV	Center Democrats		
Norway	Progress Party			
Poland	LPR			
Romania	Greater Romania Party			
Slovak Rep.	SNS			
Slovenia	SNS			
Switzerland	SVP	Lega de Tecinesi	Swiss Democrats	

EVS Analysis contains supporters of these parties.

FIGURE A3.1 Radical right parties in 20 countries

Level of attachment to commune in Switzerland

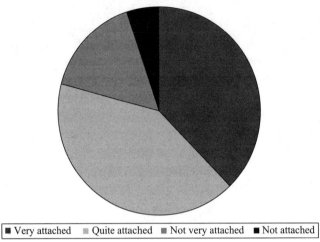

| ■ Very attached | ■ Quite attached | ■ Not very attached | ■ Not attached |

FIGURE A3.2 PANEL A
Source: Swiss Selects

Level of attachment to country in Switzerland

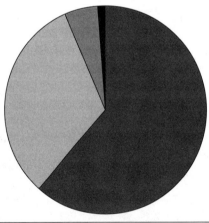

| ■ Very attached | ■ Quite attached | ■ Not very attached | ■ Not attached |

FIGURE A3.2 PANEL B
Sample = only respondents who were born in Switzerland.
Original language for options: très attaché, assez attaché, assez peu attaché, pas du tout attaché.
Source: Swiss Selects

TABLE A3.1 *Predicting Swiss People's Party support*

OLS regression models

Predictor	I		II		III	
	Coeff.	S.E.	Coeff.	S.E.	Coeff.	S.E.
Attachments/attitudes						
Local attachment	.11	(.02) *	.09	(.02) *	.04	(.02) *
National attachment					.17	(.02) *
Anti-EU					.31	(.01) *
Anti-immigrant					.10	(.01) *
Civic engagement						
(NA)						
SES/Modernization losers						
Education low			.17	(.02) *	.06	(.02) *
Education middle			.15	(.01) *	.09	(.01) *
Occupational status:						
Full-/part-time			.07	(.06)	.06	(.06)
Family business			.42	(.10) *	.32	(.09) *
Housewife/husband			.14	(.07)	.08	(.06)
Pensioner			.11	(.07)	.07	(.06)
Unemployed			.05	(.09)	.06	(.08)
In school			−.02	(.07)	.01	(.06)
Socio-demographics						
Male			.09	(.01) *	.06	(.01) *
Age			−.17	(.04) *	−.10	(.04) *
Constant	.32	(.02) *	.18	(.07) *	−.09	(.06)
R^2	.01		.06		.27	
N individuals	3,715		3,689		3,452	

* $p<.05$
Source: Swiss Selects, filter variable = born in Switzerland.

TABLE A3.2 *Local attachment and various measures of SVP support*

Predictor	SVP Sympathy Regression		SVP Probability Regression		SVP Best Logit		SVP Qualified Logit		SVP Voted 03 Logit		SVP Closest Logit	
	Coeff.	S.E.	Coeff.	S.E.	Coeff.	S.E.	Coeff.	S.E.	Coeff.	S.E.	Coeff.	S.E.
Local attachment	.15	(.03) *	.14	(.02) *	.85	(.14) *	.68	(.15) *	.50	(.19) *	.72	(.26) *
Constant	.34	(.02) *	.28	(.02) *	-1.47	(.16) *	-1.54	(.11) *	-2.24	(.15) *	-2.67	(.16) *
N individuals	1,956		3,715		1,787		3,348		3,386		3,829	
R^2	.01		.01									
LR Chi^2					19.24	*	22.29	*	7.42	*	13.62	*
-2XLog likelihood					2,169		3,210		2,650		2,550	

* p<.05
Source: Swiss Selects

TABLE A3.3 *Predicting Swiss People's Party support, OLS*

OLS regression models

Predictor	I			II			III		
	Coeff.	S.E.		Coeff.	S.E.		Coeff.	S.E.	
Attachments/attitudes									
Trust local authorities	.07	(.03)	*	.07	(.03)	*	.07	(.03)	*
Anti-EU							.33	(.01)	*
Anti-immigrant							.10	(.01)	*
Civic engagement									
(NA)									
SES/Modernization losers									
Education low				.18	(.02)	*	.06	(.02)	*
Education middle				.16	(.01)	*	.09	(.01)	*
Occupational status:									
Full-/part-time				.09	(.07)		.09	(.06)	
Family business				.46	(.11)	*	.34	(.09)	*
Housewife/husband				.16	(.07)	*	.11	(.07)	
Pensioner				.13	(.07)		.10	(.06)	
Unemployed				.09	(.09)		.05	(.08)	
In school				−.02	(.07)		.02	(.07)	
Socio-demographics									
Male				.09	(.01)	*	.06	(.01)	*
Age				−.15	(.04)	*	−.08	(.04)	*
Constant	.34	(.02)	*	.14	(.07)	*	−.03	(.04)	
R^2	.002			.06			.25		
N individuals	3,631			3,606			3,393		

* $p<.05$

Source: Swiss Selects, filter variable = born in Switzerland.

TABLE A3.4 *Predicting Swiss People's Party support, Logit*

Logit models

Predictor	I			II			III			
	Coeff.	S.E.	Sig.	Coeff.	S.E.	Sig.	Coeff.	S.E.	Sig.	Marginals
Attachments										
Communal identity	1.15	(.18)	*	.96	(.19)	*	.51	(.19)	*	.05
National identity							2.90	(.39)	*	.16
Civic engagement										
Memberships (any)							-.13	(.11)		
SES/Modernization losers										
Education low				1.81	(.24)	*	1.69	(.24)	*	.26
Education middle				1.47	(.20)	*	1.37	(.20)	*	.12
Occupational status:										
Working				-.14	(.33)		-.06	(.33)		
Retired				-.03	(.37)		-.01	(.36)		
Homemaker				.18	(.39)		.15	(.39)		
Student				-1.20	(.40)	*	-1.07	(.40)	*	-.08
Unemployed (dropped)				.32	(.50)		.48	(.51)		
Socio-demographics										
Age				-.71	(.30)	*	-1.23	(.56)	*	-.09
Male				.73	(.10)	*	.53	(.18)	*	.08
Constant	-2.50	(.14)	*	-2.78	(.41)	*	-4.89	(.52)	*	
-2XLog likelihood	3,376			3,104			3,014			
Wald Chi²	40		*	173		*	213		*	
N	4,089			3,978			3,973			

* p<.05

Marginals = Δ pr(y = 1).

Source: Swiss Household Panel, filter = Swiss born, standard errors clustered by household.

In wave 14 of the SHP (used for Table A3.4's models) the attitudinal questions about the parliament, EU, and immigrants are not asked of the same sample who respond to the community identity question.

TABLE A3.5 *Predicting National Front support*
Logit models

Predictor	I			II			III			III
	Coeff.	S.E.	Sig.	Coeff.	S.E.	Sig.	Coeff.	S.E.	Sig.	Marginals
Attitudes										
Preference: more local power	.43	(.18)	*	.38	(.19)	*	.32	(.19)		.01
Anti-immigration							3.07	(.40)	*	.10
Anti-EU							.41	(.18)	*	.01
Anti-Parliament							.38	(.34)	*	.01
Civic engagement										
(NA)										
SES/Modernization losers										
Education low				1.18	(.32)	*	.65	(.35)		.02
Education middle				.63	(.28)		.18	(.28)		
Occupational status:										
Working				-.48	(.34)		-.23	(.39)		
Retired				-.52	(.42)		-.34	(.45)		
Homemaker				-.55	(.49)		-.47	(.53)		
Student				-1.64	(.28)	*	-1.14	(.66)		-.01
Unemployed (dropped)										
Socio-demographics										
Age				-.84	(.34)	*	-1.23	(.56)	*	-.03
Male				.52	(.19)	*	.53	(.18)	*	.01
Constant	-3.46	(.46)	*	-3.45	(.46)	*	-5.45	(.55)	*	
-2XLog likelihood	1,538			1,364			1,348			
Wald Chi²	36		*	36		*	134			
N	4,291			4,291			4,158			

* p<.05
Marginals = $\Delta p(y = 1)$ for variables significant at .10.
Source: French Political Barometer, filter = French nationality/parents.

TABLE A3.6 *Predicting Jean-Marie Le Pen support*

Logit models

Predictor	I			II			III			
	Coeff.	S.E.	Sig.	Coeff.	S.E.	Sig.	Coeff.	S.E.	Sig.	Marginals
Attitudes										
Preference: more local power	.18	(.08)	*	.09	(.09)		.04	(.09)		
Anti-immigration							2.43	(.19)	*	.32
Anti-EU							.27	(.09)	*	.03
Anti-Parliament							-.54	(.18)	*	-.07
Civic engagement										
(NA)										
SES/Modernization losers										
Education low				1.16	(.17)	*	.85	(.17)	*	.12
Education middle				.99	(.14)	*	.71	(.14)	*	.09
Occupational status:										
Working				-.09	(.20)		.01	(.22)		
Retired				.07	(.23)		.06	(.25)		
Homemaker				.23	(.25)		.16	(.27)		
Student				-1.40	(.32)	*	-1.12	(.34)	*	-.10
Unemployed (dropped)										
Socio-demographics										
Age				-.02	(.004)	*	-.02	(.004)	*	-.15
Male				.14	(.09)		.16	(.09)	*	
Constant	-1.57	(.46)	*	-1.50	(.28)	*	-2.48	(.33)	*	
-2XLog likelihood	4,372			3,972			3,604			
Wald Chi^2	4			89			278			
N	4,533			4,284			4,152			

* p<.05

Marginals = Δp(y = 1).

Source: French Political Barometer, filter = French nationality/parents.

Data Appendix 3.1

Swiss Selects

Anti-EU: Are you in favor of Switzerland joining the EU or for going it alone? For joining, neither, for going it alone

Anti-immigrant: Are you in favor of a Switzerland where the foreigners have the same chances as the Swiss or for a Switzerland where the Swiss have better chances?

SVP sympathy: Can you tell me how much sympathy you have for the following political personalities on a scale going from 0 to 10 where 0 means "no sympathy" and 10 means a "great deal of sympathy"? – Christoph Blocher

SVP probability: "What is the probability that you will one day vote for [party]?" With options ranging from 0 (very small probability) to 10 (very large probability). – SVP

SVP best: Which party represents best your convictions?

SVP qualified: In your opinion, which party is most qualified to resolve that problem? (after R identifies top political problem at the moment)

SVP voted 2003: In the federal elections of 2003, for which party did you vote?

SVP closest: In general, do you feel close to a political party? Which one?

Trust local authorities: Can you tell me how much confidence you have in the following institutions and organizations? – The political authorities of your commune

Swiss Household Panel

Anti-immigrant: Are you in favour of Switzerland offering foreigners the same opportunities as those offered to Swiss citizens, or in favour of Switzerland offering Swiss citizens better opportunities? In favour of equality of opportunities, neither, in favour of better opportunities for Swiss citizens

Anti-EU: Are you in favour of Switzerland joining the European Union or are you in favour of Switzerland staying outside of the European Union? In favour of joining the EU, neither, in favour of staying outside the EU

Anti-government: How much confidence do you have in ..., if 0 means "no confidence" and 10 means "full confidence"?

Memberships: I will now read out a list of associations and organisations. Could you tell me for each of them whether you are an active member, a passive member or not a member? Sports or leisure association, organization involved in cultural activities, music or education, syndicate/employees association, political party, organization concerned with protection of the environment, charitable organization, religious organization or group, local, parents' or women's association, other interest groups such as tenants' rights association, home owners' association or consumer protection

SVP support: If there was an election for the National Council tomorrow, for which party would you vote?

Local identification: Tell me to what extent is belonging to the following locations important for your identity, if o means "not important at all" and 10 "very important"? – Belonging to the commune of [commune of residence]

National identification: Tell me to what extent is belonging to the following locations important for your identity, if o means "not important at all" and 10 "very important"? – Belonging to Switzerland as a whole

French Political Barometer

More local power: In France, would you say that the following institutions have too much power, not enough power or the right amount of power? – Les communes

Anti-immigration: Here is a list of statements. For each, can you tell me if you completely agree, mostly agree, mostly disagree or completely disagree? – There are too many immigrants in France

Anti-EU: Can you tell me, for each of these words, if it evokes for you something very positive, somewhat positive, somewhat negative or very negative? – European Union

Anti-parliament: How do you judge the action of the government of Dominique De Villepin? Would you say that it's very positive, somewhat positive, somewhat negative, very negative?

Le Pen support: Here's a list of political personalities. For each, can you tell me the probability you would vote for her, if she were candidate in the first round of the next presidential election? – Jean-Marie Le Pen?

Close to National Front: Here's a list of parties or political movements. Can you tell me to which you feel the closest or farthest? – The Front National

APPENDIX TO CHAPTER 4

TABLE A4.1 *Support for radical right in 21 countries*

Logit model

Predictor	Coeff.	S.E.	Sig.
Attachments/Attitudes			
Local attachment	.45	(.52)	
National attachment	.26	(.12)	*
Local X " "	−.15	(.19)	
Distrust parliament	1.07	(.19)	*
Local X " "	−.01	(.26)	
Distrust EU	.96	(.18)	*
Local X " "	−.32	(.24)	
Anti-immigrant	.82	(.11)	*
Local X " "	−.29	(.16)	*
Left-right ideology	2.19	(.19)	*
Local X " "	−.53	(.27)	*
Civic engagement			
Memberships (#)	−.37	(.50)	
Local X " "	−.87	(.70)	
SES/Modernization losers			
Education low	.69	(.14)	*
Local X " "	.07	(.20)	
Education middle	.38	(.11)	*
Local X " "	.10	(.17)	
Occupational status:			
Full-/part-time	−.32	(.27)	
Local X " "	.19	(.40)	
Self-employed	−.28	(.30)	
Local X " "	−.01	(.44)	
Retired	−.26	(.29)	
Local X " "	.11	(.42)	
Homemaker	−.18	(.33)	
Local X " "	−.36	(.47)	
Student	−.77	(.34)	*
Local X " "	.19	(.49)	
Unemployed	−.19	(.33)	
Local X " "	.26	(.47)	

(continued)

TABLE A4.1 *(continued)*

Predictor	Coeff.	S.E.	Sig.
Socio-demographics			
Male	.46	(.09)	*
Local X " "	−.20	(.12)	
Age	−1.19	(.26)	*
Local X " "	.41	(.36)	
Context			
Community size	−.13	(.13)	
Local X " "	.24	(.18)	
Constant	−7.87	(.42)	*
N individuals	28,282		
-2Xlog likelihood	11,304		
Wald chi²	2,023		*

* p<.05. Models include dummy variables for each country and survey year.
Source: European Values Study

TABLE A4.2 *Support for the Swiss People's Party (SVP)*

OLS regression models

Predictor	I			II		
	Coeff.	S.E.		Coeff.	S.E.	
Attachments/Attitudes						
Local attachment	.21	(.12)		.26	(.18)	
National attachment	.06	(.03)		.01	(.05)	
Local X " "	.01	(.06)		.08	(.08)	
Anti-EU	.11	(.03)	*	.15	(.03)	*
Local X " "	.19	(.04)	*	.16	(.05)	*
Anti-immigrant	.14	(.03)	*	.12	(.04)	*
Local X " "	−.16	(.04)	*	−.11	(.05)	*
Left-right ideology	.84	(.05)	*	.82	(.07)	*
Local X " "	−.18	(.08)	*	−.16	(.10)	
Civic engagement						
Memberships (#)				.02	(.05)	
Local X " "				−.11	(.08)	
SES/Modernization losers						
Education low	.08	(.05)		.13	(.07)	
Local X " "	−.02	(.07)		−.06	(.09)	
Education middle	.09	(.03)	*	.13	(.04)	*
Local X " "	−.01	(.04)		−.07	(.05)	
Occupational status:						
Full-/part-time	.13	(.09)		.13	(.13)	
Local X " "	−.19	(.10)		−.21	(.16)	
Self-employed	.07	(.23)		.23	(.20)	
Local X " "	.04	(.26)		−.16	(.24)	
Retired	.12	(.10)		.12	(.14)	
Local X " "	−.19	(.12)		−.23	(.17)	
Homemaker	.11	(.10)		.16	(.14)	
Local X " "	−.16	(.12)		−.21	(.18)	
Student	−.77	(.34)	*	.05	(.13)	
Local X " "	.19	(.49)		−.17	(.19)	
Unemployed	.00	(.10)		−.05	(.04)	*
Local X " "	.16	(.15)		.19	(.22)	
Socio-demographics						
Male	.04	(.02)		.07	(.03)	*
Local X " "	.02	(.04)		.04	(.05)	
Age	−.09	(.07)	*	−.10	(.10)	*
Local X " "	−.05	(.11)		−.03	(.14)	
Context						*
Community size	.00	(.03)		−.03	(.04)	
Local X " "	.06	(.04)		.07	(.06)	
Constant	−.33	(.09)	*	−.30	(.13)	*
N individuals	3,320			1,893		
R2	.45			.47		*

* p<.05

Source: Swiss Selects

TABLE A4.3 *Local attachment in 21 countries*

Ordered logit model

Predictor	Coeff.	S.E.	Sig
Attachments/Attitudes			
National attachment	−2.42	(.03)	*
Distrust parliament	−.31	(.06)	*
Distrust EU	.40	(.05)	*
Anti-immigrant	.15	(.04)	*
Left-right ideology	.31	(.05)	*
Civic engagement			
Memberships (#)	−.29	(.14)	*
SES/Modernization losers			
Education low	.42	(.05)	*
Education middle	.24	(.03)	*
Occupational status:			
Full-/part-time	.09	(.10)	
Self-employed	.08	(.11)	
Retired	.23	(.10)	*
Homemaker	.24	(.11)	*
Student	−.08	(.11)	
Unemployed	.13	(.11)	
Socio-demographics			
Male	−.14	(.03)	*
Age	.19	(.08)	*
Context			
Community size	−.12	(.04)	*
Cut 1	−1.17	(.14)	
Cut 2	−.02	(.14)	
N individuals	28,282		
-2Xlog pseudolikelihood	51,508		
Wald chi^2	7,285		*

* p<.05. Models include dummy variables for each country and survey year.
Source: European Values Study

TABLE A4.4 *Local attachment in Switzerland*

Ordered logit models

Predictor	I			II		
	Coeff.	S.E.		Coeff.	S.E.	
Attachments/Attitudes						
National attachment	1.61	(.14)	*	1.55	(.19)	*
Anti-EU	−.09	(.10)		−.12	(.13)	
Anti-immigrant	.13	(.10)		.07	(.13)	
Left-right ideology	.24	(.20)		.26	(.27)	
Civic engagement						
Memberships (#)				.57	(.19)	*
SES/Modernization losers						
Education low	.29	(.14)	*	.37	(.20)	
Education middle	.14	(.09)		.18	(.12)	
Occupational status:						
Full-/part-time	−.31	(.34)		−.03	(.36)	
Self-employed	.33	(.64)		.03	(.94)	
Retired	−.31	(.36)		−.22	(.40)	
Homemaker	−.03	(.37)		.42	(.41)	
Student	−.81	(.40)	*	−.57	(.45)	
Unemployed	.06	(.50)		.32	(.65)	
Socio-demographics						
Male	.16	(.09)		.23	(.11)	*
Age	1.01	(.28)	*	1.28	(.39)	*
Context						
Community size	.50	(.12)	*	.62	(.16)	*
Cut 1	.32	(.38)		.81	(.43)	
Cut 2	.50	(.12)		2.82	(.44)	
N individuals	3,385			1,917		
-2Xlog pseudolikelihood	7,064			2,400		
Wald chi²	266.60		*	156.00		*

* p<.05
Source: Swiss Selects

APPENDIX TO CHAPTER 5

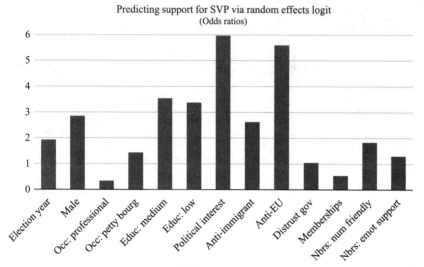

FIGURE A5.1 Based on models in Table A5.1.

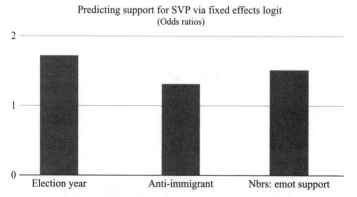

FIGURE A5.2 Based on SVP model in Table A5.3.

TABLE A5.1 *Predicting SVP support: within- and between-person analysis*

Random effects logit models

Predictor	I		II		III		IV		V	
	Coef.	S.E.	Coef.	S.E.	Coef.	S.E.	Coef.	S.E.	Coef.	S.E.
Neighboring										
Nbrs: index	.30	(.13) *								
Nbrs: emot. support			.24	(.08) *						
Nbrs: pract. support					.11	(.08)				
Nbrs: num. friendly							.71	(.30) *		
Nbrs: freq. contact									.06	(.12)
Organizations										
Memberships	-.79	(.14) *	-.78	(.14) *	-.76	(.14) *	-.79	(.14) *	-.77	(.14) *
Religious attendance	.11	(.15)	.13	(.15)	.10	(.15)	.13	(.14)	.13	(.14)
Attitudes										
Distrust gov.	.98	(.14) *	1.00	(.14) *	.98	(.14) *	.98	(.14) *	.98	(.14) *
Anti-EU	1.72	(.07) *	1.72	(.07) *	1.71	(.07) *	1.71	(.07) *	1.70	(.07) *
Anti-immigrant	.98	(.06) *	.96	(.06) *	.96	(.06) *	.94	(.06) *	.95	(.06) *
Political interest	1.49	(.14) *	1.49	(.14) *	1.51	(.14) *	1.49	(.14) *	1.48	(.14) *
SES/Modernization losers										
Education low	1.22	(.29) *	1.20	(.29) *	1.22	(.28) *	1.18	(.28) *	1.18	(.28) *
Education medium	1.27	(.11) *	1.26	(.11) *	1.28	(.11) *	1.26	(.11) *	1.26	(.11) *
Unemployed	-.21	(.27)	-.19	(.27)	-.21	(.27)	-.17	(.27)	-.15	(.27)
Occupational status:										
Employer	.41	(.36)	.41	(.26)	.45	(.35)	.43	(.35)	.43	(.35)
Petite bourgeoisie	.36	(.11) *	.36	(.11) *	.33	(.11) *	.32	(.11) *	.33	(.11) *
Manager	.03	(.11)	.03	(.11)	.02	(.11)	.01	(.11)	.01	(.11)
Professional	-1.05	(.24) *	-1.07	(.24) *	-1.03	(.24) *	-1.03	(.24) *	-1.03	(.24) *

(*continued*)

TABLE A5.1 (continued)

Predictor	I		II		III		IV		V	
	Coef.	S.E.	Coef.	S.E.	Coef.	S.E.	Coef.	S.E.	Coef.	S.E.
Semi-professional	.27	(.12) *	.26	(.12) *	.26	(.12) *	.23	(.12)	.23	(.12)
Worker	.12	(.09)	.13	(.09)	.10	(.09)	.11	(.09)	.10	(.09)
Socio-demographics										
Male	1.04	(.09) *	1.04	(.09) *	1.04	(.09) *	1.03	(.09) *	1.04	(.09) *
Age	.00	(.27)	.00	(.27)	-.01	(.27)	-.07	(.27)	-.04	(.27)
Temporal context										
Election year	.65	(.05) *	.65	(.05)	.65	(.05) *	.65	(.05) *	.65	(.05) *
Year (trend)	.44	(.10) *	.44	(.10)	.44	(.10) *	.46	(.10) *	.46	(.10) *
Constant	-8.20	(.26) *	-8.22	(.26)	-8.14	(.26) *	-8.07	(.25) *	-8.06	(.25) *
lnsig2u	2.17	(.04)	2.18	(.04)	2.17	(.04)	2.17	(.04)	2.18	(.04)
Sigma u	2.96	(.07)	2.97	(.07)	2.96	(.07)	2.97	(.06)	2.97	(.07)
Rho	.73	(.01)	.73	(.01)	.73	(.01)	.73	(.01)	.73	(.01)
N individuals	10,747		10,788		10,790		10,841		10,830	
N observations	48,779		49,308		49,809		50,515		503,211	
N years	1–11		1–11		1–11		1–11		1–11	
-2Xlog likelihood	22,142		22,364		22,498		22,822		22,754	
Wald chi²	1,769	*	1,782		1,785	*	1,802		1,788	*

* p<.05. Models include a dummy variable for each canton.

TABLE A5.2 *Predicting party support: within- and between-person analysis*

Random effects logit models

Predictor	Greens			Social Dems			Christian Dems			Radicals			SVP		
	Coeff.	S.E.		Coeff.	S.E.		Coeff.	S.E.		Coeff.	S.E.		Coeff.	S.E.	
Neighboring/Organizations															
Nbrs: index	.14	(.17)		-.05	(.12)		.35	(.16)	*	-.12	(.13)		.30	(.13)	*
Memberships	1.16	(.16)	*	.75	(.12)	*	.37	(.15)	*	-.21	(.13)		-.79	(.14)	*
Religious attendance	-.94	(.19)	*	-.90	(.14)	*	2.78	(.18)	*	-.35	(.15)	*	.11	(.15)	
Attitudes															
Distrust gov.	1.10	(.19)	*	-.33	(.14)	*	-1.87	(.18)	*	-1.40	(.15)	*	.98	(.14)	*
Anti-EU	-.59	(.09)	*	-1.29	(.06)	*	.06	(.07)		-.01	(.06)		1.72	(.07)	*
Anti-immigrant	-.62	(.10)	*	-.59	(.07)	*	.08	(.07)		.10	(.06)		.98	(.06)	*
Political interest	.76	(.19)	*	1.79	(.13)	*	.59	(.17)	*	.93	(.15)	*	1.49	(.14)	*
SES/Modernization losers															
Education low	-.42	(.34)		-.45	(.27)		-.39	(.36)		.32	(.31)		1.22	(.29)	*
Education medium	-1.05	(.13)	*	-.59	(.09)	*	.06	(.11)		-.27	(.10)	*	1.27	(.11)	*
Unemployed	.44	(.30)		.25	(.24)		-.37	(.36)		-.48	(.29)		-.21	(.27)	
Occupational status:															
Employer	.17	(.47)		-1.26	(.42)	*	-.44	(.47)		-.24	(.35)		.41	(.36)	
Petite bourgeoisie	.22	(.14)		-.18	(.09)	*	.05	(.13)		.04	(.11)		.36	(.11)	*
Manager	-.05	(.12)		-.18	(.09)	*	-.07	(.11)		.14	(.10)		.03	(.11)	
Professional	.32	(.16)	*	.05	(.12)		-.20	(.19)		-.07	(.16)		-1.05	(.24)	*
Semi-professional	-.20	(.13)		-.19	(.09)	*	-.21	(.13)	*	-.13	(.11)		.27	(.12)	*
Worker	.02	(.13)		-.08	(.09)		-.07	(.11)		-.31	(.10)	*	.12	(.09)	
Socio-demographics															
Male	-.70	(.11)	*	-.37	(.09)	*	.22	(.11)	*	.66	(.09)	*	1.04	(.09)	*
Age	-2.03	(.35)	*	-2.05	(.27)	*	-.35	(.32)		1.42	(.28)	*	.00	(.27)	

(continued)

TABLE A5.2 (continued)

Predictor	Greens		Social Dems		Christian Dems		Radicals		SVP	
	Coeff.	S.E.	Coeff.	S.E.	Coeff.	S.E.	Coeff.	S.E.	Coeff.	S.E.
Temporal context										
Election year	.80	(.06) *	-.03	(.04)	.37	(.06) *	.05	(.05)	.65	(.05) *
Year (trend)	3.02	(.14) *	-.64	(.09) *	1.49	(.12) *	-.33	(.10) *	.44	(.10) *
Constant	-5.69	(.30) *	-1.45	(.21) *	-7.67	(.30) *	-4.73	(.24) *	-8.20	(.26) *
N individuals	10,747		10,747		10,747		10,747		10,747	
N observations	48,779		48,779		48,779		48,779		48,779	
N years	1–11		1–11		1–11		1–11		1–11	
-2Xlog likelihood	13,784		29,344		17,364		23,402		22,142	
Wald chi²	959	*	1,419	*	942	*	423		1,769	*
lnsig2u	2.08	(.06)	2.48	(.04)	2.27	(.05)	2.45	(.04)	2.17	(.04)
Sigma u	2.83	(.08)	3.46	(.06)	3.11	(.08)	3.41	(.06)	2.96	(.07)
Rho	.71	(.01)	.78	(.01)	.75	(.10)	.78	(.01)	.73	(.01)

* p<.05. Models include a dummy variable for each canton.

TABLE A5.3 *Predicting party support: within-person analysis*

Fixed effects logit models

Predictor	Greens		Social Dems		Christian Dems		Radicals		SVP	
	Coeff.	S.E.	Coeff.	S.E.	Coeff.	S.E.	Coeff.	S.E.	Coeff.	S.E.
Neighboring/organizations										
Nbrs: emot. support	-.02 *	(.02)	-.01	(.01)	.19	(.19)	.08	(.17)	.34 *	(.17)
Memberships	-.02 *	(.32)	.38	(.23)	.01	(.31)	.02	(.27)	.43	(.30)
Religious attendance	.28	(.39)	.02	(.28)	.36	(.41)	-.19	(.33)	.33	(.37)
Attitudes										
Distrust gov.	1.37 *	(.39)	.18	(.27)	-.68	(.38)	-.73 *	(.32)	.21	(.32)
Anti-EU	.56 *	(.17)	-.61 *	(.12)	.34 *	(.15)	.00	(.13)	.15	(.15)
Anti-immigrant	.35 *	(.19)	-.03	(.14)	-.03	(.15)	.24	(.12)	.27 *	(.13)
Political interest	.89 *	(.43)	.60 *	(.30)	.88 *	(.41)	-.06	(.38)	.52	(.36)
SES/Modernization losers										
Education low	.61	1(.38)	-.99 *	1(.31)	y		y		y	
Education medium	-1.09 *	(.51)	.87 *	(.37)	-.61	(.50)	.04	(.39)	.19	(.46)
Unemployed	-.04	(.52)	.97	(.52)	-.53	(.73)	-1.13	(.68)	.65	(.63)
Occupational status:										
Employer	1.95 *	(.92)	-.41	(.72)	1.14	1(.04)	-.92	(.75)	-.98	(.84)
Petite bourgeoisie	.25	(.28)	-.16	(.22)	.08	(.28)	.44	(.25)	-.05	(.26)
Manager	.15	(.22)	-.30	(.16)	.17	(.24)	.05	(.22)	-.12	(.27)
Professional	.10	(.29)	-.27	(.22)	.07	(.47)	-.14	(.34)	-.60	(.57)
Semi-professional	-.10	(.24)	-.31	(.19)	-.40	(.26)	-.25	(.24)	-.03	(.29)
Worker	-.06	(.24)	.04	(.17)	.26	(.23)	-.14	(.23)	.13	(.22)

(*continued*)

TABLE A5.3 *(continued)*

Predictor	Greens		Social Dems		Christian Dems		Radicals		SVP	
	Coeff.	S.E.	Coeff.	S.E.	Coeff.	S.E.	Coeff.	S.E.	Coeff.	S.E.
Temporal context										
Election year	.38	(.10) *	.10	(.07)	.38	(.10) *	-.17	(.09)	.54	(.10) *
N individuals	299		535		288		381		322	
N observations	2,927		5,228		2,830		3,769		3,189	
N years	11		11		11		11		11	
-2Xlog likelihood	2,114		3,904		1,984		5,360		2,260	
LR chi²	76	*	93	*	52	*	38	*	84	*

* p<.05. Models include a dummy variable for each canton.
¥ Dropped due to no within-group variance.

TABLE A5.4 *Predicting SVP support: community type*

Logit models with lagged dependent variable

Predictor	Industrial/tertiary			Rural commuter		
	Coeff.	S.E.		Coeff.	S.E.	
Lagged DV (t-1)	3.39	(.07)	*	3.39	(.07)	*
Neighboring/organizations						
Nbrs: index	.16	(.12)		.31	(.12)	*
Memberships	−.58	(.11)	*	−.58	(.11)	*
Religious attendance	−.04	(.11)		−.05	(.11)	*
Attitudes						
Anti-EU	1.19	(.06)	*	1.19	(.06)	*
Anti-immigrant	.68	(.05)	*	.68	(.05)	*
Political interest	.74	(.11)	*	.74	(.11)	*
SES/Modernization losers						
Education low	.63	(.19)	*	.62	(.19)	*
Education medium	.41	(.07)	*	.41	(.07)	*
Unemployed	−.16	(.26)		−.17	(.26)	
Occupational status:						
Employer	.41	(.29)		.41	(.29)	
Petite bourgeoisie	.19	(.08)	*	.19	8(.00)	
Manager	−.05	(.08)		−.05	(.08)	
Professional	−.83	(.19)	*	−.83	(.19)	
Semi-professional	.20	(.09)	*	.20	(.09)	
Worker	.008	(.07)		.01	(.07)	
Socio-demographics						
Male	.37	(.05)	*	.37	(.05)	*
Age	.14	(.17)		.15	(.17)	
Context						
Election year	.55	(.06)	*	.55	(.06)	*
Year	−.05	(.08)		−.04	(.08)	
Commune type: industrial/tertiary	−.27	(.15)				
Commune type: rural commuter				.31	(.14)	*
Interaction						
Nbrs index X commune type	.72	(.36)	*	−.82	(.37)	*
Constant	−4.40	(.52)	*	−4.50	(.52)	*
N observations	37,294			37,294		
-2Xlog likelihood	15,290			15,288		
Wald chi²	4,663			4,337		

* p<.05. Models include a dummy variable for each canton.

Observations clustered by household.

TABLE A5.5 *Predicting SVP support: prevalence of communal councils*
Multilevel mixed effects logit model

Predictor	Coeff.	S.E.	Sig.
Lagged DV (t-1)	3.39	(.05)	*
Neighboring/organizations			
Nbrs: index	.06	(.15)	
Memberships	−.57	(.10)	*
Religious attendance	.05	(.10)	
Attitudes			
Distrust gov.	.06	(.01)	*
Anti-EU	1.13	(.06)	*
Anti-immigrant	.65	(.05)	*
Political interest	.76	(.10)	*
SES/Modernization losers			
Education low	.59	(.19)	*
Education medium	.39	(.06)	*
Unemployed	−.31	(.24)	
Occupational status:			
Employer	.38	(.27)	
Petite bourgeoisie	.17	(.08)	*
Manager	−.06	(.08)	
Professional	−.82	(.20)	*
Semi-professional	.18	(.09)	*
Worker	−.003	(.07)	
Socio-demographics			
Male	.37	(.05)	*
Age	.03	(.16)	
Context			
Election year	.56	(.05)	*
Year	−.08	(.09)	
Communal councils	−.62	(.18)	*
Interaction			
Nbrs index X communal councils	.99	(.48)	*
Constant	−5.64	(.27)	*
N individuals	8,582		
N observations	36,298		
N years	2–11		
N cantons	26		
-2Xlog likelihood	14,980		
Wald chi^2	7,140		*

* $p<.05$

APPENDIX TO CHAPTER 6

TABLE A6.1 *Predicting 2002 Le Pen support at the commune level*
OLS regression models

Predictor	Communes with CDCs			Communes without CDCs		
	No lagged DV			*Lagged DV*		
	Coeff.	S.E.	Sig.	Coeff.	S.E.	Sig.
CDC						
Established 1996–2002	.04	(.002)	*	.01	(.001)	*
Established ever (as of 2002)						
Socio-economic model						
Unemployed	.10	(.02)	*	−.05	(.01)	*
Foreign population	.31	(.02)	*	.04	(.01)	*
Modernization losers model						
Low education	.22	(.02)	*	−.01	(.01)	
High education	−.36	(.02)	*	−.11	(.01)	*
Occupational status (% employed as):						
Agriculture	−.26	(.03)	*	.00	(.01)	
Artisan	1.44	(.05)	*	.57	(.03)	*
High-skilled	.24	(.04)	*	.03	(.02)	
Intermediary	.44	(.03)	*	−.02	(.02)	
White collar	−.06	(.003)	*	−.01	(.001)	*
Manual labor	−.17	(.02)	*	−.07	(.01)	*
Controls						
Population/100,000	.03	(.001)	*	.01	(.0003)	*
Le Pen support 1995				.83	(.01)	*
Constant	.11	(.01)	*	.06	(.01)	*
R^2	.54			.86		
N	8,241			8,236		

* $p < .05$
Results based on weighted observations by communal population size.
Sample is all communes in CDCs as of 2002.

TABLE A6.2 *Predicting 2002 Le Pen support at the commune level: timing* OLS regression models

Predictor	All communes						Communes w/ CDCs					
	No lagged DV			Lagged DV			No lagged DV			Lagged DV		
	Coeff.	S.E.	Sig.	Coeff.	S.E.	Sig.	Coeff.	S.E.	Sig.	Coeff.	S.E.	Sig.
CDC												
Est. 1996	.002	(.01)		.006	(.01)		.006	(.01)		.008	(.004)	
Est. 1997	.03	(.01)	*	.004	(.01)		.02	(.01)	*	.001	(.005)	
Est. 1998	.02	(.01)		.01	(.01)		.017	(.01)		.01	(.05)	*
Est. 1999	.03	(.01)	*	.016	(.004)	*	.04	(.002)	*	.02	(.002)	*
Est. 2000	.02	(.01)	*	-.001	(.003)		.02	(.003)	*	-.003	(.002)	
Est. 2001	.06	(.003)	*	.02	(.002)	*	.05	(.002)	*	.02	(.001)	*
Est. 2002	.03	(.003)	*	.02	(.002)	*	.02	(.002)	*	.01	(.001)	*
Established ever (as of 2002)	-.03	(.003)	*	-.01	(.002)	*						
Socio-economic model												
Unemployed	.20	(.01)	*	.07	(.01)	*	.05	(.02)	*	-.06	(.01)	*
Foreign population	.11	(.01)	*	-.09	(.01)	*	.33	(.01)	*	.05	(.01)	*
Modernization losers model												
Low education	.40	(.01)	*	-.005	(.01)		.15	(.01)	*	-.02	(.01)	
High education	-.13	(.01)	*	-.10	(.01)	*	-.39	(.02)	*	-.10	(.01)	*
Occupational status (% employed as):												
Agriculture	-.37	(.02)	*	.04	(.02)		-.26	(.03)	*	.01	(.02)	
Artisan	.92	(.03)	*	.51	(.02)	*	1.37	(.04)	*	.55	(.03)	*

	Model 1		Model 2		Model 3		Model 4	
High-skilled	−.34	(.02) *	.02	(.01)	.32	(.04) *	−.01	(.02)
Intermediary	.50	(.02) *	.02	(.01)	.37	(.03) *	−.03	(.02) *
White collar	−.04	(.001) *	−.002	(.001) *	−.05	(.003) *	−.005	(.001) *
Manual labor	−.26	(.01) *	−.07	(.01) *	−.15	(.02) *	−.07	(.01) *
Controls								
Population/100,000	.0006	(.0001) *	.0002	(.0001) *	.02	(.001) *	.01	(.0003) *
Le Pen support 1995			.82	(.01) *			.83	(.01) *
Constant	.09	(.01) *	.07	(.01) *	.12	(.01) *	.06	(.01) *
R²	.60		.76		.57		.86	
N	34,610		34,595		8,241		8,236	

* $p < .05$

Results based on weighted observations by communal population size.

TABLE A6.3 *Predicting 2002 Le Pen support at the commune level: CDC detail* OLS regression models

Predictor	Aquitaine communes w/ CDCs as of 2002								
	CDC detail			IntX: CDC power			IntX: biggest		
	Coeff.	S.E.	Sig.	Coeff.	S.E.	Sig.	Coeff.	S.E.	Sig.
CDC									
CDC established 1996–2002	.02	(.001)	*	−.03	(.006)	*	.01	(.002)	*
CDC power	.003	(.0004)	*	−.004	(.002)	*	.00	(.0004)	*
Commune biggest in CDC	−.01	(.001)	*	−.007	(.002)	*	−.01	(.003)	*
Interaction									
CDC 96-02 X CDC power				.01	(.001)	*			
CDC 96-02 X biggest in CDC							.01	(.003)	*
Socio-economic model									
Unemployed	.37	(.03)	*	.40	(.03)	*	.37	(.03)	*
Foreign population	.14	(.04)	*	.12	(.04)	*	.12	(.04)	*
Modernization losers model									
Low education	.15	(.02)	*	.15	(.02)	*	.16	(.02)	*
High education	−.19	(.03)	*	−.17	(.03)	*	−.19	(.03)	*
Occupational status (% employed as):									
Agriculture	.06	(.02)		.06	(.03)		.07	(.03)	*
Artisan	.27	(.03)		.31	(.05)	*	.30	(.06)	*
High-skilled	.49	(.04)	*	.46	(.06)	*	.48	(.07)	*
Intermediary	.38	(.03)	*	.35	(.04)	*	.37	(.04)	*
White collar	−.01	(.00)	*	−.004	(.004)		.00	(.004)	
Manual labor	.07	(.02)		.070	(.03)	*	.08	(.003)	*
Control									
Population/100,000	−.01	(.01)	*	−.020	(.01)	*	.01	(.003)	*
Constant	−.07	(.01)		(.03)	(.01)	*	−.01	(.01)	
R²	.34			.36			.34		
N	1,932			1,932			1,932		

* p < .05
Results based on weighted observations by communal population size.

TABLE A6.4 *Predicting 2002 Le Pen support at the commune level: foreigners and unemployment*

OLS regression models

Predictor	Foreign X CDC						Unemp X CDC					
	No lagged DV			Lagged DV			No lagged DV			Lagged DV		
	Coeff.	S.E.	Sig.	Coeff.	S.E.	Sig.	Coeff.	S.E.	Sig.	Coeff.	S.E.	Sig.
CDC												
Established 1996–2002	.03	(.003)	*	.01	(.002)	*	.06	(.004)	*	.02	(.003)	*
Established ever (as of 2002)	-.03	(.003)	*	-.01	(.002)	*	-.04	(.003)	*	-.01	(.002)	*
Socio-economic model												
Unemployed	.20	(.01)	*	.08	(.01)	*	.21	(.01)	*	.08	(.01)	*
Foreign population	.06	(.01)	*	-.12	(.01)	*	.13	(.01)	*	-.09	(.01)	*
Interactions												
Unemployed X CDC							-.07	(.01)	*	-.03	(.01)	*
Foreign population X CDC	.37	(.02)	*	.19	(.01)	*						
Modernization losers model												
Low education	.40	(.01)	*	-.007	(.01)		.40	(.01)	*	-.01	(.01)	
High education	-.14	(.01)	*	-.11	(.01)	*	-.11	(.01)	*	-.10	(.01)	*
Occupational status (% employed as):												
Agriculture	-.37	(.02)	*	.04	(.02)	*	-.38	(.01)	*	.04	(.02)	*
Artisan	.96	(.03)	*	.52	(.02)	*	.94	(.02)	*	.51	(.02)	*
High-skilled	-.34	(.02)	*	.05	(.02)	*	-.40	(.03)	*	.02	(.02)	
Intermediary	.52	(.02)	*	.030	(.01)	*	.48	(.02)	*	.010	(.01)	

(continued)

TABLE A6.4 (continued)

Predictor	Foreign X CDC						Unemp X CDC					
	No lagged DV			Lagged DV			No lagged DV			Lagged DV		
	Coeff.	S.E.	Sig.	Coeff.	S.E.	Sig.	Coeff.	S.E.	Sig.	Coeff.	S.E.	Sig.
White collar	-.04	(.001)	*	-.002	(.001)		-.04	(.02)	*	-.002	(.001)	*
Manual labor	-.26	(.01)	*	-.07	(.01)	*	-.27	(.001)	*	-.07	(.01)	*
Controls												
Population/100,000	.001	(.0001)	*	-.0002	(.0001)	*	.001	(.0001)	*	.0001	(.0001)	*
Le Pen support 1995	.09	(.01)	*	.82	(.01)	*	.08	(.01)	*	.82	(.01)	*
Constant				.06	(.004)	*				.06	(.004)	*
R^2	.59			.76			.59			.76		
N	35,209			35,194			35,209			35,194		

* $p < .05$
Results based on weighted observations by communal population size.

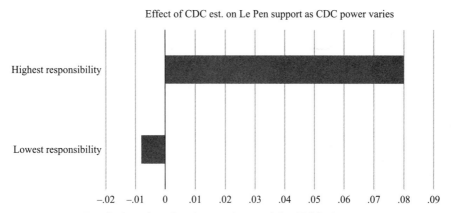

FIGURE A6.1 Results based on first interaction model in Table A6.3.

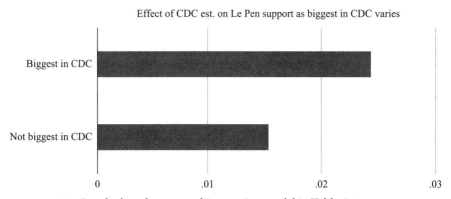

FIGURE A6.2 Results based on second interaction model in Table A6.3.

TABLE A6.5 *Predicting 2002 Le Pen support at the commune level: Gironde* OLS regression models

Predictor	Gironde communes					
	Social capital			Interaction		
	Coeff.	S.E.	Sig.	Coeff.	S.E.	Sig.
CDC est.						
Established 1996–2002	.001	(.003)		.01	(.003)	
Social capital						
Local activities	−.12	(.02)	*	−.03	(.04)	
Interaction						
CDC 96-02 X Local activities				−.11	(.05)	*
Socio-economic model						
Unemployed	.09	(.05)		.10	(.05)	*
Foreign population	−.07	(.06)		−.04	(.06)	
Modernization losers model						
Low education	.01	(.04)		.01	(.04)	
High education	−.13	(.04)	*	−.12	(.04)	*
Occupational status (% employed as):						
Agriculture	.18	(.06)	*	.18	(.06)	*
Artisan	.38	(.09)	*	.36	(.09)	*
High-skilled	−.13	(.09)		−.13	(.09)	
Intermediary	−.05	(.05)		−.04	(.05)	
White collar	.003	(.01)		.002	(.006)	
Manual labor	.07	(.04)		.08	(.04)	
Control						
Population/100,000	−.004	(.003)		−.004	(.003)	
Constant	.16	(.02)	*	.16	(.02)	*
R²	.71			.71		
N	551			551		

* p < .05

Results based on weighted observations by communal population size.

TABLE A6.6 *Use of French census variables: commune level 1999*

Population	PSCD99
Foreign population	RD99ETR/PSDC99
Unemployed	CHOM99/TNS15PP99
Low education	TDSP00/TNS15PP99
High education	(TBACBPP99 + TBAC2P99 + TSUBAC2P99)/TNS15PP99
Agricultural	AGR99/TNS15PP99
Artisan	ART99/ TNS15PP99
High skilled	CAD99/ TNS15PP99
Intermediary	PIN99/ TNS15PP99
White collar	EMP99/ TNS15PP99
Manual labor	OUV99/ TNS15PP99
Rootedness	((RA99AOCO/POPACT99)+(PROPRP99/RPD99) +((1-PAUTCOMP99)/PSDC99))/3

TABLE A6.7 *Original wording for interview quotations*

commune A, quotation 1:

JF: Commenter les changements des derniers 10, 20, 30 ans. Quand est-ce qu'ils ont été les plus forts ?

RESPONDENT: Ah oui, depuis 10 ans, oui. Ça se rapproche un peu à la [recording garbled]. Oui, on cherche à regrouper … Parce que le problème, la France, sur la communauté européenne, c'est le pays qui a le plus de communes. On a 36,000 communes en France. Enorme ! On aime bien nos petites communes. Et on aime beaucoup notre clocher. Vous savez qu'on est un petit peu chauvin et on aime bien son chez-soi. Pour nous c'est toujours un petit peu difficile d'accepter justement ces regroupements de communes, parce qu'on est tous très attaché à notre commune. Oui, beaucoup. C'est assez typique. En général, les Français, c'est « mon clocher ». Voilà. Pas nécessairement par conviction au milieu. Parce que la commune, pour les Français, c'est quelque chose de familiale. Un repaire. C'est pas comme ça [aux Etats-Unis, implied] ? Moins ? Vous bougez beaucoup plus, peut-être. Le Français a tendance à pas trop vouloir bouger. C'est un petit peu son défaut. Nous, on est attaché à nos origines.

commune A, quotation 2:

JF: Qu'est-ce que vous aimez ici ?

RESPONDENT: C'est ma commune.

JF: Vous êtes chez vous.

RESPONDENT: Voilà. C'est tout. Après c'est un tout, hein ? L'église, la mairie, c'est un tout. C'est notre commune. C'est important. Ça, on le retrouve chez les anciennes familles, les familles, les nouveaux, beaucoup moins. Peut-être ça viendra.

commune A, quotation 3:

JF: Diriez-vous que [commune A] est moins social que l'autre commune que vous décriviez ? On ne voit pas les gens dans la rue … ?

RESPONDENT: Oui. Parce que [commune A], c'est peut-être pas représentatif des villages de France, on n'a pas vraiment de bourg, on s'est très dispersé, beaucoup de petits hameaux, des petits quartiers, quoi, qui sont, voilà, alors on ne se retrouve pas. Les gens ne passent pas, 84% de la commune n'a aucune raison de passer devant la mairie. On ne voit pas beaucoup de monde, quoi. Ils sont dispersés. Il y a des villages comme ça en France, mais il est pas représentatif des villages de France.

commune A, quotation 4:

JF: Est-ce que les nouveaux sont intégrés ?

RESPONDENT: Quelques-uns, mais il y en a si vous voulez, c'est comme une dortoire. Ils travaillent à l'extérieur, et ils viennent après, le week-end, le soir. Ils arrivent, il est 18h ou 19h, ils restent chez eux. Ils viennent dormir ici [mais pour participer à la vie sociale] ils n'ont pas le temps.

commune A, quotation 5:

RESPONDENT: Et je le découvre de plus en plus. Ma ville, mon clocher. C'est ça – on revient au clocher. Les gens ont besoin d'une identité communale, même s'ils ne participent pas.

(continued)

commune B, quotation 1:

JF: Est-ce que vous diriez que cette ville a beaucoup changé depuis dix ans ? ...
Est-ce que ces changements sont difficiles pour les habitants ?"

RESPONDENT: C'est la vie, hein, mais par rapport à l'identité communale, il y a
moins de liens de relation entre les habitants qu'il y en avait autrefois. Autrefois,
il y avait un soutien quand quelqu'un avait des difficultés, il avait un voisin, des
amis qui venaient les aider etc.

commune C, quotation 1:

JF: Quelles sont les sources de la fierté dans cette ville ? Qu'est-ce que ça veut dire
d'être [commune C] ais ?

RESPONDENT: Ça veut dire que vous êtes Médocaine, et Médocain, c'est une
tradition, c'est une, il y a une histoire, il y a, voilà, on est là. C'est, en fait, on
le dit souvent, je compare souvent les Médocains, et j'en suis un, un peu aux
Corses. Nous sommes dans une presqu'île, donc nous ne sommes pas une
île, mais nous sommes, voilà. C'est très difficile de rentrer dans une famille
Médocaine. Très difficile, Le Médocain est assez frileux. Voilà. Quand je dis
frileux, ça veut dire qu'il ne va pas vous accueillir à bras ouverts. Il va chercher
à savoir, il va mettre de la distance, et rentrer dans une famille Médocaine, c'est
très difficile. Maintenant, le jour où vous avez été accepté, vous êtes vraiment de
la famille. Mais il faut que vous y rentriez. C'est très très difficile.

commune D, quotation 1:

RESPONDENT: Il y a une très forte activité associative sur [commune D], mais
qui repose essentiellement sur un noyeau de bénévoles qui est assez réduit,
qui s'occuper de plusieurs associations. Donc il n'y a pas un gros engagement
bénévole ou associatif ou civique. Globalement, plutôt faible, même.

commune E, quotation 1:

RESPONDENT: Si vous voulez il ya des anciens qui votent Le Pen qui je connais, ce
sont des paysans qui ont leur truc, le nouveau qui fait peur; il y en a qui votent
Le Pen parce qu'ils ont été déçus de tout le monde de droite et de gauche donc
ils vont voter Le Pen. Donc, des racistes purs, il y en a très peu, mais il y a plus
de mécontents du système. Et puis ils se disent voilà, la droite nous a dit ça ils le
font pas, la gauche nous a dit ça ils le font pas, est-ce que c'est Le Pen qui ... ?
... Il y a ces gens qui ont une mentalité très ancrée, très spécifique, que c'est sa
terre, c'est son truc, là, oui, pour beaucoup c'est un reflexe de protection. Et puis
après il y a les gens qui ont marre que, de la politique, qui vont ou à l'extrême
droite, ou à l'extrême gauche.

APPENDIX TO CHAPTER 7

Figure A7.1 details the trajectories of radical right support in the most recent national legislative election and percentage of tax revenues controlled by the central government (OECD 2011). Thirty OECD countries are examined in each year across sixteen years.[1] The federal authority measure remains relatively steady during this time period, with periods of slight rises balanced out by slight falls. The average percentage of central government control of these resources is .602 in 1995 and .585 in 2010. For these countries, the average radical right support grows during this time period from approximately 5 percent to 8 percent.

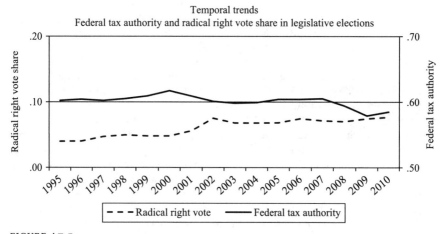

FIGURE A7.1

[1] These are: Australia, Austria, Belgium, Canada, Czech Rep., Denmark, Estonia, Finland, France, Germany, Greece, Hungary, Iceland, Ireland, Israel, Italy, Japan, Luxembourg, Netherlands, New Zealand, Norway, Poland, Portugal, Slovakia, Slovenia, Spain, Sweden, Switzerland, UK, and USA.

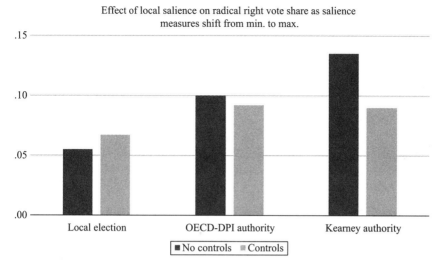

FIGURE A7.2 Estimates based on models in Tables 7.1, 7.2 and 7.3.

TABLE A7.1 *List of parties included in data*

Country	Party 1	Party 2	Party 3	Party 4	Party 5
Australia	One Nation				
Austria	FPÖ	BZÖ			
Belgium	Vlaams Blok/Balang	Front National			
Bulgaria	Attack				
Canada	Reform party				
Croatia	Party of Rights				
Czech Rep.	Republicans	National Party	Workers' Party		
Denmark	Progress Party	People's Party			
Estonia	Independence Party				
Finland	True Finns				
France	National Front	Movement for France	National Republican Mvmt		
Germany	Republikaner	National Democratic Party	German People's Union		
Greece	Golden Dawn	Greek Front	Populist Orthodox Rally		
Hungary	MIEP	MIEP/Jobbik			
Iceland					
Ireland					
Israel	Mafdal National Relig				
Italy	MSI-National Alliance	Northern League	Tri-Color		
Japan					
Latvia	All for Latvia	National Alliance			
Lithuania	Lithuanian Freedom Union				
Luxembourg					
Netherlands	List Pim Fortuyn	Center Democrats	Party for Freedom		

Country					
New Zealand	New Zealand First				
Norway	Progress Party				
Poland	National Rebirth	Fatherland Party	Polish National Party		
		League of Polish Families			
Portugal					
Romania	Greater Romania Party	National Unity Party			
Slovakia	Slovak National Party				
Slovenia	Slovene National Party				
Spain	Falangistas				
Sweden	Sweden Democrats	New Democracy			
Switzerland	Swiss People's Party	Federal Democratic Union	Swiss Democrats	Ticino League	Freedom Party
UK	British National Party	National Front	UKIP		
USA					

TABLE A7.2 *Cases and years included in models*

Country	Table 7.1		Table 7.2		Table 7.3		Table A7.4
	Baseline	Full	Baseline	Full	Baseline	Full	
Australia	x	x	x	x	x	x	
Austria					x	x	x
Belgium					x		
Bulgaria					x		
Canada	x		x		x		
Croatia					x		
Czech Rep.			x	x	x		
Denmark	x	x			x	x	x
Estonia					x		
Finland	x	x			x	x	x
France	x	x	x	x	x	x	x
Germany	x	x	x	x	x	x	
Greece	x	x	x	x	x	x	
Hungary	x	x	x	x	x		
Iceland	x				x		
Ireland	x	x			x	x	
Israel					x		
Italy	x	x	x	x	x	x	x
Japan	x				x		
Latvia					x		
Lithuania					x		
Luxembourg					x	x	
Netherlands	x	x	x	x	x	x	x
New Zealand	x				x	x	x
Norway	x	x			x	x	x
Poland	x	x	x	x	x		
Portugal	x	x			x	x	
Romania			x	x	x		
Slovakia	x	x			x		
Slovenia					x		
Spain	x	x			x	x	
Sweden	x	x			x	x	x
Switzerland	x				x		
UK	x		x		x		
USA	x				x		
Years	*1995– 2010*	*1995– 2010*	*1980– 2012*	*1980– 2010*	*1980– 2012*	*1980– 2010*	*1980– 2010*

TABLE A7.3 *Kearney local authority index components and radical right vote across countries and over time*

Tobit models

Predictor	Local executive		Education		Infrastructure		Policing	
	Coeff.	S.E.	Coeff.	S.E.	Coeff.	S.E.	Coeff.	S.E.
Local exec. elected	.15	(.05) *						
Education authority			.08	(.04) *				
Infrastructure authority					.08	(.05)		
Policing authority							.08	(.04) *
Constant	-.14	(.05) *	-.06	(.05)	-.04	(.04)	-.02	(.03)
N (country-years)	102		102		102		102	
-2Xlog likelihood	110		100		98		101	
LR chi²	43		33		30		33	

* p < .05. All models contain country fixed effects.

Note: Loading these factors into one model reveals that the policing authority variable is the strongest independent predictor among these four.

TABLE A7.4 *Local election timing X decentralization platform: effects on radical right vote in legislative elections across countries and over time*

Tobit models

Predictor	Coeff.	S.E.	Sig.
Local election year	.04	(.03)	
Decentralization platform	−.003	(.00)	
Elect X Decent	.30	(.14)	*
Regional election year	−.001	(.03)	
Unemployment rate	.000	(.42)	
Immigration level	.70	(.34)	*
Electoral threshhold	.02	(.19)	
Polarization	.05	(.03)	
Federalism	.09	(.10)	
Turnout	−.24	(.12)	
Constant	.04	(.17)	
N (country-years)	52		
-2Xlog likelihood	178		
LR chi²	54		

* p < .05. Model contains country fixed effects.

References

AdCF. 2009. "État de l'intercommunalité: la France intercommunale 2009." Assemblée des communautés de France. www.intercommunalites.com.

Agnew, John A. [1987] 2014. *Place and Politics: The Geographical Mediation of State and Society*. New York: Routledge.

Akkerman, Tjitske. 2015. "Gender and the radical right in Western Europe: a comparative analysis of policy agendas." *Patterns of Prejudice* 49(1–2): 37–60.

Alidières, Bernard. 2004. "Anciens et nouveaux territoires du vote Front national: le cas du Nord-Pas-de-Calais." *Hérodote* 2(113): 48–67.

Allen, Trevor J. 2017. "All in the party family? Comparing far right voters in Western and Post-Communist Europe." *Party Politics* 23(3): 274–285.

Allen, William Sheridan. 1965. *The Nazi Seizure of Power: The Experience of a Single German Town*. Danbury, CT: Franklin Watts.

Almond, Gabriel, and Sidney Verba. 1963. *The Civic Culture: Political Attitudes and Democracy in Five Countries*. Princeton, NJ: Princeton University Press.

Alonso, Sonia. 2012. *Challenging the State: Devolution and the Battle for Partisan Credibility: A Comparison of Belgium, Italy, Spain and the United Kingdom*. Oxford, UK: Oxford University Press.

Andersen, Jørgen Goul. 2004. "The Danish People's Party and new cleavages in Danish politics." Working paper, Centre for Comparative Welfare Studies, Aalborg University.

Andersen, Jørgen Goul, and Tor Bjørklund. 1990. "Structural changes and new cleavages: the progress parties in Denmark and Norway." *Acta Sociologica* 33(3): 195–217.

Anderson, Benedict. 1983. *Imagined Communities: Reflections on the Origin and Spread of Nationalism*. London: Verso Books.

Anderson, Christopher J. 1996. "Economics, politics, and foreigners: populist party support in Denmark and Norway." *Electoral Studies* 15(4): 497–511.

Anderson, Mary R. 2009. "Beyond membership: a sense of community and political behavior." *Political Behavior* 31: 603–627.

Andeweg, Rudy B. 1982. *Dutch Voters Adrift: On Explanations of Electoral Change (1963–1977)*. Dissertation, Leiden University,.

Arendt, Hannah. [1951] 1973. *The Origins of Totalitarianism*. New York, NY. Harvest Books, Harcourt. Inc.

Armingeon, Klaus, David Weisstanner, Sarah Engler, Panajotis Potolidis, and Marlène Gerber. 2012. *Comparative Political Data Set I 1960–2010*. Bern: Institute of Political Science, University of Bern.

Art, David. 2011. *Inside the Radical Right: The Development of Anti-Immigrant Parties in Western Europe*. New York: Cambridge University Press.

Arter, David. 2010. "The breakthrough of another West European populist radical right party? The case of the true Finns." *Government and Opposition* 45(4): 484–504.

Arzheimer, Kai. 2009. "Contextual factors and the extreme right vote in Western Europe, 1980–2002." *American Journal of Political Science* 53(2): 259–275.

Arzheimer, Kai, and Elisabeth Carter. 2006. "Political opportunity structures and right-wing extremist party success." *European Journal of Political Research* 45: 419–443.
2009. "How (not) to operationalise subnational political opportunity structures: a critique of Kestilä and Söderlund's study of regional elections." *European Journal of Political Research* 48(3): 335–358.

Astor, Avi. 2016. "Social position and place-protective action in a new immigration context: understanding anti-mosque campaigns in Catalonia." *International Migration Review* 50(1): 95–132.

Ayres, Jeffrey, and Michael J. Bosia. 2011. "Beyond global summitry: food sovereignty as localized resistance to globalization." *Globalizations* 8(1): 47–63.

Baker, Andy, Barry Ames, and Lucio R. Renno. 2006. "Social context and campaign volatility in new democracies: networks and neighborhoods in Brazil's 2002 elections." *American Journal of Political Science* 50(2): 382–399.

Baldersheim, Herald and Lawrence E. Rose, Eds. 2010. *Territorial Choice: The Politics of Boundaries and Borders*. London: Palgrave MacMillan.

Bale, Tim. 2003. "Cinderella and her ugly sisters: the mainstream and extreme right in Europe's bipolarizing party systems." *West European Politics* 26(3):67–90.

Barber, Benjamin. 1996. *Jihad vs. McWorld: How Globalism and Tribalism are Reshaping the World*. New York: Ballantine Books.

Barthel, Michael, Jesse Holcomb, Jessica Mahone, and Amy Mitchell. 2016. "Civic engagement strongly tied to local news Habits." Pew Research Center, November 3. www.journalism.org/2016/11/03/civic-engagement-strongly-tied-to-local-news-habits/ Accessed April 14, 2017.

Baym, Nancy K., Yan Bing Zhang, and Mei-Chen Lin. 2004. "Social interactions across media: interpersonal communication on the internet, telephone and face-to-face." *New Media and Society* 6(3): 299–318.

Beck, Thorsten, George Clarke, Alberto Groff, Philip Keefer, and Patrick Walsh. 2001. "New tools in comparative political economy: the Database of Political Institutions." *World Bank Economic Review* 15(1): 165–176.

Beggs, John J., Jeanne S. Hurlbert, and Valerie A. Haines. 1996. "Community attachment in a rural setting: a refinement and empirical test of the systemic model." *Rural Sociology* 61(3): 407–426.

Berelson, Bernard R., Paul F. Lazarsfeld, and William N. McPhee. 1954. *Voting: A Study of Opinion Formation in a Presidential Campaign*. Chicago, IL: University of Chicago Press.

Berning, Carl C., and Conrad Ziller. 2017. "Social trust and radical right populist party preferences." *Acta Politica* 52(2): 198–217.

Bess, Kimberly D., Adrian T. Fisher, Christopher C. Sonn, and Brian J. Bishop. 2002. "Psychological sense of community: theory, research, and application." In Adrian T. Fisher, Christopher C. Sonn, and Brian J. Bishop, Eds., *Psychological Sense of Community*, pp. 3–22. New York: Kluwer Academic/Plenum Publishers.

Betz, Hans-Georg. 1993. "The new politics of resentment: radical right-wing populist parties in Western Europe." *Comparative Politics* 25(4): 413–427.

1994. *Radical Right-Wing Populism in Western Europe*. New York: St. Martin's Press.

Billiet, Jaak, and Hans De Witte. 1995. "Attitudinal dispositions to vote for a 'new' extreme right party: the case of the 'Vlaams Blok.'" *European Journal of Political Research* 27(2): 181–202.

Blöchliger, Hansjörg, and Oliver Petzold. 2009. "Taxes and grants: on the revenue mix of sub-central governments." OECD Network on Fiscal Relations Across Levels of Government. COM/CTPA/ECO/GOV/WP.

Blume, Lorenz, and Stefan Voigt. 2008. "Federalism and decentralization: a critical survey of frequently used indicators." Joint Discussion Paper Series in Economics, No. 2008–21. Marberg, Germany.

Body-Gendrot, Sophie. 2007. "France upside down over a headscarf?" *Sociology of Religion* 68(3): 289–304.

Books, John W., and Charles L. Prysby. 1991. *Political Behavior and the Local Context*. New York: Praeger.

Boonen, Joris, and Marc Hooghe. 2014. "Do nationalist parties shape or follow sub-national identities? A panel analysis of the rise of the nationalist party in the Flemish region of Belgium, 2006–2011." *Nations and Nationalism* 20(1): 56–79.

Botterman, Sarah, and Marc Hooghe. 2012. "Religion and voting behavior in Belgium: an analysis of the relation between religious beliefs and Christian Democratic voting." *Acta Politica* 47(1): 1–17.

Botterman, Sarah, Marc Hooghe, and Tim Reeskins. 2012. "'One size fits all'? An empirical study into the multidimensionality of social cohesion indicators in Belgian local communities." *Urban Studies* 49(1): 185–202.

Boulianne, Shelley. 2015. "Social media use and participation: a meta-analysis of current research." *Information, Communication and Society* 18(5): 524–538.

Boulianne, Shelley, and Michelle Brailey. 2014. "Attachment to community and civic and political engagement: a case study of students." *Canadian Review of Sociology* 52(4): 375–388.

Bourdieu, Pierre. 1986. "The forms of capital." In J. Richardson, Ed., *Handbook of Theory and Resarch for the Sociology of Education*, pp. 46–58. Trans. Richard Nice. New York: Greenwood.

Bowyer, Benjamin. 2008. "Local context and extreme right support in England: the British national party in the 2002 and 2003 local elections." *Electoral Studies* 27(4): 611–620.

Brancati, Dawn. 2006. "Decentralization: fueling the fire or dampening the flames of ethnic conflict and secessionism?" *International Organization* 60(3): 651–685.

Brand, Jack, James Mitchell, and Paula Surridge. 1993. "Identity and the vote: class and nationality in Scotland." *British Elections and Parties Yearbook* 3(1): 143–157.

Braunthal, Gerard. 2009. *Right-Wing Extremism in Contemporary Germany*. London: Palgrave Macmillan.

Bréchon, Pierre, and Subrata Kumar Mitra. 1992. "The national front in France: the emergence of an extreme right protest movement." *Comparative Politics* 25(1): 63–82.

Brehm, John, and Wendy Rahn. 1997. "Individual-level evidence for the causes and consequences of social capital." *American Journal of Political Science* 41(3): 999–1023.

Brubaker, Rogers. 2004. *Ethnicity Without Groups*. Cambridge, MA: Harvard University Press.

Bulli, Giorgia, and Filippo Tronconi. 2012. "Regionalism, right-wing extremism, populism: the elusive nature of the Lega Nord." In Andrea Mammone, Emmanuel Godin, and Brian Jenkins, Eds., *Mapping the Extreme Right in Contemporary Europe: From Local to Transnational*, Ch. 5. New York: Routledge.

Bulliard, Pascal. 2005. "Local government in Switzerland." In Nico Steytler, Ed., *The Place and Role of Local Government in Federal Systems*, pp. 123–148. Konrad-Adenauer-Stiftung, Occasional Papers: Johannesburg, South Africa.

Burbank, Matthew J. 1995. "The psychological basis of contextual effects." *Political Geography* 14: 621–635.

Bustikova, Lenka. 2014. "Revenge of the radical right." *Comparative Political Studies* OnlineFirst: http://cps.sagepub.com/content/early/2014/02/07/0010414013516069

Bustikova, Lenka, and Herbert Kitschelt. 2009. "The radical right in post-communist Europe: comparative perspectives on legacies and party competition." *Communist and Post-Communist Studies* 42(4): 459–483.

Callois, Jean-Marc, and Francis Aubert. 2007. "Towards indicators of social capital for regional development issues: the case of French rural areas." *Regional Studies* 41(6): 809–821.

Campbell, Angus, Philip E. Converse, Warren E. Miller, and Donald E. Stokes. 1960. *The American Voter*. New York: John Wiley and Sons, Inc.

Caramani, Daniele. 2004. *The Nationalization of Politics: The Formation of National Electorates and Party Systems in Western Europe*. Cambridge, UK: Cambridge University Press.

Carter, Elisabeth. 2005. *The Extreme Right in Western Europe: Success or Failure?* Manchester: Manchester University Press.

Chambers, Simone, and Jeffrey Kopstein. 2001. "Bad civil society." *Political Theory* 29: 837–865.

Cherni, Julie. 2001. "Social-local identities." In Tim O'Riordan, Ed., *Globalism, Localism and Identity: New Perspectives on the Transition of Sustainability*, pp. 61–80. Abingdon: Taylor & Francis.

Cigler, Allan, and Mark R. Joslyn. 2002. "The extensiveness of group membership in social capital: the impact on political tolerance attitudes." *Political Research Quarterly* 55: 7–25.

Citrin, Jack, and David O. Sears. 2014. *American Identity and the Politics of Multiculturalism*. New York: Cambridge University Press.

Coffé, Hilde, Bruno Heyndels, and Jan Vermier. 2007. "Fertile grounds for extreme right-wing parties: explaining the Vlaams Blok's electoral success." *Electoral Studies* 26(1): 142–155.

Coffé, Hilde, and Marieke Voorpostel. 2010. "Young people, parents and radical right voting: the case of the Swiss People's Party." *Electoral Studies* 29(3): 435–443.

Converse, Philip E., Warren E. Miller, Jerrold G. Rusk, and Arthur G. Wolfe. 1969. "Continuity and change in American politics: parties and issues in the 1968 election." *American Political Science Review* 63: 1083–1105.

Corcoran, Mary P. 2002. "Place attachment and community sentiment in marginalised neighbourhoods: a European case study." *Canadian Journal of Urban Research* 11(1): 201–221.

Cotterill, Lesley, and Diane Taylor. 2001. "Promoting health and well-being amongst housebound older people." *Quality in Ageing* 2(1): 32–46.

Cowell, Alan. 2010. "The British voter, adrift." *The New York Times*, May 8. Accessed through University of Colorado Boulder, June 3, 2017. www.nytimes.com/2010/05/09/weekinreview/09cowell.html

Cox, Ed, and Charlie Jeffery. 2014. "The future of England: the local dimension." Newcastle, UK: Institute for Public Policy Research-North.

Cox, Kevin. 1969. "The voting decision in a spatial context." *Progress in Geography* 1: 83–117.

Cox, Kevin, and A. Mair. 1988. "Locality and community in the politics of local economic development." *Annals of the Association of American Geographers* 78(2), 307–320.

Cramer, Katherine J. 2016. *The Politics of Resentment: Rural Consciousness in Wisconsin and the Rise of Scott Walker*. Chicago, IL: University of Chicago Press.

Crosby, Faye. 1976. "A model of egotistical relative deprivation." *Psychological Review* 83: 85–113.

Cutts, David, Robert Ford, and Matthew J. Goodwin. 2011. "Anti-immigrant, politically disaffected or still racist after all? Examining the attitudinal drivers of extreme right support in Britain in the 2009 European elections." *European Journal of Political Research* 50(3): 418–440.

Dalton, Russel J. 1984. Cognitive mobilization and partisan dealignment in advanced industrial democracies. *Journal of Politics* 46(1): 264–284.

Dalton, Russell J., and Martin P. Wattenberg, Eds. 2000. *Parties Without Partisans: Political Change in Advanced Industrial Democracies*. New York: Oxford University Press.

Dancygier, Rafeala M. 2010. *Immigration and Conflict in Europe*. Cambridge, UK: Cambridge University Press.

Dassonneville, Ruth, and Marc Hooghe. 2018. "Indifference and alientation: diverging dimensions of electoral dealignment in Europe." *Acta Politica* 53(1): 1–23.

De Lange, Sarah L., and Liza M. Mügge. 2015. "Gender and right-wing populism in the Low Countries: ideological variations across parties and time." *Patterns of Prejudice* 49(1–2): 61–80.

De Winter, Lieven, and Huri Türsan, Eds. 2003. *Regionalist Parties in Western Europe*. London: Routledge.

Dekker, Karien. 2007. "Social capital, neighborhood attachment and participation in distressed urban areas: a case study in The Hague and Utrecht, the Netherlands." *Housing Studies* 22(3): 355–379.

Deutscher, Irwin. 1966. "Words and deeds: social science and social policy." *Social Problems* 13: 235–254.

DeVos, Sjoerd, and Rinus Deurloo. 1999. "Right extremist votes and the presence of foreigners: an analysis of the 1994 elections in Amsterdam." *Tijdschrift voor economische en sociale geografie* 90(2): 129–141.

DiPasquale, Denise, and Edward L. Glaeser. 1999. "Incentives and social capital: are homeowners better citizens?" *Journal of Urban Economics* 45(2): 354–384.

Dixon, John, and Kevin Durrheim. 2000. "Displacing place-identity: a discursive approach to locating self and other." *British Journal of Social Psychology* 39(1): 27–44.

Djupe, Paul A., and Christopher P. Gilbert. 2008. *The Political Influence of Churches.* New York: Cambridge University Press.

Doggett, Gina. 2017. "French voters adrift as unconventional election looms." Agence France-Presse, March 21. Accessed via Yahoo News through University of Colorado, June 4, 2017. www.yahoo.com/news/french-voters-adrift-unconventional-election-looms-040226255.html

Dollery, Brian, and Lorenzo Robotti. 2008. *The Theory and Practice of Local Government Reform.* Cheltenham: Edward Elgar Publishing.

Dostie-Goulet, Eugénie, André Blais, Patrick Fournier, and Elizabeth Gidengil. 2012. "L'abstention selective, ou pourquoi certains jeunes qui votent au federal boudent les élections municipals." *Canadian Journal of Political Science* 45(4): 909–927.

Dougherty, Michael Brendan. 2016. "This is who votes Donald Trump." *The Week,* Opinion: January 28, 2016. http://theweek.com/articles/601671/who-votes-donald-trump

Downs, Anthony. 1957. *An Economic Theory of Democracy.* New York: Harper & Row.

Dülmer, Hermann, and Markus Klein. 2005. "Extreme right-wing voting in Germany in a multilevel perspective: a rejoinder to Lubbers and Scheepers." *European Journal of Political Research* 44(2): 243–263.

Duncan, Lauren. 2010. "Using group consciousness theories to understand political activism: case studies of Barak Obama, Hillary Clinton, and Ingo Hasselbach." *Journal of Personality* 78(6): 1601–1636.

Duncan, Lauren, and Abigail J. Stewart. 2007. "Personal political salience: the role of personality in collective identity and action." *Political Psychology* 28(2): 143–164.

DuPuis, E. Melanie, and David Goodman. 2005. "Should we go 'home' to eat?: toward a reflexive politics of localism." *Journal of Rural Studies* 21(3): 359–371.

Durkheim, Émile. [1897] 1951. *Suicide: A Study in Sociology.* Glencoe, IL: Free Press.

Eatwell, Roger. 1998. "The dynamics of right-wing electoral breakthrough." *Patterns of Prejudice* 32(3): 3–31.

2000. "The rebirth of the 'extreme right' in western Europe?" *Parliamentary Affairs* 53(3): 407–425.

Elff, Martin. 2007. "Social structure and electoral behavior in comparative perspective: the decline of social cleavages in Western Europe revisited." *Perspectives on Politics* 5(2): 277–294.

Eliasoph, Nina. 1998. *Avoiding Politics: How Americans Produce Apathy in Everyday Life.* Cambridge, UK: Cambridge University Press.

Ellinas, Antonis A. 2014. *The Media and the Far Right in Western Europe.* New York: Cambridge University Press.

Ennser, Laurenz. 2012. "The homogeneity of West European party families: the radical right in comparative perspective." *Party Politics* 18(2): 151–171.

Erk, Jan, and Lawrence Anderson. 2009. "The paradox of federalism: does self-rule accommodate or exacerbate ethnic divisions?" *Regional and Federal Studies* 19(2): 191–202.

Ethier, Kathleen A., and Kay Deaux. 1994. "Negotiating social identity when contexts change: maintaining identification and responding to threat." *Interpersonal Relations and Group Processes* 67(2): 243–251.

Evans, Jocelyn A. J. 2005. "The dynamics of social change in radical right-wing populist party support." *Comparative European Politics* 3(1): 76–101.

Evans, Jocelyn A. J., and Gilles Ivaldi. 2000–2002. "Extreme right electorates and party success." Institut fur Politikwissenschaft, University Mainz. www.politik.uni-mainz.de/ereps/electoral_results.htm. Accessed July 7, 2005.

Ezro, Lawrence, Margit Tavits, and Jonathan Homola. 2014. "Voter polarization, strength of partisanship, and support for extremist parties." *Comparative Political Studies* 47(11): 1558–1583.

Faiola, Anthony. 2012. "Anti-immigrant Golden Dawn rises in Greece." *The Washington Post*, October 20, 2012. www.washingtonpost.com/world/europe/anti-immigrant-golden-dawn-rises-in-greece/2012/10/20/e7128296-17a6-11e2-a346-f24efc680b8d_story.html?utm_term=.6082304e52a5

Falter, Jürgen W., and Siegfried Schumann. 1988. "Affinity towards right-wing extremism in Western Europe." *West European Politics* 11(2): 96–110.

Festinger, Leon. 1947. "The role of group belongingness in a voting situation." *Human Relations* 1(2): 154–180.

Fisher, Stephen D. 2000. "Class contextual effects on the Conservative vote in 1983." *British Journal of Political Science* 30(2): 347–361.

Fitzgerald, Jennifer. 2011. "Family dynamics and Swiss parties on the rise: exploring party support in a changing electoral context." *Journal of Politics* 73(3): 783–796.

2012. "Social engagement and immigration attitudes: panel survey evidence from Germany." *International Migration Review* 46(4): 941–970.

2013. "What does 'political' mean to you?" *Political Behavior* 35(3): 453–479.

Fitzgerald, Jennifer, K. Amber Curtis, and Catherine L. Corliss. 2012. "Anxious publics: concerns about crime and immigration." *Comparative Political Studies* 45(4): 477–506.

Fitzgerald, Jennifer, and Duncan Lawrence. 2011. "Local cohesion and radical right support: the case of the Swiss People's Party." *Electoral Studies* 30(4): 834–847.

Fitzgerald, Jennifer, and Jennifer Wolak. 2016. "The roots of trust in local government in Western Europe." *International Political Science Review* 37(1): 130–146.

Flecker, Jorge, Ed. 2007. *Changing Working Life and the Appeal of the Extreme Right.* Aldershot, UK: Ashgate Publishing.

Fontana, Marie-Christine, Andreas Sidler, and Sibylle Hardmeier. 2006. "The 'New Right' vote: an analysis of the gender gap in the vote choice for the SVP." *Swiss Political Science Review* 12(4): 243–271.

Ford, Robert, and Matthew J. Goodwin. 2010. "Angry white men: individual and contextual predictors of support for the British National Party." *Political Studies* 58(1): 1–25.

Forrest, Ray, and Ade Kearns. 2001. "Social cohesion, social capital and the neighbourhood." *Urban Studies* 38(12): 2125–2143.

Fowler, James, and Cindy D. Kam. 2007. "Beyond the self: social identity, altruism, and political participation." *Journal of Politics* 69(3): 813–827.

Franklin, Mark N., Thomas T. Mackie, Henry Valen et al. 1992. *Electoral Change: Response to Evolving Social and Attitudinal Structures in Western Countries.* Cambridge, UK: Cambridge University Press.

Frémy, Dominique, and Michèle Frémy. 2001. *Quid 2002: tout sur tout et un peu plus que tout.* Fixot.

Friedman, Thomas L. 2000. *The Lexus and the Olive Tree.* New York: Anchor Books.

Frusetta, James, and Anca Glont. 2009. "Interwar fascism and the post-1989 radical right: ideology, opportunism and historical legacy in Bulgaria and Romania." *Communist and Post-Communist Studies* 42(4): 551–571.

Fukuyama, Francis. 1999. *The Great Disruption: Human Nature and the Reconstitution of Social Order.* London: Profile Books.

Geys, Benny. 2006. "Explaining voter turnout: a review of aggregate-level research." *Electoral Studies* 25(4): 637–663.

Gieryn, Thomas F. 2000. "A space for place in sociology." *Annual Review of Sociology* 26: 463–496.

Gindengil, Elisabeth, Matthew Hennigar, André Blais, and Neil Nevitte. 2005. "Explaining the gender gap in support for the New Right: the case of Canada." *Comparative Political Studies* 38(10): 1171–1195.

Givens, Terri E. 2004. "The radical right gender gap." *Comparative Political Studies* 37(1): 30–54.

2005. *Voting Radical Right in Western Europe.* Cambridge, UK: Cambridge University Press.

2017. "The radical right gender gap." In Cas Mudde, Ed., *The Populist Radical Right: A Reader,* pp. 290–307. New York: Routledge.

Golder, Matt. 2003a. "Electoral institutions, unemployment and extreme right parties: a correction." *British Journal of Political Science* 33(3): 525–534.

2003b. "Explaining variation in the success of extreme right parties In Western Europe." *Comparative Political Studies* 36(4): 432–466.

2016. "Far right parties in Europe." *Annual Review of Political Science* 19: 477–497.

Golebiowska, Ewa A. 1999. "Gender gap in political tolerance." *Political Behavior* 21(1): 43–66.

Goodhart, David. 2017. *The Road to Somewhere: The Populist Revolt and the Future of Politics.* London: C. Hurst and Company.

Goodliffe, Gabriel. 2012. *The Resurgence of the Radical Right in France: From Boulangisme to the Front National.* New York: Cambridge University Press.

Goodwin, Matthew J. 2008. "Backlash in the 'hood: determinants of support for the British National Party (BNP) at the local level." *Journal of Contemporary European Studies* 16(3): 347–361.

2012. "Exploring support for the British National Party (BNP) at the local level." In Andrea Mammone, Emmanuel Godin, and Brian Jenkins, Eds., *Mapping the Extreme Right in Contemporary Europe,* pp. 17–32. London: Routledge.

Graff, Thibault Fleury. 2015. "Le Front national est un parti anti-régional." Slate.fr., July 12, 2015. www.slate.fr/story/111131/le-front-national-est-un-parti-anti-regional

Green, Anne E., and Richard J. White. 2007 "Attachment to place, social networks, mobility and prospects of young people." Joseph Rowntree Foundation,

October 29. Warwick University. www.jrf.org.uk/report/attachment-place-social-networks-mobility-and-prospects-young-people

Green, Eva G.T., Oriane Sarrasin, Robert Baur, and Nicole Fasel. 2015. "From stigmatized immigrants to radical right voting: multilevel study on the role of threat and contact." *Political Psychology* 37(4): 465–480.

Guilluy, Christophe. 2015. *La France périphérique: comment on a sacrifié les classes populaires*. Paris: Flammarion.

Gurr, Ted Robert. 1970. *Why Men Rebel*. Princeton, NJ: Princeton University Press.

Haeberle, Steven H. 1987. "Neighborhood identity and citizen participation." *Administration and Society* 19(2): 178–196.

Hainsworth, Paul. 1992. "The extreme right in post-war France: the emergence and success of the Front National." In Paul Hainsworth, Ed., *The Extreme Right in Europe and the United States*, pp. 29–60. London: Pinter Publishers.

2000. "The Front National: from ascendency to fragmentation on the French extreme right." In Paul Hainsworth, Ed., *The Politics of the Extreme Right: From the Margins to the Mainstream*, pp. 18–32. New York: Pinter Publishers.

2004. "The extreme right in France: the rise and rise of Jean-Marie Le Pen's Front National." *Representation* 40(2): 101–114.

2008. *The Extreme Right in Western Europe*. New York: Routledge.

Halikiopoulou, Daphne, Kyriaki Nanou, and Sofia Vasilopoulou. 2012. "The paradox of nationalism: the common denominatory of radical right and radical left euroskepticism." *European Journal of Political Rsearch* 51(4): 504–539.

Hamilton, Richard F. 1982. *Who Voted for Hitler?* Princeton, NJ: Princeton University Press.

Heinen, Jacqueline. 1997. "Public/private: gender – social and political citizenship in Eastern Europe." *Theory and Society* 26(4): 577–597.

Helms, Ludger. 1997. "Right-wing populist parties in Austria and Switzerland: a comparative analysis of electoral support and conditions of success." *West European Politics* 20(2): 37–52.

Hess, David J. 2009. *Localist Movements in a Global Economy: Sustainability, Justice, and Urban Development in the United States*. Cambridge, MA: MIT Press.

Hetherington, Marc J. 2001. "Resurgent mass partisanship: the role of elite polarization." *American Political Science Review* 95(3): 619–631.

Hiro, Airo. 2012. *New Challenger Parties in Western Europe*. London: Routledge.

Hirschfield, Alex, and Kate J. Bowers. 1997. "The effect of social cohesion on levels of recorded crime in disadvantaged areas." *Urban Studies* 34(8): 1275–1295.

Hix, Simon, and Michael Marsh. 2011. "Second-order effects plus pan-European political swings: an analysis of European Parliament elections across time." *Electoral Studies* 30(1): 4–15.

Hobsbawm, Eric J. 1994. "The nation as invented tradition." Ch. 12 in John Hutchinson and Anthony D. Smith, Eds., *Nationalism*. New York, NY: Oxford University Press: 76–82.

2007. *Globalisation, Democracy and Terrorism*. New York: Little, Brown.

Hollifield, James F., and George Ross, Eds. 1991. *Searching for the New France*. New York: Routledge, Chapman and Hall, Inc.

Hooghe, Liesbet, Gary Marks, and Arjan H. Schakel. 2010. *The Rise of Regional Authority: A Comparative Study of 42 Democracies*. New York: Routledge.

Hooghe, Marc. 2003. "Participation in voluntary associations and value indicators: the effect of current and previous participation experiences." *Nonprofit and Voluntary Sector Quarterly* 32(1): 47–69.

Hooghe, Marc, and Ellen Quintelier. 2013. "Do all associations lead to lower levels of ethnocentrism? A two-year longitudinal test of the selection and adaptation model." *Political Behavior* 35(2): 289–309.

Hopkins, Daniel J. 2010. "Politicized places: explaining where and when immigrants provoke local opposition." *American Political Science Review* 104(1): 40–60.

2011. "National debates, local responses: the origins of local concern about immigration in Britain and the United States." *British Journal of Political Science* 41(3): 499–524.

Horowitz, Donald L. 1985. *Ethnic Groups in Conflict.* Berkeley: University of California Press.

Huber, John, and Ronald Inglehart. 1995. "Expert interpretations of party space and party locations in 42 societies." *Party Politics* 1(1): 73–111.

Huckfeldt, Robert, Eric Plutzer, and John Sprague. 1993. "Alternative contexts and political behavior: churches, neighborhoods, and individuals." *Journal of Politics* 55(2): 365–381.

Huckfeldt, Robert, and John Sprague. 1995. *Citizens, Politics, and Social Communication: Information and Influence in an Election Campaign.* Cambridge, UK: Cambridge University Press.

Huddy, Leonie. 2001. "From social to political identity: a critical examination of social identity theory." *Political Psychology* 22(1): 127–156.

2003. "Group identity and political cohesion." In David O. Sears, Leonie Huddy, and Robert Jervis, Eds., *Oxford Handbook of Political Psychology*, pp. 511–558. Oxford, UK: Oxford University Press.

Huddy, Leonie, and Nadia Khatib. 2007. "American patriotism, national identity, and political involvement." *American Journal of Political Science* 51(1): 63–77.

Hug, Simon, and Tobias Schulz. 2007. "Left-right positions of political parties in Switzerland." *Party Politics* 13(3): 305–330.

Huici, Carmen, María Ros, Ignacio Cano, Nicholas Hopkins, Nicholas Emler, and Mercedes Caarmona. 1997. "Comparative identity and evaluation of sociopolitical change: perceptions of the EC as a function of the salience of regional identities." *European Journal of Social Psychology* 27(1): 97–113.

IDHEAP/BADAC. 2001. "Base de données cantons, Collaborations: Concordats, RPT, Communes: Communes et fusions des communes: Communes avec parlement communal 2001 (C4.21)." Accessed May 2, 2016.

Ignazi, Piero. 2003. *Extreme Right Parties in Western Europe.* New York: Oxford University Press.

Immerzeel, Tim, Hilde Coffé, and Tanja van der Lippe. 2015. "Explaining the gender gap in radical right voting: a cross-national investigation in 12 Western European countries." *Comparative European Politics* 13(2): 263–286.

Immerzeel, Tim, Eva Jaspers, and Marcel Lubbers. 2013. "Religion as catalyst or restraint of radical right voting?" *West European Politics* 36(5): 946–968.

Inglehart, Ronald. 1977. *The Silent Revolution: Changing Values and Political Styles Among Western Publics.* Princeton, NJ: Princeton University Press.

1997. *Modernization and Postmodernization: Cultural, Economic and Political Change in 43 Societies.* Cambridge University Press.

Inglehart, Ronald, and Pippa Norris. 2000. "The developmental theory of the gender gap: women's and men's voting behavior in global perspective." *International Political Science Review* 21(4): 441–463.

2016. "Trump, Brexit, and the rise of populism: economic have-nots and cultural backlash." Harvard Kennedy School of Government, Faculty Research Working Paper Series RWP16-026.

Ivaldi, Gilles, and Joël Gombin. 2015. "The Front National and the new politics of the rural in France." HAL archives-ouvertes.fr. HAL ID: halshs-01245081. https://halshs.archives-ouvertes.fr/halshs-01245081

Ivarsflaten, Elisabeth. 2008. "What unites right-wing populists in Western Europe? Reexamining grievance mobilization models in seven successful cases." *Comparative Political Studies* 41(1): 3–23.

Jackman, Robert W., and Karin Volpert. 1996. "Conditions favouring parties of the extreme right in Western Europe." *British Journal of Political Science* 26(4): 501–521.

Jeffery, Charlie. 2006. "Devolution and local government." *Publius* 36(1): 57–73.

Jennings, M. Kent. 1983. "Gender roles and inequalities in political participation: results from an eight-nation study." *The Western Political Quarterly* 36(3): 364–385.

Jesuit, David K., Piotr R. Paradowski, and Vincent A. Mahler. 2009. "Electoral support for extreme right-wing parties: a subnational analysis of western European elections." *Electoral Studies* 28(2): 279–290.

John, Peter, Helen Margetts, David Rowland, and Stuart Weir. 2006. "The BNP: the roots of its appeal." Democratic Audit, Human Rights Centre, University of Essex, Colchester, UK.

Johnston, Ronald J. 1972. "Spatial elements in voting patterns at the 1968 Christchurch city council election." *Political Science* 24(1): 49–61.

Johnston, Ronald, and Charles Pattie. 2006. *Putting Voters in Their Place: Geography and Elections in Great Britain.* Oxford, UK: Oxford University Press.

Karácsony, Gergely, and Dániel Róna. 2011. "The secret of Jobbik: reasons behind the ries of the Hungarian radical right." *Journal of East European and Asian Studies* 2(1): 61–92.

Kasarda, John D., and Morris Janowitz. 1974. "Community attachment in mass society." *American Sociological Review* 39(3): 328–339.

Katz, Richard S., and Peter Mair. 1995. "Changing models of party organization and party democracy: the emergence of the cartel Party." *Party Politics* 1(1): 5–28.

Kawachi, Ichiro, and Lisa F. Berkman. 2001. "Social ties and mental health." *Journal of Urban Health* 78 (3): 458–467.

Kearney, Christine. 1999. "Decentralization index." Henderson Faculty Papers. Brown University, Providence, RI. www.econ.brown.edu/faculty/henderson/decentraliza-tion.pdf.

Keefer, Philip. 2010. DPI2010. *Database of Political Institutions: Changes and Variable Definitions.* Development Research Group, World Bank.

2012. *Database of Political Institutions: Changes and Variable Definitions.* Research on Macroeconomics and Growth, Development Research Group, The World Bank. Issued: December 2012

Keefer, Philip E., and David Stasavage. 2003. "The limits of delegation: veto players, central bank independence and the credibility of monetary policy." *American Political Science Review* 97(3): 407–423.

Keele, Luke. 2007. "Social capital and the dynamics of trust in government." *American Journal of Political Science* 51: 241–254.

Kerrouche, Eric. 2010. "France and its 36,000 communes: an impossible reform?" In Herald Baldersheim and Lawrence E. Rose, Eds., *Territorial Choice: The Politics of Boundaries and Borders*, pp. 160–179. London: Palgrave MacMillan.

Kessler, Alan E., and Gary P. Freeman. 2005. "Support for extreme right-wing parties in Western Europe: individual attributes, political attitudes, and national context." *Comparative European Politics* 3: 261–288.

Kestilä, Elina, and Peter Söderlund. 2007. "Subnational political opportunity structures and the success of the radical right: evidence from the March 2004 regional elections in France."*European Journal of Political Research* 46(6): 773–796.

Kingston, Sharon, Roger Mitchell, Paul Florin, and John Stevenson. 1999. "Sense of community in neighborhoods as a multi-level construct." *Journal of Community Psychology* 27(6): 681–694.

Kitschelt, Herbert. 2007. "Growth and persistence of the radical right in postindustrial democracies: advances and challenges in comparative research." *West European Politics* 30(5): 1176–1206.

Kitschelt, Herbert (in collaboration with Anthony McGann). 1995. *The Radical Right in Western Europe: A Comparative Analysis*. Ann Arbor, MI: University of Michigan Press.

Klandermans, Bert. 2002. "How group identification helps to overcome the dilemma of collective action." *American Behavioral Scientist* 45(5): 887–900.

Klandermans, Bert, and Nonna Mayer, Eds. 2006. *Extreme Right Activists in Europe. Through the Magnifying Glass*. London: Routledge.

Knack, Stephen. 1992. "Civic norms, social sanctions, and voter turnout." *Rationality and Society* 4(2): 133–156.

Knapp, Andrew, and Vincent Wright. 2001. *The Government and Politics of France*. 5th edition. London: Routledge.

Knigge, Pia. 1998. "The ecological correlates of right-wing extremism in Western Europe." *European Journal of Political Research* 34(2): 249–279.

Kolinsky, Eva. 1993. "Party change and women's representation in United Germany." In Joni Lovenduski and Pippa Norris, Eds., *Gender and Party Politics*, pp. 113–146. Sage Publications: London.

Koopmans, Ruud, and Paul Statham. 1999. "Ethnic and civic conceptions of nationhood and the differential success of the extreme right in Germany." In Marco Guigni, Doug McAdam, and Charles Tilly, Eds., *How Social Movements Matter*, pp 225–251. Minneapolis, MI: University of Minnesota Press.

Kornhauser, William. 1960. *The Politics of Mass Society*. Glencoe, IL: Free Press.

Kriesi, Hanspeter, Edgar Grande, Romain Lachat, Martin Dolezal, Simon Bornschier, and Timotheos Frey. 2008. *West European Politics in the Age of Globalization*. New York: Cambridge University Press.

Kriesi, Hanspeter, and Alexander Trechsel. 2008. *The Politics of Switzerland: Continuity and Change in a Consensus Democracy*. Cambridge, UK: Cambridge University Press.

Kuhn, Ursina. 2009. "Stability and change in party preference." *Swiss Political Science Review* 15(3): 463–494.

La Due Lake, Ronald, and Robert Huckfeldt. 1998. "Social capital, social networks, and political participation." *Political Psychology* 19(3): 567–584.

Ladner, Andreas. 2001. "Swiss political parties: between persistence and change." *West European Politics* 24(2): 123–144.

2007. "Local government and metropolitan regions in Switzerland." Paper prepared for the international roundtable "Local Government and Metropolitan Regions in Federal Countries," Johannesburg, April 19–22. Working paper de L'IDHEAP No. 2.2007, March 2007.

Laitin, David D. 1986. *Hegemony and Culture: Politics and Change Among the Yoruba.* Chicago, IL: University of Chicago Press.

1998. *Identity in Formation: The Russian-Speaking Populations in the Near Abroad.* New York: Cambridge University Press.

Lamprianou, Iasonas, and Antonis A. Ellinas. 2017. "Institutional grievances and right-wing extremism: voting for Golden Dawn in Greece." *South European Society and Politics* 22(1): 43–60.

Lane, Robert E. 2000. *The Loss of Happiness in Market Democracies.* New Haven, CT: Yale University Press.

LaPiere, Richard T. 1934. "Attitudes vs. actions." *Social Forces* 13(2): 230–237.

Lazarsfeld, Paul F., Bernard Berelson, and Hazel Gaudet. [1948] 1968. *The People's Choice: How the Voter Makes up His Mind in a Presidential Campaign.* 3rd edition. New York and London: Columbia University Press.

Le Pen, Jean-Marie. 1993. *300 mesures pour la renaissance de la France: Front National, programme de gouvernement.* Paris: Editions nationales.

Lee, Jo, Arnar Árnason, Andrea Nightingale, and Mark Shucksmith. 2005. "Networking: social capital and identities in European rural development." *Sociologica Ruralis* 45(4): 269–283.

Lehmann, Pola, Theres Matthieß, Nicolas Merz, Sven Regel, and Annika Werner. 2015. Manifesto Corpus. Version: MPDS2015-a. Berlin: WZB Berlin Social Science Center.

Lewicka, Maria. 2005. "Ways to make people active: the role of place attachment, cultural capital, and neighborhood ties." *Journal of Environmental Psychology* 25(4): 381–395.

Lewis-Beck, Michael S. 1983. "Economics and the French voter: a microanalysis." *Public Opinion Quarterly* 47(3): 193–205.

Li, Yaojun, Andrew Pickles, and Mike Savage. 2005. "Social capital and social trust in Britain." *European Sociological Review* 21: 109–123.

Lijphart, Arend. 1977. *Democracy in Plural Societies: A Comparative Exploration.* New Haven, CT: Yale University Press.

1997. "Unequal participation: democracy's unresolved dilemma." *American Political Science Review* 91(1): 1–14.

1999. *Patterns of Democracy: Government Forms and Performance in Thirty-six Countries.* New Haven, CT: Yale University Press.

Linder, Wolf. 1997. *Possible Solutions to Conflict in Multicultural Societies.* London: Palgrave Macmillan.

Lipset, Seymour Martin. 1960. *Political Man: The Social Bases of Politics.* Garden City, NY: Doubleday.

1981. *Political Man: The Social Bases of Politics.* Expanded and updated edition. Baltimore, MD: Johns Hopkins University Press.

Lipset, Seymour Martin, and Stein Rokkan. 1967. *Party Systems and Voter Alignments: Cross-national Perspectives.* New York: Free Press.

Livingston, Mark, Nicky Bailey, and Ade Kearns. 2008. "People's attachment to place – the influence of neighbourhood deprivation." Glasgow University. Chartered Institute of Housing/Joseph Rowntree Foundation, York, UK.

Loughlin, John, Ed. 2001. *Subnational Democracy in the European Union: Challenges and Opportunities*. Oxford, UK: Oxford University Press.

Low, Setha M., and Irwin Altman. 1992. "Place attachment: a conceptual inquiry." In Irwin Altman and Setha M. Low, Eds., *Place Attachment*, pp. 1–12. Springer US.

Lowndes, Vivien, and Lawrence Pratchett. 2012. "Local governance under the coalition government: austerity, localism and the 'Big Society.'" *Local Government Studies* 38 (1): 1–20.

Lubbers, Marcel. 2000. "Expert judgment survey of West-European political parties 2000." Dataset. Nijmegen, Netherlands: NOW, Department of Sociology, University of Nijmegen.

Lubbers, Marcel, and Marcel Coenders. 2017. "Nationalistic attitudes and voting for the radical right in Europe." *European Union Politics* 18(1): 98–118.

Lubbers, Marcel, Mérove Gijsberts, and Peer Scheepers. 2002. "Extreme right-wing voting in Western Europe." *European Journal of Political Research* 41(3): 345–378.

Lubbers, Marcel, and Peer Scheepers. 2000. "Individual and contextual characteristics of the German extreme right-wing vote in the 1990s: a test of complementary theories." *European Journal of Political Research* 38: 63–94.

2001. Explaining the trend in extreme right-wing voting: Germany 1989–1998. *European Sociological Review* 17(4): 431–449.

Lubbers, Marcel, P. Scheepers, and J. Billiet. 2000. "Individual and contextual characteristics of the Vlaams Blok vote." *Acta Politica* 35: 363–398.

Luther, Kurt Richard. 2009. "The revival of the radical right: the Austrian parliamentary election of 2008." *West European Politics* 32(5): 1049–1061.

Maloney, William A., Graham Smith, and Gerry Stoker. 2000. "Social capital and associational life." In S. Baron, J. Field, and T. Schuller, Eds., *Social Capital: Critical Perspectives*, pp. 212–225. Oxford, UK: Oxford University Press.

Mann, Peter H. 1954. "The concept of neighborliness." *American Journal of Sociology* 60(2): 163–168.

Manzo, Lynne C. 2003. "Beyond house and haven: toward a revisioning of emotional relationships with places." *Journal of Environmental Psychology* 23(1): 47–61.

Markoff, John. 1985. "The social geography of rural revolt at the beginning of the French Revolution." *American Sociological Review* 50(6): 761–781.

Marks, Gary. 1999. "Territorial identities in the European Union." In Jeffrey J. Anderson, Ed., *Regional Integration and Democracy: Expanding on the European Experience*, Ch. 4. Lanham, MD: Rowman and Littlefield.

Massey, Doreen. 1994. *Space, Place and Gender*. Cambridge, UK: Policy Press, pp. 1–14.

Mayer, Nonna. 1992. "Presence of immigrants and National Front vote: the case of Paris (1984–1989)." In Lucius J. Barker, Ed., *Ethnic Politics and Civil Liberties*, pp. 103–126. New Brunswick, NJ: Transaction Publishers.

1998. "The front national vote in the plural." *Patterns of Prejudice* 32(1): 3–24.

1999. *Ces Français qui votent FN*. Paris: Flammarion.

2002. *Ces Français qui votent Le Pen*. Paris: Flammarion.

2005. "Radical right populism in France: how much of the 2002 Le Pen votes does populism explain?" Symposium: Globalization and the Radical Right Populism.

Center for the Study of European Politics and Society, Ben Gurion University of the Neguev, April, 11–12, 2005.

2014. "The electoral impact of the crisis on the French working class: more to the right?" In Nancy Bermeo and Larry M. Bartels, Eds., *Mass Politics in Tough Times: Opinions, Votes, and Protest in the Great Recession*, pp. 266–296. Oxford, UK: Oxford University Press.

Mayer, Nonna, and Pascal Perrinneau. 1992. "Why do they vote for Le Pen?" *European Journal of Political Research* 22(1): 123–141.

1996/1989. *Le Front national à découvert*. Paris: Presses de la Fondation nationale des sciences politiques.

Mayer, Nonna, and Vincent Tiberj. 2004. "Do issues matter? Law and order in the 2002 French presidential election." In Michael Lewis-Beck, Ed., *The French Voter: Before and After the 2002 Elections*, pp. 33–46. London: Palgrave Macmillan.

McClurg, Scott D. 2006. "Political disagreement in context: the conditional effect of neighborhood context, disagreement and political talk on electoral participation." *Political Behavior* 28: 349–366.

McGann, Anthony J., and Herbert Kitschelt. 2005. "The radical right in the Alps: evolution of support for the Swiss SVP and Austrian FPÖ." *Party Politics* 11(2): 147–171.

McLaughlin, Eric S. 2007. "Beyond the racial census: the political salience of ethnolinguistic cleavages in South Africa." *Comparative Political Studies* 40(4): 435–456.

Meaney, Thomas. 2016. "The new star of Germany's far right." *The New Yorker*, October 3, 2016. www.newyorker.com/magazine/2016/10/03/the-new-star-of-germanys-far-right

Merton, Robert K. 1957. *Social Theory and Social Structure*. Glencoe, IL: Free Press.

Middendorp, Cees P., and Jos D. Meloen. 1990. "The authoritarianism of the working class revisited." *European Journal of Political Research* 18(2): 257–267.

Middleton, Alan, Alan Murie, and Rick Groves. 2005. "Social capital and neighbourhoods that work." *Urban Studies* 42(10): 1711–1738.

Miller, Arthur H., Patricia Gurin, Gerald Gurin, and Oksana Malanchuk. 1981. "Group consciousness and political participation." *American Journal of Political Science* 25(3): 494–511.

Minkenberg, Michael. 2000. "The renewal of the radical right: between modernity and anti-modernity." *Government and Opposition* 35(2): 170–188.

2017. "Organizational patterns and ideological profiles." In Michael Minkenberg, Ed., *The Radical Right in Eastern Europe: Democracy under Seige?*, pp. 67–98. New York: Palgrave Macmillan.

Minkenberg, Michael, and Pascal Perrineau. 2007. "The radical right in the European elections 2004." *International Political Science Review* 28(1): 29–55.

Mitchell, Stacy. 2007. *Big-Box Swindle: The True Cost of Mega-retailers and the Fight for America's Independent Business*. Boston, MA: Beacon.

Mondak, Jeffery J., Diana C. Mutz, and Robert Huckfeldt. 1996. "Persuasion in context: the multilevel structure of economic evaluations." In Diana C. Mutz, Paul M. Sniderman, and Richard A. Brody, Eds., *Political Persuasion and Attitude Change*. Ann Arbor, MI: University of Michigan Press.

Mondon, Aurélien. 2013. *The Mainstreaming of the Extreme Right in France and Australia: A Populist Hegemony?* Farnham, UK: Ashgate Publishing.

Moody, James, and Douglas R. White. 2003. "Structural cohesion and embeddedness: a hierarchical concept of social groups." *American Sociological Review* 68(1): 103–127.

Morgenstern, Scott, and Stephen M. Swindle. 2005. "Are politics local? An analysis of voting patterns in 23 democracies." *Comparative Political Studies* 38(2): 143–170.

Morrow, Duncan. 2000. "Jörg Haider and the new FPÖ: beyond the democratic pale?" In Paul Hainsworth, Ed., *The Politics of the Extreme Right: From the Margins to the Mainstream*, pp. 33–63. New York: Pinter.

Mudde, Cas. 1996. "The war of words: defining the extreme right party family." *West European Politics* 19(2): 225–248.

1999. "The single-issue party thesis: extreme right parties and the immigration issue." *West European Politics* 22(3): 182–197.

2004. "The populist zeitgeist." *Government and Opposition* 39(4): 541–563.

2007. *Populist Radical Right Parties in Europe*. Cambridge, UK: Cambridge University Press.

Mughan, Anthony, and Pamela Paxton. 2006. "Anti-immigrant sentiment, policy preferences and populist party voting in Australia." *British Journal of Political Science* 36(2): 341–358.

Nagel, Joane. 1998. "Masculinity and nationalism: gender and sexuality in the making of nations." *Ethnic and Racial Studies* 21(2): 242–269.

New York Times, The. 2016. "Europe's rising far right: a guide to the most prominent parties." December 4, 2016. www.nytimes.com/interactive/2016/world/europe/europe-far-right-political-parties-listy.html

Newton, Kenneth. 1997. "Social capital and democracy." *American Behavioral Scientist* 40(5): 575–586.

Nie, Norman H., D. Sunshine Hillygus, and Lutz Erbring, 2002. "Internet use, interpersonal relations, and sociability: a time diary study." In Barry Wellman and Caroline Haythornthwaite, Eds.,*The Internet in Everyday Life*, pp. 215–243. Malden, MA: Blackwell Publishers.

Norris, Pippa. 1999. "A gender-generation gap?" In Geoffrey Evans and Pippa Norris, Eds., *Critical Elections: British Parties and Voters in Long-term Perspective*. London: SAGE.

2005. *Radical Right: Voters and Parties in the Electoral Market*. New York: Cambridge University Press.

Oakes, Penelope J. 1987. "The salience of social categories." In J. C. Turner, M. A. Hogg, P. J. Oakes, S. D. Reicher, and M. S. Weatherell, Eds., *Rediscovering the Social Group: A Self-categorization Theory*, pp. 117–141. Oxford, UK: Blackwell.

OECD. 2010a. "International migration database." *OECD International Migration Statistics* (database). Accessed August 7, 2013. doi: 10.1787/data-00342-en

2010b. "Revenue statistics: comparative tables." *OECD Tax Statistics* (database). Accessed August 7, 2013. doi: 10.1787/data-00262-en

2011. "Fiscal decentralisation: tax autonomy." *OECD Tax Statistics* (database). Accessed August 7, 2013. doi: 10.1787/data-00582-en

2013. "Main economic indicators – complete database." *Main Economic Indicators* (database). Accessed August 7, 2013. doi: 10.1787/data-00052-en

Oesch, Daniel. 2008. "Explaining workers' support for right-wing populist parties in Western Europe: evidence from Austria, Belgium, France, Norway, and Switzerland." *International Political Science Review* 29(3): 349–373.

O'Loughlin, John, C. Flint, and L. Anselin. 1994. "The geography of the Nazi vote: context, confession and class in the Reichstag elections of 1930." *Annals of the American Society of Geographers* 84(3): 351–380.

Parsons, Talcott. 1968. *The Structure of Social Action*, Vol. 2. New York: Free Press.

Pattie, Charles, and Ron Johnston. 1998. "The role of regional context in voting: evidence from the 1992 British General Election." *Regional Studies* 32(2): 249–263.

　2000 "'People who talk together vote together': an exploration of contextual effects in Great Britain." *Annals of the Association of American Geographers* 90(1): 41–66.

Paxton, Pamela. 1999. "Is social capital declining in the United States? A multiple indicator assessment." *American Journal of Sociology* 105(1): 88–127.

Perrineau, Pascal. 1997. *Le Symptôme Le Pen*. Paris: Fayard.

Pichler, Florian, and Claire Wallace. 2007. "Patterns of formal and informal social capital in Europe." *European Sociological Review* 23(4): 423–435.

Pollack, Detlef. 2008. "Religious change in Europe: theoretical considerations and empirical findings." *Social Compass* 55(2): 168–186.

Portes, Alejandro, and Patricia Landolt. 1996. "The downside of social capital." *The American Prospect* 26:18–21.

Posner, Daniel N. 2004. "The political salience of cultural difference: why Chewas and Tumbukas are allies in Zambia and adversaries in Malawi." *American Political Science Review* 98(4): 529–545.

　2005. *Institutions and Ethnic Politics in Africa*. Cambridge, UK: Cambridge University Press.

Powell, G. Bingham, and G. D. Whitten. 1993. "A cross-national analysis of economic voting: taking account of the political context." *American Journal of Political Science* 37: 391–414.

Poznyak, D., K. Abts, and M. Swyngodouw. 2011. "The dynamics of the extreme right support: a growth curve model of the populist vote in Flanders-Belgium in 1987–2007." *Electoral Studies* 30(4): 672–688.

Proshansky, Harold M. 1978. "The City and Self-Identity." *Environment and Behavior* 10(2): 147–169.

Proshansky, Harold M., Abbe K. Fabian, and Robert Kaminoff. 1983. "Place-identity: physical world socialization of the self." *Journal of Environmental Psychology* 3: 57–83.

Puddifoot, John E. 1996. "Some initial considerations in the measurement of community identity." *Journal of Community Psychology* 24(4): 327–336.

Putnam, Robert D. 1993. *Making Democracy Work: Civic Traditions in Modern Italy*. Princeton, NJ: Princeton University Press.

　2000. *Bowling Alone: The Collapse and Revival of American Community*. New York: Simon and Schuster.

Quentin, David, and Gilles Van Hamme. 2011. "Pillars and electoral behavior in Belgium: the neighborhood effect revisited." *Political Geography* 30(5): 250–262.

Redfield, Robert. 1960. *The Little Community and Peasant Society and Culture*. Chicago, IL: University of Chicago Midway Reprint.

Rink, Nathalie, Karen Phalet, and Marc Swyngedouw. 2009. "The effects of immigrant population size, unemployment, and individual characteristics on voting for the Vlaams Blok in Flanders 1991–1999." *European Sociological Review* 25(4): 411–424.

Rodriguez-Pose, Andrés, and Nick Gill. 2003. "The global trend towards devolution and its implications." *Environment and Planning C: Government and Policy* 21(3): 333–351.

Rydgren, Jens. 2004. *The Populist Challenge: Political Protest and Ethno-nationalist Mobilization in France.* Oxford, UK: Berghahn Books.

2006. "Immigration skeptics, xenophobes, or racists? Radical right-wing voting in six West European countries." Working paper, Department of Sociology, Stockholm University.

2008. "Immigration, skeptics, xenophobes or racists? Radical right-wing voting in six West European countries." *European Journal of Political Research* 47(6): 737–765.

2009. "Social isolation? Social capital and radical right-wing voting in Eastern Europe." *Journal of Civil Society* 5(2): 129–150.

2011. "A legacy of 'uncivicness'? Social capital and radial right-wing voting in Western Europe." *Acta Politica* 46(2): 132–157.

Rydgren, Jens, and Patrick Ruth. 2011. "Voting for the radical right in Swedish municipalities: social marginality and ethnic competition?" *Scandinavian Political Studies* 34(3): 202–225.

2013. "Contextual explanations of radical right-wing support in Sweden: socioeconomic marginalization, group threat, and the halo effect." *Ethnic and Racial Studies* 36(4): 711–728.

Sampson, Robert J. 1991. "Linking the micro- and macrolevel dimensions of community social organization." *Social Forces* 70(1): 43–64.

Sandford, Mark. 2016. "Devolution to local government in England." Briefing paper No. 07029, April 5. House of Commons Library.

Särlvik, Bo, and Ivor Crewe. 1983. *Decade of Dealignment.* Cambridge, UK: Cambridge University Press.

Satyanath, Shanker, Nico Voigtlaender, and Hans-Joachim Voth. 2013. "Bowling for Fascism: social capital and the rise of the Nazi Party." NBER working paper No. 19201.

Savelkoul, Michael, and Peer Scheepers. 2017. "Why lower educated people are more likely to cast their vote for radical right parties: testing alternative explanations in The Netherlands." *Acta Politica* 52(4): 544–573.

Scala, Dante J., and Kenneth M. Johnson. 2017. "Polarization along the rural-urban continuum? The geography of the presidential vote, 2000–2016." *ANNALS, AAPSS,* 672(1): 162–184.

Schain, Martin A. 2006. "The extreme-right and immigration policy-making: measuring direct and indirect effects. *West European Politics* 29(2): 270–289.

Schain, Martin A., Aristide Zolberg, and Patrick Hossay. 2002. "The development of radical right parties in Western Europe." In M. A. Schain, A. R. Zolberg, and P. Hossay, Eds., *Shadows Over Europe: The Development and Impact of the Extreme Right in Western Europe,* pp. 3–17. New York, NY. Palgrave Macmillan.

Schakel, Arjan H. 2011. "Congruence between regional and national elections." *Comparative Political Studies* 46(5): 631–662.

Schakel, Arjan H., and Régis Dandoy. 2014. "Electoral cycles and turnout in multilevel electoral systems." *West European Politics* 37(3): 605–623.

Schlueter, Elmar, and Eldad Davidov. 2013. Contextual sources of perceived group threat: negative immigration-related news reports, immigrant group size and their interaction, Spain 1996–2007. *European Sociological Review* 29(2): 179–191.

Schuler, Martin, Pierre Dessemontet, Dominique Joye, and Manfred Perlik. 2005. *Recensement fédéral de la population 2000. Les niveaux géographiques de la Suisse.* Neuchâtel, Switzerland: Office fédéral de la statistique.

Schurr, Carolin. 2013. "Towards an emotional electoral geography: the performativity of emotions in electoral campaigning in Ecuador." *Geoforum* 49: 114–126.

Sellers, Jefferey, and Anders Lidström. 2012. "The localization of territorial identity: citizen attachment in an era of globalization." Paper presented at American Political Science Association Annual Meeeting, New Orleans, LA, August 29–September 2, 2012.

Shields, James G. 2007. *The Extreme Right in France: From Pétain to Le Pen.* Routledge: New York.

Simon, Bernd, and Bert Klandermans. 2001. "Politicized collective identity: a social psychological analysis." *American Psychologist* 56(4): 319–331.

Skenderovic, Damir. 2009. *The Radical Right in Switzerland: Continuity and Change, 1945–2000.* Oxford, UK: Berghahn Books.

Smith, Sandy G. 1994. "The essential qualities of a home." *Journal of Environmental Psychology* 14: 31–46.

Spierings, Neils, and Andrej Zaslove. 2015a. "Gendering the vote for populist radical-right parties." *Patterns of Prejudice* 49(1–2): 135–162.

2015b. "Conclusion: dividing the populist radical right between 'liberal nativism' and traditional conceptions of gender." *Patterns of Prejudice* 49(1–2): 163–173.

2017. "Gender, populist attitudes, and voting: explaining the gender gap in voting for populist radical right and populist radical left parties." *West European Politics* 40(4): 821–847.

Spinner-Haley, Jeff, and Elizabeth Theiss-Morse. 2003. "National identity and self-esteem." *Perspectives on Politics* 1(3): 515–532.

Starr, Amory, and Jason Adams. 2003. "Anti-globalization: the global fight for local autonomy." *New Political Science* 25(1): 19–42.

Statham, Paul, and Ruud Koopmans. 2009. "Political party contestation over Europe in the mass media: who criticizes Europe, how, and why?" *European Political Science Review* 1(3): 435–463.

Steiner, Reto. 2003. "The causes, spread, and effects of intermunicipal cooperation and municpal mergers in Switzerland." *Public Management Review* 5(4): 551–571.

Stone, Walter J. 2017. *Candidates and Voters: Ideology, Valence, and Representation in U.S. Elections.* Cambridge, UK: Cambridge University Press.

Stubager, Rune. 2008. "Education effects on authoritarian-libertarian values: a question of socialization." *The British Journal of Sociology* 59(2): 327–350.

Swank, Duane, and Hans-Georg Betz. 2003. "Globalization, the welfare state and right-wing populism in Western Europe." *Socio-Economic Review* 1(2): 215–245.

Swyngedouw, Marc. 1998. "The extreme right in Belgium: of a non-existent Front National and an omnipresent Vlaams Blok." In H.-G. Betz and S. Immerfall, Eds., *The New Politics of the Right: Neo-populist Parties and Movements in Established Democracies*, pp. 59–76. Basingstoke, UK: Macmillan.

2000. "Belgium: explaining the relationship between Vlaams Blok and the city of Antwerp." In Paul Hainsworth, Ed., *The Politics of the Extreme Right: From the Margins to the Mainstream*, pp. 121–134. New York: Pinter.

2001. "The subjective cognitive and affective map of extreme right voters: using open-ended questions in exit polls." *Electoral Studies* 20: S217–S241.

Tajfel, Henri. 1981. *Human Groups and Social Categories: Studies in Social Psychology.* Cambridge University Press.

Tajfel, Henri, and John C. Turner. 1979. "An integrative theory of intergroup conflict." In W. G. Austin and W. Worchel, Eds., *The Social Psychology of Intergroup Relations,* pp. 33–48. Monterey, CA: Brooks/Cole.

Taylor, Shelley E., and Susan T. Fiske. 1978. "Salience, attention and attribution: top of the head phenomena." In L. Berkowitz, Ed., *Advances in Experimental Social Psychology,* Vol. 11. New York: Academic Press.

 Téney, Céline, Onawa Promise Lacewell, and Pieter de Wilde. 2014. "Winners and losers of globalization in Europe: attitudes and ideologies." *European Political Science Review* 6(4): 575–595.

Tilly, Charles. 1961. "Local conflicts in the Vendée before the rebellion of 1793." *French Historical Studies* 2(2): 209–231.

1964. *The Vendée.* Cambridge, UK: Cambridge University Press.

Timpone, Richard J. 1998. "Ties that bind: measurement, demographics, and social connectedness." *Political Behavior* 20(1): 53–77.

Tingsten, Herbert L. G. 1937. *Political Behavior: Studies in Election Statistics.* London: P. S. King.

Tomz, Michael, Jason Wittenberg, and Gary King. 2003. "CLARIFY: Software for interpreting and presenting statistical results." *Journal of Statistical Software* 8(1): 130. Version 2.1. Stanford University, University of Wisconsin, and Harvard University. http://gking.harvard.edu/

Tönnies, Ferdinand. [1887] 1957. *Community and Society [Gemeinschaft und Gesellschaft].* Lansing, MI: Michigan State University Press.

Travis, Alan. 2016. "Fear of immigration drove the leave victory – not immigration itself." *The Guardian.* Friday, June 24. www.theguardian.com/politics/2016/jun/24/voting-details-show-immigration-fears-were-paradoxical-but-decisive

Trentelman, Carla Koons. 2009. "Place attachment and community attachment: a primer grounded in the lived experience of a community sociologist." *Society and Natural Resources* 22(3): 191–210.

Turner, John C., Penelope J. Oakes, S. Alexander Haslam, Craig McGarty. 1994. Self and collective: cognition and social context. *Personality and Social Psychology Bulletin* 20, 454–463.

UDC. 2015. "Programme du parti: 2015–2019 UDC – le parti de la Suisse." www.udc.ch/positions/programme-politique/

Unger, Donald, and Abraham Wandersman. 1985. "The importance of neighbors: the social, cognitive, and affective components of neighboring." *American Journal of Community Psychology* 13(2): 139–169.

Uzzell, David, Enric Pol, and David Badenas. 2002. "Place identification, social cohesion, and environmental sustainability." *Environment and Behavior* 34(1): 26–53.

Valdez, Sarah. 2014. "Visibility and votes: a spatial analysis of anti-immigrant voting in Sweden." *Migration Studies* 2(2): 162–188. doi: 10.1093/migration/mnu029.

Van den Hende, Anthe. 2015. "Settling and dwelling in the Swiss peri-urban areas: residential trajectories and life course events." Doctoral thesis, University of Geneva, No. SdS 6. URN: urn:nbn:ch:unige-554885. http://archive-ouverte.unige.ch/unige:55488

Van der Brug, Wouter, and Meindert Fennema. 2003. "Protest or mainstream? How European anti-immigrant parties have developed into two separate groups by 1999." *European Journal for Political Research* 42(1): 55–76.

2007. "What causes people to vote for a radical right party? A review of recent work." *International Journal of Public Opinion Research* 19(4): 474–487.

Van der Brug, Wouter, Meindert Fennema, and Jean Tillie. 2000. "Anti-immigrant parties in Europe: ideological or protest vote?" *European Journal of Political Research* 37(1): 77–102.

2005. "Why some anti-immigrant parties fail and others succeed: a two-step model of aggregate electoral support." *Comparative Political Studies* 38(5): 537–573.

Van der Eijk, Cees, Mark Franklin, and Michael Marsh. 1996. "What voters teach us about Europe-wide elections: what Europe-wide elections teach us about voters." *Electoral Studies* 15(2): 149–166.

Van der Meer, Tom W. G., Erika van Elsas, Rozemarijn Lubbe, and Wouter van der Brug. 2013. "Are volatile voters erratic, whimsical or seriously picky? A panel study of 58 waves into the nature of electoral volatility (The Netherlands 2006–2010)." *Party Politics* 21(1): 100–114.

Van der Pas, Daphne, Catherine de Vries, and Wouter van der Brug. 2011. "A leader without a party: exploring the relationship between Geert Wilders' leadership performance in the media and his electoral success." *Party Politics* 19(3): 458–476.

Van Hiel, Alain, and Ivan Mervielde. 2002. "Explaining conservative beliefs and political preferences: a comparison of social dominance orientation and authoritarianism." *Journal of Applied Social Psychology* 32(5): 965–976.

Vanhoutte, Bram, and Marc Hooghe. 2013. "The influence of social structure, networks and community on party choice in the Flemish region of Belgium: a multilevel analysis." *Acta Politica* 48: 209–236.

Verba, Sidney, Nancy Burns, and Key Lehman Schlozman. 1997. "Knowing and caring about politics: gender and political engagement." *Journal of Politics* 59(4): 1051–1072.

Veugelers, John. 2012. "After colonialism: local politics and far-right affinities in a city of southern France." In Andrea Mammone, Emmanuel Godin, and Brian Jenkins, Eds., *Mapping the Extreme Right in Contemporary Europe: From Local to Transnational*, Ch. 2. New York: Routledge.

Veugelers, John, and André Magnan. 2005. "Conditions of far-right strength in contemporary Western Europe: an application of Kitschelt's theory." *European Journal of Political Research* 44(6): 837–860.

Vidal, Tomeu, Hector Berroeta, Andrés de Masso, Sergi Valera, and Maribel Peró. 2013. "Place attachment, place identity, sense of community, and local civic participation in an urban renewal context." *Studies in Psychology* 34(3): 275–286.

Voorpostel, Marieke, Robin Tillmann, Florence Lebert, Ursina Kuhn, Oliver Lipps, Valérie-Anne Ryser, Flurina Schmid, Erika Antal, Gian-Andrea Monsch and Boris Wernli. 2016. *Swiss Household Panel Userguide (1999–2015)*, Wave 17, December 2016. Lausanne, Switzerland: FORS.

Vossen, Koen. 2011. "Classifying Wilders: the ideological development of Geert Wilders and his party for freedom." *Politics* 31(3): 179–189.

Walsh, Kathy Cramer. 2012. "Putting inequality in its place: rural consciousness and the power perspective. *American Political Science Review* 106(3): 517–532.

Weatherell, Charlotte, Angela Tregear, and Johanne Allinson. 2003. "In search of the concerned consumer: UK public perceptions of food, farming and buying local." *Journal of Rural Studies* 19(2): 233–244.

Weatherford, M. Stephen. 1982. "Interpersonal networks and political behavior." *American Journal of Political Science* 26(1): 117–143.

Weber, Max. [1922] 1978. *Economy and Society*. Guenther Roth and Claus Wittich, Eds. Berkeley: University of California Press.

Werts, Han, Peer Scheepers, and Marcel Lubbers. 2013. "Euro-scepticism and radical right-wing voting in Europe, 2002–2008: social cleavages, socio-political attitudes and contextual characteristics determining voting for the radical right." *European Union Politics* 14(2): 183–205.

Widfeldt, Anders. 2015. *Extreme Right Parties in Scandinavia*. London: Routledge.

Wilkinson, Kenneth P. 1986. "In search of the community in the changing countryside." *Rural Sociology* 51(1): 1–17.

Wilson, Georjeanna, and Mark Baldassare 1996. "Overall 'sense of community' in a suburban region: the effects of localism, privacy and urbanization." *Environmental Studies* 28(1): 27–43.

Wilton, Robert D. 1998. "The constitution of difference: space and psyche in landscapes of exclusion." *Geoforum* 29(2): 173–185.

Winter, Michael. 2003. "Embeddedness, the new food economy and defensive localism." *Journal of Rural Studies* 19(1): 23–32.

Wirth, Louis. [1938] 1969. "Urbanism as a way of life." In Richard Sennett, Ed., *Classic Essays on the Culture of Cities*, pp. 143–164. Englewood Cliffs, NJ: Prentice-Hall.

Wolfinger, Raymond E. 1965. "The development and persistence of ethnic voting." *American Political Science Review* 59(4): 896–908.

Wong, Cara. 2010. *Boundaries of Obligation in American Politics: Geographic, National and Racial Communities*. New York: Cambridge University Press.

Wylie, Laurence. 1957. *Village in the Vaucluse*. Cambridge, MA: Harvard University Press.

Zaller, John R. 1992. *The Nature and Origins of Mass Opinion*. Cambridge, UK: Cambridge University Press.

Zaslove, Andrej. 2004. "The dark side of European politics: unmasking the radical right." *Journal of European Integration* 26(1): 61–81.

2011. *The Reinvention of the European Radical Right: Populism, Regionalism, and the Italian Lega Nord*. McGill-Queen's University Press.

Zuckerman, Alan S. 2005. "Returning to the social logic of political behavior." In Alan S. Zuckerman, Ed., *The Social Logic of Politics: Personal Networks as Contexts for Political Behavior*, Ch. 1. Philadelphia, PA: Temple University Press.

Zuckerman, Alan S., Josip Dasović, and Jennifer Fitzgerald. 2007. *Partisan Families: The Social Logic of Bounded Partisanship in Germany and Britain*. Cambridge, UK: Cambridge University Press.

Zuckerman, Alan S., Nicholas A. Valentino, and Ezra W. Zuckerman. 1994. "A structural theory of vote choice: social and political networks and electoral flows in Britain and the United States." *Journal of Politics* 56(4): 1008–1033.

Index

Cambridge Studies in Public Opinion and Political Psychology